COMPETING FOR CUSTOMERS AND CAPITAL

VICTOR J. COOK, JR.

THOMSON

SOUTH-WESTERN

Australia · Brazil · Canada · Mexico · Singapore · Spain · United Kingdom · United States

Competing for Customers and Capital
Victor J. Cook, Jr.

COPYRIGHT © 2006 by Victor J. Cook, Jr. Thomson and the Star logo are trademarks used herein under license.

Composed by: Interactive Composition Corporation

Printed in the United States of America by RR Donnelley—Crawfordsville

1 2 3 4 5 09 08 07 06
This book is printed on acid-free paper.

ISBN 0-324-40597-9

This publication is designed to provide accurate and authoritative information in regard to the subject matter covered. It is sold with the understanding that the publisher is not engaged in rendering legal, accounting, or other professional services. If expert assistance is required, the services of a competent professional person should be sought.

ALL RIGHTS RESERVED.
No part of this work covered by the copyright hereon may be reproduced or used in any form or by any means—graphic, electronic, or mechanical, including photocopying, recording, taping, Web distribution, or information storage and retrieval systems, or in any other manner—without the written permission of the publisher.

The names of all companies or products mentioned herein are used for identification purposes only and may be trademarks or registered trademarks of their respective owners. Texere disclaims any affiliation, association, connection with, sponsorship, or endorsements by such owners.

For permission to use material from this text or product, submit a request online at http://www.thomsonrights.com.

Library of Congress Cataloging in Publication Number is available. See page 258 for details.

For more information about our products, contact us at:

Thomson Learning Academic Resource Center
1-800-423-0563

Thomson Higher Education
5191 Natorp Boulevard
Mason, Ohio 45040
USA

To my sons,
Victor, William, and Christopher

and to my other teachers,
Kenneth Boulding
Paul McCracken
Maynard Phelps
Bernard Sliger
Allen Spivey

TABLE OF CONTENTS

INTRODUCTION	xii
1 A Bridge to Tomorrow	**1**
Sources of Shareholder Value	2
Some Technical Details	2
A Few Examples	3
A Trip to Philly	4
Intangible Value in Industrials	5
Consumer Product Intangibles	6
The Big Picture	6
The Knowledge Gap	8
The Pacioli Factor	8
The Silo Problem	9
The Cobbler's Children	10
Lost in the Ivory Tower	11
The 4Ps and the Big P	12
What Does Tomorrow Look Like?	12
The Goal	13
The Competitive Enterprise Matrix	14
Domains of Executive Action	16
Performance Is Relative	18
Enterprise Market Shares	18
Value-Sales Differentials	19
Risk-Adjusted Differentials	19
Relative Earnings Productivity	20
Baker Takes the Gold Ring	24
Why Doesn't Able Line Up?	24
Errors in the Variables	25
On Building That Bridge to Tomorrow	26
References	26
End Notes	28
2 Y'all Buckle That Seat Belt	**30**
Value-Sales Principles	31
Who Competes with *LUV*?	32
The Back of an Envelope	32
Share of Value and Share of Revenue	34
Is *LUV* the Market Share Leader?	34
More Bang per Buck	35

The Value-Sales Differential	36
Will the Winner Please Stand Up?	37
What Does the Value-Sales Differential Mean?	37
Tangible Value Intuition	39
Intangible Value Intuition	40
Formalizing the Intuition	41
Is the Mean VSD Zero?	43
Adjusting for Enterprise Marketing Risk	44
Another Useful Property	45
Interpreting Risk-Adjusted Differentials	45
Properties of RAD	46
High-Flyers	47
Average Joes	48
Bottom-Feeders	48
Burning the Candle at Both Ends?	49
The Bottom Line	50
References	50
End Notes	51
3 Who's in *My* Strategic Group?	**52**
The Shifting Competitive Landscape	52
Different Views of Competition	54
A Pure Industrial Play	56
Value/Revenue Ratios	58
Limits of Free Online Services	59
Values Are More Volatile Than Revenues	59
Risk-Adjusted Differentials	60
Global Industry Classification Standard	61
Defining Strategic Groups in Volatile Markets	63
Market Commonality	63
Resource Equivalence Guidelines	70
These Are Just Guidelines	71
Strategic Groups in Stable Markets	72
Market Commonality	72
Deleted Firms	72
High Resource Equivalence	73
Medium Resource Equivalence	74
Low Resource Equivalence	75
Potential and Indirect Competitors	75
A Longer View	76
Other Considerations	77
Financial Analysts' Reports	78
Robust in Number of Competitors	79
A Final Word on Strategic Groups	82
References	82
End Notes	83

4 Enterprise Marketing Expenses — 84
Who Creates Shareholder Value? — 84
Ongoing Costs — 85
    Accounting for Enterprise Marketing Expenses — 86
    Are Accounting Costs Enterprise Marketing Expenses? — 86
    Is Financial Management An Enterprise Marketing Expense? — 87
    Where Does Traditional Marketing Fit? — 87
Enterprise Marketing Expenses in Autos — 90
    Some Cautionary Notes — 91
    From Storefront to Superstar — 92
A Really Big Picture — 93
Enterprise Marketing Expenses in Banking — 95
    Interest Expense — 96
    Large Value/Revenue Ratio — 97
    Enterprise Marketing Expenses Differences — 97
    Your Banking Dollar — 97
Old-Line and New-Wave Supermarket Chains — 99
    Your Grocery Dollar — 101
    Trends in Your Grocery Dollars — 102
    Risk-Adjusted Differentials in Grocery Chains — 104
Measuring Enterprise Marketing Expenses Can Be Tricky — 105
Four Marketing Mysteries — 106
References — 106
End Notes — 107

5 The Rule of Maximum Earnings — 109
Surround *IBM* — 109
The Principle of Force — 110
    Us Against Them? — 111
    How Do We Know This Is True? — 112
    How Does x Behave? — 112
    Incremental Force — 113
    New Orleans to West Palm Beach — 113
    Hubs and Spokes in a New Light — 114
    A Route Less Traveled — 115
    Jump to the Enterprise Level — 116
    Revenue per Share Point — 116
    First Bite of the Revenue Dollar — 117
    Profit per Share Point — 118
Maximum Earnings Market Share — 119
    Efficient Factor Markets — 119
    LUV's Enterprise Marketing Expenses — 120
    What Should *LUV* Have Spent? — 121
    Share Point Cost at the Margin — 122
    The Ante in a Poker Game — 122

Maximum Earnings Market Share Formula	123
Enterprise Marketing Performance	123
Enterprise Marketing Expenses and EBITDA	124
A Result That Makes Sense	125
On the Upside of the Curve	125
Dramatic Tumble on the Downside	125
Are Incremental Cost and Profits Equal?	125
The Incremental Profit Function	126
The Incremental Cost Function	127
Graph *LUV's* Incremental Profits and Costs	127
Follow the Money	128
Aggressive Competitive Response?	128
What If *UAL* Downsized?	129
It's All About People	130
Appendix 5-A Domestic Airline Income Statements	130
Appendix 5-B *LUVs* Maximum Earnings Market Share Formula	131
References	133
End Notes	133

6 The Battle for Your Desktop — 136

Your Desktop	136
David and Big Blue	137
The Last Thing *IBM* Needs Is a Vision	139
IBM's Market Share	140
IBM's Incremental Profit and Cost Per Basis Point	141
IBM's Achilles' Heel	142
What a Difference 11 ¢ Can Make	144
Was Less Really More for *IBM*?	145
Always a Bridesmaid	145
HPQ's Bottom Line	147
Hewlett-Packard Lost Its Marketing Edge	148
Compaq Was Way Off the Mark	149
Bow-Shaped Market Response	151
Hard as *Dell*	152
A Recent Look at *Dell*	153
Dell's Incredible Marketing Machine	155
Desktop Differential Performance	155
Why Did *Dell* Fall Short?	158
It's a Different Ball Game	158
Tapping the Corporate Market	159
Roadblocks in the Consumer Market	159
Dell in Another Strategic Group	160
Are the Markets Finally Catching UP?	160
Summing It Up	160
Remember the Rule of Maximum Earnings	161

Appendix 6-A: Desktop Data 1991–2000	162
Appendix 6-B: Periodicity in the Desktop Space	163
References	163
End Notes	164

7 In Search of Maximum Earnings — 165

I Gotta Check My Auction	166
Porous Boundaries	167
Out of Nowhere	167
Share of Revenues	169
Share of Market Value	170
Value-Sales Differentials	170
Risk-Adjusted Differentials	171
After the Bubble Burst	171
Lost Profit Opportunities	172
Amazon Overspending	173
AMZN's Marketing Efficiencies	174
Closing the Earnings Gap	174
What Happened to *eBay?*	177
The Sundown Rule	178
Amazing Value	179
Enterprise Marketing Efficiency	179
Maximum Earnings Market Share	179
Profit and Cost per Basis Point	180
Competitors' Enterprise Marketing Resources	182
What Was Left on the Table?	182
Scale Efficiencies in Enterprise Marketing?	183
All the News That Fits	184
Low Tide in Communications	184
Gannett's Maximum Earnings Market Share	185
Cumulative Earnings Shortfall	186
Differences in Key Operating Ratios	187
Combined Company Performance	188
Buy on the Rumor, Sell on the News	188
The Players	189
Enterprise Marketing Efficiency	189
AWE's Maximum Earnings Market Share	189
The Medicine Men	190
Market Share Attraction in Pharmaceuticals	191
Relative Earnings Productivity	193
Higher Order Effects	195
The Sum Constraint	195
The Revenue-Multiplier Effect	196
Carryover Effects	196

Any Added Information?	197
References	197
End Notes	198

8 High-Flyers and Bottom-Feeders — 199

The *MSI* Sample	199
Calibration Sample	199
Analysis Sample	200
The Big Picture	201
Life in the Ad Lane	201
Toyota's on Top	203
It's Easier to Fall Then Fly	204
The Best a Man Can Get	204
The Scorecard of High-Flyers	205
The Bottom-Feeders	208
Did The Big Players Always Win?	208
Group Size Has No Big Effect	210
Market Cap Has No Effect	210
What It Adds Up To	214
Financial Forces Mediate	214
Constant Growth Model	214
Is the Glass Half-Empty or Half-Full?	215
Descriptive Statistics in the *MSI* Study	215
Regression Results in the *MSI* Study	217
What's Up Next?	218
Appendix 8-A: *MSI* Sample Frame	218
References	219
End Notes	219

9 Competitive Stock Valuation — 221

Competitive Stock Valuation Model	222
The Missing Link	223
Anecdotal Evidence	224
I Gotta Check My Auction—Revisited	225
Strategic Group Revenues	225
Company Maximum Earnings Market Share	226
Earnings After Enterprise Marketing Expenses	227
Risk-Adjusted Differential and Earnings Productivity	228
Confidence Interval Estimates	230
Freehand Directional Vectors	231
Strategic Group Market Value	232
Amazon's Competitive Valuation	233
The Price of Market Leadership	234
Taking Stock	234
Risk-Adjusted Differentials and Relative Earnings Productivity	235
Novartis' Topped-Out Performance	236

Hewlett-Packard's Northwest Drift	238
Yahoo's Northeast Drift	239
Wal*Mart's Southwest Drift	240
Honda's Southeast Drift	241
PriceLine's Martingale	242
A Closer Look at Directional Vectors	244
Longer-Term Shareholder Value	245
Annual Data	246
Forecasting Methodology	246
Present Value Discounting	246
Value Added	247
References	248
End Notes	249
APPENDIX A: Definitions and Derivations	**250**
INDEX	**253**
About Texere	**258**

INTRODUCTION

The golden egg of business mythology probably can be found in the spaces between the markets that serve customers and those that create capital. The managers of product and stock markets speak different languages, rely on different theories, and use different data. These markets are separate, but equally important. Yet, they share a fundamental force—both are driven by competition.

Competition drives managers to create the greatest possible net value per dollar of expenditure. Investors evaluate a company's future productivity and risk to price its common stock. They also compare systematically the performance of one company with its peers. Other things being equal, those companies that are expected to be the more productive, lower-risk ones within a group of peer companies will be more highly valued by investors. Those that are expected to be higher risk and less productive than their peers will be valued less. This leads to a new approach to stock pricing—competitive stock valuation.

Some companies make more efficient use of their resources than others. Some maximize earnings while others don't. Companies that maximize earnings after the cost of sales return the largest possible residual to the bottom line. Understanding this profit—maximizing behavior leads to metrics that blend financial and marketing processes together. When these metrics are combined, the result is the rule of maximum earnings.

The competition for customers and capital leads to systematic interactions between product and stock markets. While subtle and complex, this interaction can be explained by value-sales principles. Applying these principles to the way we assess company performance leads to new and surprising insights about investment risk and the impact of enterprise marketing expenses on shareholder value.

This book introduces and applies competitive stock valuation, the rule of maximum earnings, and value-sales principles to a wide range of public enterprises. These concepts were developed and tested in my research over the last twenty-five years using financial data to bridge the gaps between corporate finance and enterprise marketing. The gaps remain wide and the bridge is still under construction. But I've made enough progress to share these ideas with you here in this first edition of *Competing for Customers and Capital*.

Both marketing and finance are about maximizing returns. Since corporate finance operates at the enterprise level, so must marketing if the two disciplines are to join in an ongoing and productive relationship. The link between them comes from corporate financial accounting—selling, general, and administrative expenses capture the costs of the people involved in creating and managing intangible market value. These expenses may properly be called "enterprise marketing resources." Even though they are reported in the income statement, after filtering through accounting rules and market evaluation, a residual eventually appears on the balance as "intangible assets."

Students at *Tulane University's Freeman School of Business* took several courses using early manuscripts of this book. Ten students attended the first graduate offering in the fall of 2003. I am grateful to Caryl Ewing, Lauren King, David Jackson, Erin Murphy, Kellie Newton, Joe Nguyen, and Jim Warrenfeltz for the *Bottom Line Marketing Reports* they produced in that class. The first undergraduate course was offered in the spring of 2004 with thirty-six students in attendance. I want to thank Stephen Jacobson, Shawn Pederson, and Kevan Rayden for their meaningful contributions.

The second graduate offering was in the fall of 2004. I thank all thirty-five MBA students in that class for their dedication to mastering the material. I owe special thanks to Alexander Oeing for his assistance in representing my concepts graphically and to Michael Dodson for his evocative questions. I also wish to thank Julie Bruton, Michael Calabrese, and Supasith Chonglerttham for serving as teaching assistants in the fourth offering of this class in the spring of 2005.

I began to write this book on July 3, 2003 and finished it on August 24, 2003. The second revision of the manuscript was completed just in time to go to press for the fall 2004 class. This version was finished in time for the fall semester on August 15, 2005. Unfortunately, that semester was cancelled. On August 29, only days after I received fifty copies of the perfect-bound manuscript, Katrina struck New Orleans a near-fatal blow. Fortunately, the uptown campus of Tulane University suffered relatively little flooding and no irreparable damage. We were back in business on January 7, 2006.

The course of the same name that I developed for this book is the only one in the *Freeman School* that is cross-listed for credit toward concentrations in both finance and marketing. It may be the only one in the world. I believe the academy should lead the way in filling the empty spaces between these disciplines with knowledge. With this in mind, I hope my book stimulates integrative research in finance and marketing. It is badly needed. Authors writing for the five leading academic journals in these two fields rarely cite the work of those in the other discipline. One would think these scholars believe they have nothing to learn from each other. It is also my hope that the faculties of other colleges, universities, and centers of corporate education will find this book a catalyst that drives the cross-listing of courses in their organizations.

I want to thank my friends, former students, and colleagues for the contributions they have made over the last two decades to the development of this material. In particular, I am grateful to Tim Ambler, Suman Banerjee, Ken Boudreaux, Barbara Brainard, Jeff Carr, Denise Dahlhoff, Harry Davis, John D'Angelo, Harvey Dodgson, Meyer Feldberg, Marji Fox, David Forlani, Rob Hansen, Chris Ittner, Prem Jain, Jevons Lee, David Lesmond, Bill Moult, Beau Parent, Mehmet Paşa, Margie Peteraf, David Reibstein, Raul Sanabria, Tom Robertson, Ed Strong, Dave Sutton, John Trapani, and Jianan Wu. This book would not have been written without the academic freedom and technical support provided by Tulane University. I'm also sure it would never have seen the light of day without the patience and support of my editor, Steve Momper, and my production team at Thomson Learning, especially Michelle Gaudreau, my Copy Editor and Jennifer Zeigler, my Production Project Manager. I hope the encouragement I received from all these people is justified by the insights you take away from applying the theories in this book to your own investments.

Victor J. Cook, Jr., Ph.D.
February 3, 2006

CHAPTER 1

A BRIDGE TO TOMORROW

You've heard a lot about *Southwest Airlines* in recent years. It's that low-cost, point-to-point carrier that serves peanuts. You can fly from West Palm Beach to Los Angeles for just ninety-nine dollars every day except Friday and Sunday. Along the way you get to stop in Tampa, New Orleans, Houston, and Las Vegas at no extra charge.

Chances are your knowledge of *Southwest* is based on personal experience. You may have visited the company's Web site. You've likely flown on one of its *Boeing 737s*, because the airline carried more passengers in 2004 than any other domestic carrier. If you have flown *Southwest*, you know its planes are usually on time and almost always full.

But what do you know about *Southwest's* shareholder value? For openers, you may not know its ticker symbol is *LUV*. A company's ticker symbol is its brand name on stock exchanges. Metaphorically, a ticker is the symbol of a company's Wall Street credit card. Want to know how much "credit" a company has on the street? Enter its ticker symbol in a search engine and look up its market cap. If you look at its competitors too, you'll discover that *LUV's* shareholder value is greater than the combined market value of them all.

Stop and think about this. *LUV* is the brand name for *Southwest Airlines* on Wall Street. Okay, then why didn't you know this? The answer is simple. *Southwest's* management itself apparently isn't aware of this "hidden" asset. How could they capitalize on it? Well, why not put *LUV* in the heart of their logo? How could management overlook such a powerful option? It's just one example of the separation between enterprise marketing and corporate finance. This is your first lesson in how to use enterprise marketing to create shareholder value. Stock markets and product markets interact. So, tie your Wall Street brand name to your corporate logo.

Courtesy of Southwest Airlines

Investors know more about the financial details than customers. They also know a lot less about enterprise marketing. That's because two separate—but equally important—markets exist for the buyers of products and stocks. In a nutshell, the conventional wisdom goes something like this:

- Product and service markets generate sales revenues.
- Only capital markets can create shareholder value.

Sources of Shareholder Value

There are two kinds of shareholder value—the value of **tangible** assets and the value of **intangible** assets. Most of the value creators in finance are based on tangible assets. These are assets that have either a physical or financial form. Most of these assets appear in a company's balance sheet.

> Linda Tan, a recent MBA graduate and financial news reporter, was given an assignment to analyze the financial performance of various Asian and American companies. It was her job to present her findings in a front-page feature on "identifying value creators." To assess which company created or destroyed value for investors, Linda would make use of several financial criteria. (Ho, Chan, and Wang, 2002)

In this case, a number of public Asian and American companies were compared on the basis of sixteen value creators—including sales revenues, net income, earnings per share, return on capital, return on assets, market value of equity, share price, price-earnings ratio, financial risk beta, and debt-to-equity ratio. Notice that the lion's share of these value creators is found on a company's balance sheet. Sales revenue was the only marketing measure included in the list. The implication is that customers' brand experiences and market share, for example, are not among the value creators.

By definition, intangible assets have neither a physical nor a financial form. To say the least, this makes them difficult to measure. But intangibles can have a huge impact on shareholder value. Recognizing this, accountants try to measure the value of intangibles and report that number in the balance sheet. The trouble is, accounting measures of the **book value** of intangibles often underestimate the **shareholder value** of these assets. This is no surprise. But it is surprising just how big this underestimate can be.

Some Technical Details

Total shareholder value (v) equals the sum of a company's tangible market value (v_1) and intangible market value (v_2). We can get an estimate of the market price of a tangible asset by measuring its replacement cost. But this is a complex process. It can be especially tricky for older assets like airplanes.

A simpler and more meaningful approximation is to estimate the market value of tangible assets by assuming the book value of an asset equals its replacement cost (Rao et al., 2004, 130). The total book value of assets[1] includes current assets like cash, plus physical assets like property, plants, and equipment, plus intangible assets, investments, and advances.

In some industries, enterprise marketing plays a very small role. As a rule, intangible assets have less impact on shareholder value in industries that are extremely dependent on tangible assets. Petroleum refining is one example. Intangible assets accounted for only 2.4% of *British Petroleum's* $177.6 billion total shareholder value in 2003. Its sister industry—offshore drilling rigs—is another example where shareholder value is driven almost totally by tangible assets.

A Few Examples

In companies across a broad range of industries you will see that intangible assets play a significant role in determining shareholder value. One example is the mail-order industry.

Beginning with "Online Services" which include *eBay, Yahoo, America OnLine* and similar players, Chart 1-1 shows the split between tangibles and intangibles. This industry had a total value of $79 billion in 2003. Intangible market value was $70 billion, or 88% of total value.

The picture is reversed in the airline market. The next chart tells the story. Only the four leading low-fare carriers were included in this market space (*Southwest, Jet Blue, AirTran,* and *ExpressJet*).

The assumption that book value is a good proxy for replacement value probably doesn't hold for the big legacy carriers like *United* and *American*.

The market value of the four low-fare airlines was $17.3 billion in 2003. The book value of tangible assets was $13.43 billion. The value of intangibles was $4.0 billion, or 23% of total value as shown in Chart 1-2.

Intangibles are not as important in low-fare airlines as they are in mail-order, but 22% is still a big number. The book value of intangibles reported

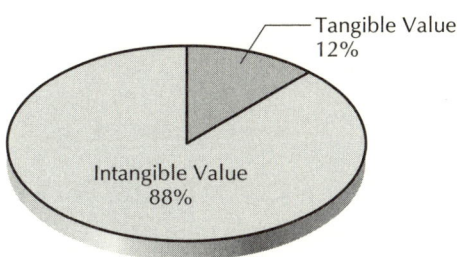

Chart 1-1   Online Services

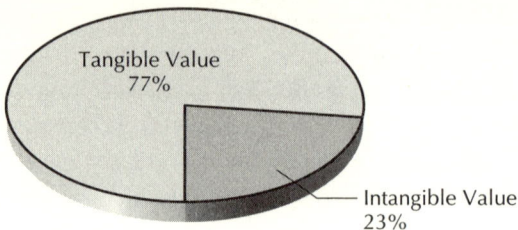

Chart 1-2   Low-Fare Airlines

by these four airlines in 2003 was $109 million. That's only 3% of the market value of intangibles.

A Trip to Philly

Even though the service provided by an airline is based on an expensive capital asset, that asset has surprisingly little to do with the brand experience.

> Every single step in a customer's relationship with your company goes into forming aspects of the brand experience. (Sutton and Klein 2003, 65)

Last week a friend of mine made a business trip to Philadelphia. Price wasn't a factor since the company was paying his expenses. Otherwise he might have flown on *Southwest*. He decided to book a *U.S. Airways* nonstop flight with an upgrade to first class using "Dividend Miles." He went to the Web site and got the phone number for frequent-flyer services because he couldn't find his number or password. He couldn't remember how many miles he had in his account, either.

After punching through several levels of voice screening, he waited five minutes, listening to recorded messages about how important his call was. He finally got a service rep on the line. He asked her if she would please give him his number and password so he could book an upgrade.

> *"I'm sorry sir, we don't have that information here."*
> *"What do you mean, isn't this Dividend Miles?"*
> *"Yes sir, it is. But we don't keep that information here."*
> *"Well, where can I get it?"*
> *"You have to call another number, sir."*
> *"May I have the number?"*
> *"Sir, I don't have that number here."*
> *"Why don't you have that number? This is Dividend Miles, for Pete's sake!"*
> *"Sir, I don't have that number here."*
> *"OK, will you just tell how many miles I have in my account?"*
> *"No sir, I can't give out that information without your account number."*
> *"Never mind, I think I won't fly U.S. Air **ever** again."*

It turns out he had to fly *U.S. Air* anyway because it had the only nonstop flight that arrived in Philly at 2:00 p.m. And it was the same price as the nonstop *Southwest* flight. But he didn't get that first class upgrade and he probably will never get to use his "Dividend Miles" because he still can't find his number and password. So much for their frequent-flyer loyalty program. Next time, he says, he'll take *Southwest* to Philly.

The telephone representative did nothing wrong. She couldn't help it that the company information system she used didn't have the information my friend wanted. Was anyone responsible for his bad brand experience? Yes, enterprise marketing was responsible. Enterprise marketing was responsible for not ensuring that the Information Technology (IT) department linked *Dividend Miles* redemption to membership records.

Can such a small thing hurt the company's market value? Yes, if it happens to enough customers. How many passengers does *U.S. Airways* lose every day because of poor brand experiences caused by this "little" slip-up? *U.S. Airways* management doesn't know the answer to this question because they don't have that information.

Intangible Value in Industrials

Are brand experiences as important to industrial product and service users as they are to consumers? As the complexity of a product or service increases, does the brand experience become more important? If so, we should find that intangible value is as large a percentage of total market value for pure industrial plays as it is for consumer products and services.

Let's see: the "Electro-medical Apparatus" industry sounds pretty complex and risky. The combined shareholder value of the sixteen players in this market space was $22.5 billion in 2003. The biggest company was *St. Jude Medical* with a market value of $8.1 billion. The second-biggest player was *Varian Medical Systems* with a market cap of $3.6 billion.

The smallest company in the group—with a market cap of $155 million—was *Endocardial Solutions Inc.* Not exactly a household name imprinted on our minds with a billion-dollar ad budget—but the company name sure sounds like it sells very high-risk products and services. Here's a product description from the company Web site[2]:

> The EnSite System's *surface electrode technology—called* **EnSite NavX™**—*allows physicians to create real-time, three-dimensional graphical displays of all four heart chambers and navigate the heart using any manufacturer's catheter.*

If the *EnSite NavX* system were to crash, you can bet it would become a bad brand experience if it weren't fixed in a hurry. The intangible value of the company was 81% of its total market value in 2003. As it happens,

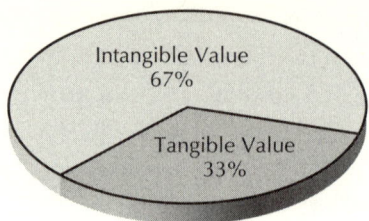

Chart 1-3 Industrial Machinery

St. Jude Medical acquired the company early in 2005. The ratio of intangible value to total value in this space ranged from 96.7% for *Imagining Diagnostics Systems Inc.* to a low of 7.2% for *Datascope Corp.* Overall, the ratio was 77%.

But, you say, "These are just computer companies disguised as industrials." Okay; take a look at Industrial Machinery in Chart 1-3. The companies in this space had a combined shareholder value of $72.2 billion in 2003. The leader was *Applied Materials*. Its intangible value was $27.6 billion. This represented 3.4% of *Applied Materials'* $37.6 billion in total shareholder value. The combined value of **intangibles** for the sixteen companies in this strategic group was $48.6 billion. That amounted to 67% of combined shareholder value.

Consumer Product Intangibles

Next, consider a strategic group with *Proctor & Gamble, Dial Corporation, Church & Dwight, Clorox Company,* and *Ecolab Inc.* This should be the mother lode of intangible value. But it isn't that different from industrial machinery. The household-products space had a market cap of $151.4 billion in 2003. Intangible market value was $115.0 billion. That 76% of packaged-goods total shareholder value is only nine points greater than industrial machinery!

Alternatively, take the packaged-food companies *Campbell Soup, H. J. Heinz,* and *Kellogg.* Their combined market cap was $39.4 billion. Of this total, $23.8 billion was made up of intangibles. That's 60.4% of the total.

The Big Picture

As you might expect from these examples, there's a lot of variation in the percent of intangible value from one industry to another. The following bar chart shows the value of intangibles as a percent of total market value in thirty industries.

Total shareholder value in this sample of 479 companies in 2003 was $4.412 trillion. The total value of intangibles was $2.950 trillion, or 67%. Look over the list of industries. Both Online Services and Computer Communications equipment manufacturers have a high percentage of intangible-to-total value. Ditto for Biotechs, Electromedical Apparatus,

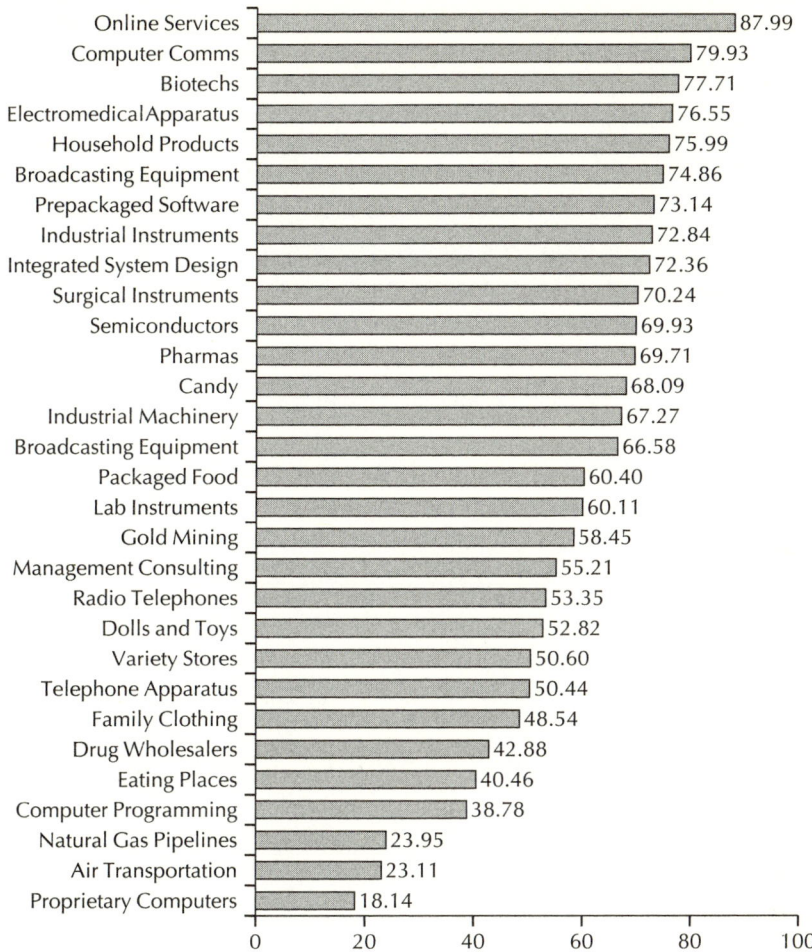

Chart 1-4 Percent Intangible Shareholder Value in Thirty Industries

Household Products, and TV Broadcasting industries. Candy, Industrial Machinery, and Broadcasting Equipment companies have two-thirds their value in intangibles. Management Consulting, Radio Telephone, and Doll and Toy companies have over one-half their total shareholder value in intangibles. Proprietary Computer makers like Apple and Sun Microsystems have the lowest percentage of their value in intangibles.

Intangible value is a significant part of shareholder wealth in most of these thirty industries. It's also true that the intangible value of these industries is based on different drivers. For example, in software, semiconductors, and electromedical apparatus, intangible values may be driven by patents—while intangibles in candy and household products are driven more by brands.

In any event, since this wealth is so important, why don't we know more about how shareholder value is created with intangible assets?

The Knowledge Gap

Specialists in finance and marketing are so focused on their disciplines that they tend to miss an important fact. Product and stock markets **interact**. The result is that senior managers on both sides of the aisle overlook opportunities for creating shareholder value with enterprise marketing, not to mention opportunities for discovering the best way to maximize the return on these expenses. This is critical because "you can't touch or copy the sources of intangible value and intangibles play an effective role in sustaining a firm's competitive advantage . . ." (Villalogna 2004, 205).

Does enterprise marketing have an impact on shareholder value?[3] Yes, product and stock markets interact. But the relationships are complex and subtle. In the next chapters we will untangle the complexities and highlight the subtleties. But before that can happen, we need to explore some of the reasons for the knowledge gap that exists between marketing and finance. There are at least five historical reasons for this gap: *The Pacioli Factor, The Silo Problem, The Cobbler's Children, Lost in the Ivory Tower,* and *The 4Ps and the Big P.*

The Pacioli Factor

Marketing managers are driven by segment **p**rofit-and-**l**oss (P&L) statements. They plan and track a market segment's income statement. The segment P&L is a marketing manager's money map. Unfortunately, there is no such thing as a segment balance sheet.

The balance sheet accounts for the company's assets and liabilities. It's the financial manager's instrument of control and the source of Linda Tan's *tangible value creators* listed at the beginning of this chapter. You can blame King Richard's crusades, the merchants of Venice who provisioned the crusaders, and the Franciscan monk Luca Pacioli for inventing double-entry accounting to protect the King's assets. But you can't deny the impact of the Pacioli Factor on diminishing marketing's role in the management of an enterprise.

Here's a short version of Pacioli's impact on modern financial accounting: The interaction between the income statement and the balance sheet is one-sided. It tends to take place only at the highest levels of financial management. Many marketing managers in corporations are shielded from this interaction since their income statements are not charged interest for the capital invested in product markets.

There are two important implications of this practice. First, marketing managers will quite properly think money is free. If you're spending ten million bucks on an ad campaign in a company with a 12% weighted average cost of capital, the cost of that capital does not appear on your P&L statement. This sends the wrong signal to all marketing professionals. But, you say, you didn't actually borrow the money. True, but *someone* is paying the $120,000 cost of that capital. If the bank isn't paying for it, then your shareholders are. Second, if marketing managers were charged the cost of the capital they use, you would find them giving much more serious attention to "return on investment" (ROI). And senior managers would take their plans more seriously.

The Silo Problem

The historical difference in focus is exaggerated by an academic curriculum that has become increasingly specialized and compartmentalized. This is the well-known "silo" problem. Students who concentrate in marketing live in its "silo" and know too little about finance. Conversely, those who concentrate in finance learn too little about marketing.

Students in each silo speak different languages, use different measures, and rely on different theories. Their work is carefully designed by the "disciplinary architects" who preserve operational integrity. That operational integrity is important and should be maintained—but not at the expense of creating a knowledge gap between these two critical business functions.

Over the past three decades, the knowledge gap between marketing and finance has generated a deep division between the corporate marketing and finance groups.

> *Most companies and CFOs will tell you that there is an adversarial relationship between finance and marketing. . . . The CFO is viewed as the person who wants to cut the [marketing] budget . . . and marketing as the person that fails to effectively explain the return on investment for communications. . . . The result is a wall between the two departments.* (Banham 1998, 36)

The gap between marketing and finance is reinforced by our underlying assumptions about competition in product and capital markets. You might be thinking: "Competition in capital markets? What's that? I know what you mean by competition in product markets, but what do you mean by competing for capital in equity markets?"

In academic circles, teachers and students too often assume that financial mangers are more-or-less free to ignore the effects of competition on investor demand for their stocks. This assumption is based on the "efficient markets" hypothesis. Many academics not only buy into the notion that capital markets are cleared by price alone, they teach it in finance classes.

Students in finance learn that capital markets are driven by the capital asset pricing model (CAPM). In this model, the expected return, and hence the price of a stock, is determined by three factors: the overall demand for stocks, the risk-free cost of capital, and the riskiness of the company's stock compared with the market.

It's significant that the CAPM actually doesn't explain much of the variation in stock returns. The leading theorists concluded "our tests do not support the most basic prediction of the ... (CAPM) ... model, that average stock returns are related positively to market βs." (Fama and French 1992, 428) It's also significant that the CAPM does not include a marketing metric. Even though we believe that marketing contributes to shareholder value, little is known about the specific links. This is the reason you will find surprisingly few chief marketing officers (CMOs) in company rosters of C-level executives.[4]

Students in marketing learn to incorporate the actions of competitors in their plans to sell products and services to customers. They are taught that customer markets are not cleared by price alone. Decisions are driven by the customer's motives, needs, wants, and budget constraints, as well as other forces. Yet they are affected by companies' marketing-mix decisions. This mix of the four Ps is a loose assemblage of: **p**roduct quality, **p**romotions, **p**rice, and the **p**laces products are sold. The marketing mix says that customer decisions are affected by product quality, the degree to which they are exposed to advertising and promotion campaigns, product availability, and price.

The Cobbler's Children

Of course, this all comes right back to the marketing professionals who march to the beats of the same old drummers. One of the ironies of the marketing profession is:

> *its inability to position itself effectively and compete for market share in the boardroom. You might think that marketers who dispense costly strategic advice on how to position businesses and create competitive advantage would be particularly adept at positioning the practice of marketing, locking down its taxonomy, and building the profession's credibility. Unfortunately, the cobbler's children have no shoes. . . . This is marketing's fault. This is the fault of a profession that has simply lost its bearings in a world that changed too rapidly. . . . We need to understand the notion of profit as central to the meaning of marketing.* (Kenton 2003, 1)

When financial managers ask marketing managers how their plans will affect shareholder value, too often all they get is a kiss and a promise. The promises take many forms. For example, it was reported recently that:

> *For the average firm in our sample, a one-point increase in customer satisfaction translates into a $55 million increase in net operating cash flow in the next year. That same*

one point in customer satisfaction results in a reduction in the variance of future cash flows of more than 4%. Such outcomes boost the value of a firm to its shareholders. (Gruca and Rego 2005, 127)

How does management create a one-point increment in a firm's customer satisfaction score? Does the company spend more money on advertising or research and development? Does it increase the number of sales training courses or does it cut prices? Does it offer customers double-their-money-back if they're not completely satisfied? How much will these initiatives cost? This book does not answer questions about specific marketing initiatives like this, but without answers to these questions, Chief Financial Officers (CFOs) will quickly lose interest in the finding that customer satisfaction is linked to shareholder value.

Marketing today faces myriad challenges, among them the pressure to meet short-term financial goals, an inability to quantify marketing's contributions to the firm, and a shift of responsibility for marketing strategy from corporate to the SBU level. As one CMO put it, 'Marketing has lost its seat at the table.' (Webster, Malter, and Ganesan 2003)

Lost in the Ivory Tower

Once upon a time, marketing ruled strategic thinking in academic circles and board rooms. The **P**rofit **I**mpact of **M**arketing **S**trategy (PIMS) studies led to powerful conclusions about the impact of market share on profitability: profits are a function of market share. Other things being equal, the more market share, the greater are company profits. These conclusions were given credibility in three ways. First, one of the most profitable companies in the world, *General Electric,* conceived of PIMS and focused management's attention on strategic business units. Second, the *Marketing Science Institute,* a not-for-profit think tank that was affiliated with the *Harvard Business School,* assumed responsibility for maintaining and updating the PIMS database. Third, the *Harvard Business School's* marketing faculty became the intellectual advocates of the concept. Professor Robert D. Buzzell and his colleagues published articles in the leading journals that were widely read (Buzzell and Bradley 1987). In the 1970s these articles became a cornerstone in strategic management and marketing.

Marketing's clout in the ivory tower ended in the 1980s when two things happened almost at the same time. The PIMS findings were challenged by marketing scholars, and Michael Porter (1989) published his five forces model.

The 4Ps and the Big P

Recently, marketing scholars have reached deep into their analytical tool kit to establish important links between the lifetime value of customers and shareholder value:

> *If customers are the key generators of revenue and profit—the big P—then the cumulative value of all current and future customers should be a strong proxy for the firm's market value.* (Gupta 2004)

This approach is particularly useful for companies in new markets where historical financial accounting data are not available, or where the data fail to capture potential market growth, or the firm suffers from negative earnings. In each of these instances, traditional financial models of valuation are problematic at best.

> *The underlying premise of our model is that customers are important intangible assets of a firm, and their value should be measured and managed as is any other asset. . . . by using DCF at a customer level, we are able to provide a useful method for forecasting the stream of future earnings, which is a key input to any valuation model.* (Gupta, Lehmann, and Stuart 2004)

Linking customer lifetime value to market value is a significant step toward making enterprise marketing metrics relevant to financial analysts. This research direction is important for two other reasons—it focuses on the enterprise rather than individual brands, and it takes a long-term rather than a short-term perspective. These steps indicate a new and important direction for marketing.

What Does Tomorrow Look Like?

The current gaps between marketing and finance boil down to three critical dimensions: core metrics, level of aggregation, and time horizon. These dimensions provide a roadmap for the evolution of marketing illustrated in Chart 1-5 (adapted from Agres et al. 2003, 21).

Historically, marketing has focused on a short-term analysis of brand sales. The lower left-hand corner of Chart 1-5 defines this perspective. The "brand-enterprise" dimension deserves special attention here. It's easy to add up the sales of all the brands in a corporate portfolio to the enterprise level. That's not the point. It's not just an aggregation problem. It's a question of orientation. Adding up past sales is backward looking. What we need is a forward-looking orientation toward the impact of enterprise marketing expenses on future market share, earnings, and shareholder value. Recently, the focus of marketing has begun to evolve in this way. Linking customer lifetime value to future shareholder value is the first step toward the practice of enterprise marketing.

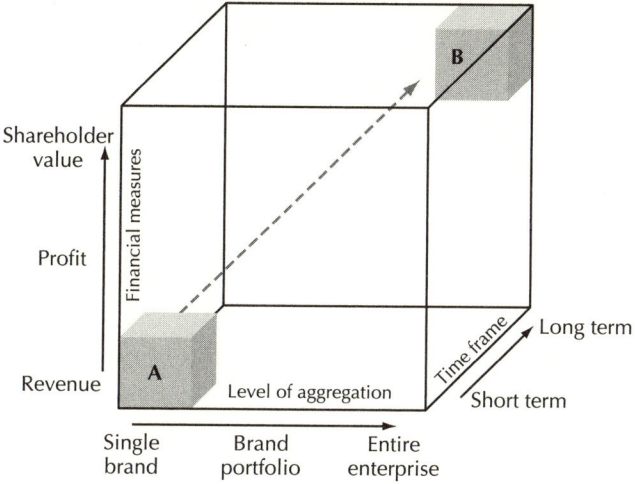

Chart 1-5 From Brand to Enterprise Marketing

But these metrics . . . are also best employed, not one brand at a time, as is typical today, but for categories, brand portfolios, and even the total enterprise. (Agres et al. 2003, 21)

This book is a roadmap for the evolution of traditional marketing as it moves from today's narrow brand-sales perspective to embrace tomorrow's enterprise marketing expenses, earnings, and shareholder value.

The Goal

The goal of this book is to develop links between the cost of enterprise marketing and the creation of shareholder value.

More successful companies have attacked this problem by choosing their performance measures on the basis of causal models, also called value driver maps, which lay out the plausible cause-and-effect relationships that may exist between the chosen drivers of strategic success and outcomes. (Ittner and Larcker 2003, 3)

The purpose of this book is to articulate a cause-and-effect model of the relationships between market share and shareholder value, based on common language, economic theory, and financial accounting data. This model directly links enterprise marketing expenses to shareholder value[5] through the profit-maximizing behavior of each firm in a strategic group.

This approach doesn't require that we estimate statistically a set of industry-specific simultaneous equations. Nor will it be necessary to engage in complex dynamic programming exercises (Ross 1978). Instead, we calculate directly from financial accounting data the incremental cost of market share, and compare it with the incremental profit of market share.

The development of market share cost and profit functions extends the classic work of Dorfman and Steiner (1954) to strategic groups. Viewed from this perspective, management's job is "to equate the changing marginal cost of market share with its shifting marginal value. The task is complicated by the unexpected behavior of competitors." (Cook 1985, 56) These marginal cost and profit functions are driven by the Market Share Attraction model. "This model, prevalent in the marketing literature, is the simplest representation of customer reaction to competition among firms that we know." (Farris et al. 2001, 3)

We calibrate interactions among operations, marketing, and finance by linking the profit and cost per market share point to earnings and shareholder value in a strategic group. Then we assess the actions management can take to increase the price of their stock by increasing (or decreasing) enterprise marketing expenses.

This story is told in a variety of industries—from airline travel to banks, from desktop to supermarkets—using real data. These data are found in the financial statements of well-known public companies.

You'll discover untold and surprising stories based on the financial statements of a wide range of companies. For example, *Amazon.com, AT&T Wireless, Dell, Dow Jones, DuPont, Harrah's, IBM, Johnson & Johnson, Southwest Airlines, Toyota Motors, Wal*Mart,* and *Whole Foods Market* are studied in depth, along with many of their competitors. Most of these competitors are also household names.

In some cases, the data are recent, taken from the period between the first quarter of 2001 and the second quarter of 2004. Where quarterly data are used—for example, in the analysis of supermarket chains—short-term influences like seasonality are important. In other cases, like the desktop industry where epochal evolution occurs over long time-periods, annual data are necessary.

In every case, *Standard & Poor's COMPUSTAT* database provides easy access to the historical data used throughout this book.[6] In a few examples, based on just one reporting period—or in cases where only the most recent quarterly data will do—reports are taken off financial statements available from the company or the Security and Exchange Commission's (SEC) online files.

The Competitive Enterprise Matrix

The competitive matrix is the foundation of enterprise marketing. Financial managers typically make two big mistakes in their efforts to create shareholder value. The first is to ignore the potential impact of enterprise marketing. The second is to heavily discount the impact of competitors.

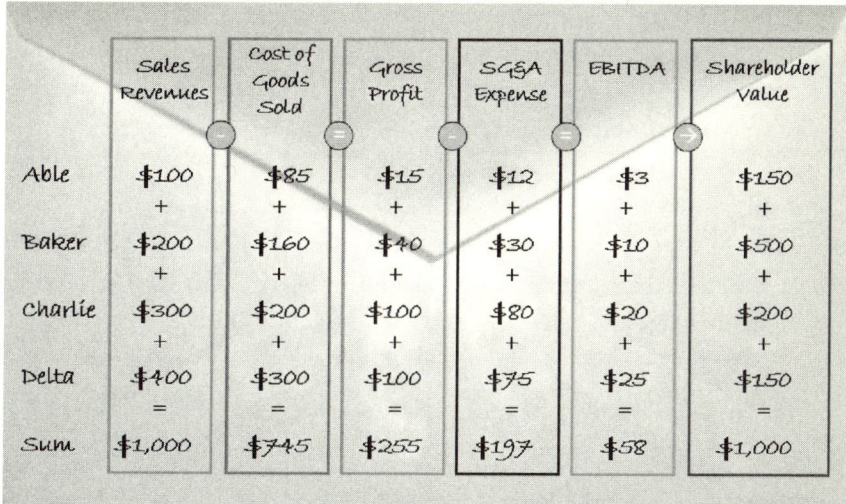

Chart 1-6 The Back of an Envelope

Tracking the components of the competitive enterprise matrix makes it unlikely that these mistakes will be made.

Chart 1-6 defines a hypothetical matrix. It shows where the dollars come and go for a set of hypothetical competitors. The relationships are so simple you can write them on the back of an envelope.

Each of the columns in the matrix represents a unique enterprise marketing metric: sales revenues; cost of goods sold; gross profit; selling, general, and administrative expenses; earnings before interest, taxes, depreciation, and amortization; and market value.

A company's performance depends on the performance of its rivals. Companies with the greatest market value often will be those that "anticipate the combination of strategic resources that yield the greatest earnings, and pay less for them in strategic factor markets than do their competitors." (Barney 1986)

The rows in the chart include four hypothetical competitors—*Able, Baker, Charlie,* and *Delta*—that define a **strategic group** within an industry. A strategic group is a set of companies that can (or might) serve common customer needs and have (or might acquire) equivalent resources. In short, firms that have a high degree of market commonality and resource equivalence may be viewed as *direct competitors in a strategic group* (Bergen and Peteraf 2002, 162).

The competitive enterprise cycle begins with sales revenues and ends with shareholder value. Think of these beginning and end points as the "sales space" and "value space."

The members of a strategic group execute their strategies in a market place that is both dynamic and evolutionary. The companies in a strategic group may change abruptly through merger, acquisition, or failure. Alternatively, the strategic group may evolve gradually over time as a result of product innovations, changes in served geographic market segments, and the creation of new supply chains.

Domains of Executive Action

If you take a company's historical income statement and reconstruct the way it's presented in financial accounting data files, every dollar of sales revenue is divided into three parts:[7]

1. cost of goods sold;
2. selling, general, and administrative expenses; and
3. earnings before interest, tax, depreciation, and amortization.

Operations Management. The cost of goods sold (COGS) is primarily the domain of operations. For manufacturing companies, this is a flow measure reported in the income statement after the current stocks of finished goods inventories are sold. A company's gross profits[8] signal its operational efficiency through its gross margin.[9] The costs of goods sold in manufacturing include plant, equipment, and raw materials. The cost of goods sold in retailing is literally the cost of products bought for resale in arm's-length transactions.

Beyond manufacturing and retailing, the cost of goods sold varies from business to business. For example, in restaurants it's the cost of food and beverages. In banks it's the cost of money.

Enterprise Marketing. The soul of enterprise marketing is a cross-functional perspective where "every member of your sales force, every customer service rep, every email, every invoice, every voice mail, every interaction with every customer at any time" (Sutton and Kline 2003, 215) is a part of the practice of enterprise marketing. Selling, general, and administrative (SG&A) expenses capture the costs of all these events and interactions. These are the costs of enterprise marketing. Looking at these expenses as a whole breaks down the silos and opens the analysis to how the company should operate if it is to maximize earnings.

The SG&A expense category includes the current costs of technology-based "assets" (R&D expenses); customer-based "assets" (sales operation expenses); market-based "assets" (advertising and promotion expenses); talent-based organizational "assets" (employee compensation); and contract-based statutory "assets" (legal expenses).[10] Each of these expenses affects the way customers and investors feel, think, and act toward your company.

| COGS ≈ Operations Management | SG&A ≈ Enterprise Marketing | EBITDA ≈ Corporate Finance |

Chart 1-7 Domains of Executive Action

Conceptually, the management of these expenses is the domain of enterprise marketing.

Reporting of SG&A expenses often follows different conventions in company income statements for different types of businesses. For example, R&D expenses may be reported separately or combined with other expenses in a manufacturer's income statement. In pure service businesses, such as restaurants, operating expenses sometimes are included in the COGS.

In these industries, operating expenses, which include the people that play a vital role in shaping customers' perceptions, must be moved into the category of enterprise marketing expenses. Another example is banks. Banking companies typically report the cost of operations in COGS even though the true cost of the goods is simply the interest they pay for money.

Corporate Finance. The main reason financial managers overlook the potential of enterprise marketing for creating shareholder value is their focus on earnings. Earnings before interest, taxes, depreciation, and amortization (EBITDA) is what's left over after operations management and enterprise marketing expenses are subtracted from sales revenues. Management of EBITDA is the domain of corporate finance, but financial managers need to look further back up the income stream for new opportunities for creating shareholder value.

Financial Accounting. The plus, minus, and equal signs in Chart 1-6 identify the financial accounting relationships among the rows and columns. For example, the sales revenues of *Able* ($100) are added to those of *Baker* ($200), *Charlie* ($300), and *Delta* ($400) to create the total sales space. Reading across the rows, sales revenues less cost of goods sold equals gross profits, and so on.

The sum of selling, general, and administrative expenses for the four companies is the dollar value of all the enterprise marketing expenses in this strategic group. These are the *critical resources* that contribute to (or detract from) competitive advantages among the players (Peteraf and Barney 2003, 316). These resources are evaluated by investors relative to those of other firms in a strategic group. The results of their evaluations imply (=>) the *future* shareholder value of each firm.

Performance Is Relative

Performance in a strategic group is relative. Management's belief in the superiority of their performance matters far less than how their operational capacity, marketing efficiency, and earnings productivity stack up against competitors. To amplify this point, take a closer look at the sales and value spaces in the hypothetical matrix illustrated by Chart 1-8.

Enterprise Market Shares

We've got to transform the dollar data from Chart 1-6 so that it highlights the relative performance of each player. To do this, we use two basic measures of market share. These are share of value (**SOV**) and share of revenue (**SOR**). The results are shown in Chart 1-8.

Delta was the sales leader, hands-down. It generated 40% of the sales revenue (**SOR**) in its strategic group. But *Delta* created only 15% of the capitalized value (**SOV**) in the group. Its value/revenue ratio was just 0.375. *Baker* company, on the other hand, generated only 20% of sales revenues, but created 50% of the market value. Its value/revenue ratio was 2.50. Sales of *Delta* were twice this follower, yet its shareholder value was less than a third of

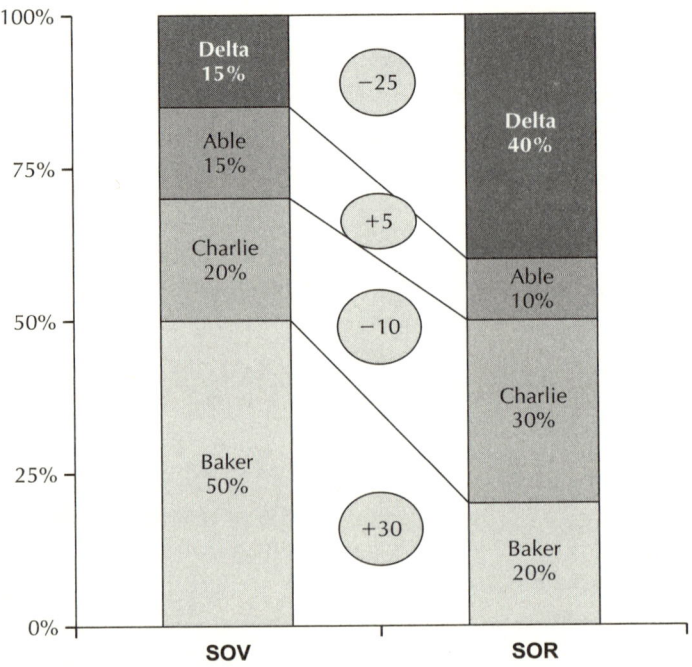

Chart 1-8 Performance Is Relative

Baker's. Is something wrong with this picture? Are these data atypical? Are the product market and stock markets out of sync? No, there are missing links between sales revenues and shareholder value.

Value-Sales Differentials

The "**v**alue-**s**ales differential" is the first of the missing links. The VS differential is the difference between a company's share of value and its share of revenues. The numbers in the circles in Chart 1-8 are the VS differentials of each company in this hypothetical competitive matrix. *Able's* differential is −25 points—its share of value is 25 percentage points ***less*** than its share of revenue. *Baker's* differential is +30 points—its share of value is 30 percentage points ***greater*** than its share of revenue.

Is it better to have a positive or a negative differential? Positive is better. A positive differential means that investors have rewarded the company with a market value in excess of its sales revenue. This is a good thing. Remember, market value is a company's credit card on Wall Street. A negative differential means that investors have discounted the company's market value relative to its sales revenue. This is a bad thing. The stock of shareholder value is less than the churn in sales revenues.

Risk-Adjusted Differentials

As with all performance measures, we've got to account for volatility. We can create a risk-adjusted measure by dividing a company's VS differentials by its standard deviation. It turns out that the standard deviation of VS differentials in a large sample of companies is about 6.6 (Cook 2003, new calculation based on MSI sample data). Of course, volatility varies from company to company as well as over time.

To simplify things, for now let's assume all four companies have a standard deviation of 6.6. In this case, the **r**isk-**a**djusted **d**ifferentials (RAD) are the ones reported in Table 1-1. *Baker* is +4.5 and *Delta* is −3.8. Now we have a standardized measure of the interaction between product and stock markets. This is an important step.

Table 1-1 Risk-Adjusted Differentials

	SOV	SOR	VSD	RAD
Able	15.00	10.00	5.00	0.8
Baker	50.00	20.00	30.00	4.5
Charlie	20.00	30.00	(10.00)	−1.5
Delta	15.00	40.00	(25.00)	−3.8

Relative Earnings Productivity

Another key measure is relative earnings productivity. The concept itself is simple. It's the difference between a company's actual earnings (EBITDA) and what it would have earned if management had achieved maximum potential earnings. EBITDA comes straight from the income statement; but, we can't look up **r**elative **e**arnings **p**roductivity (REP) in the income statement. The calculation is a bit complicated. Relative earnings productivity depends on four fundamental measures of enterprise marketing performance.

Enterprise Marketing Efficiency. There are two ways to measure efficiency of enterprise marketing expenses. The first measure is intuitive and linear: **s**ales **p**er **d**ollar (SPD) enterprise marketing expenses. *Baker* company's SPD is significantly greater than its competitors'. Management generates $6.67 in revenues for every dollar spent on SG&A expenses.[11] Its three competitors on average generate only $4.89 per dollar of SG&A expense.[12] Based on linear differences, *Baker* is about 36% more efficient than its competitors.

The second measure is theoretical and nonlinear: the enterprise **m**arketing **e**fficiency **r**atio (MER). Given the strategic marketing cost function (Cook 1983, 72), if management spends *less* than required to maintain current share of revenues, they're more efficient. In this case, the enterprise MER is less than one. If management spends *more* than is needed to maintain current share of revenues, the company is less efficient. In this case their MER is greater than one. If a company spends no more or less than is necessary to support current share of revenues, its efficiency ratio is one.

This concept of enterprise marketing efficiency works only if we assume a high correlation between sales revenues and selling, general, and administrative expenses. There is strong evidence to support this assumption. For example, in the calendar year 2003, the mean correlation between sales and selling, general, and administrative expenses for the thirty industries examined in this chapter—was 0.96, with a standard deviation of 0.07. Individual correlation coefficients for each of these industries are shown in Chart 1-9.

The high correlations between these two enterprise marketing variables demonstrate that when a marketing efficiency ratio departs significantly from 1.0 in either direction, the company is more (or less) efficient than its competitors.[13]

Baker company is far more efficient than its competitors, with an MER of 0.72. Theoretically, *Baker* would spend $41.75 to maintain a revenue share of 20%. The company spends only $30.00. The marketing efficiency ratio of its three competitors combined is 1.39. They spent $167 to maintain a

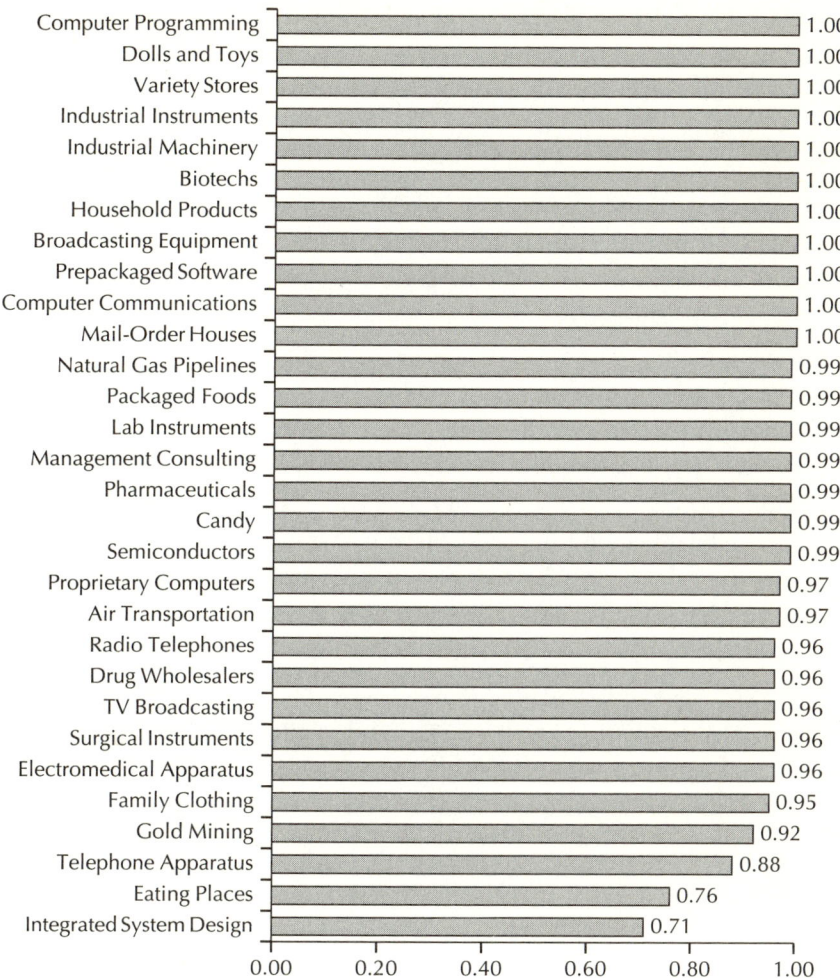

Chart 1-9 Correlations Between Sales Revenues and Selling, General, and Administrative Expenses

combined share of 80% when they should have spent only $120.[14] Based on this nonlinear measure of marketing efficiency, *Baker* is almost twice as efficient as its competitors.

Cost per Point. The second indicator upon which relative earnings productivity depends is the table stakes required to play the game. The table stakes a company must put up in the competitive strategy game is the money required to buy the first market share point. This amount depends both on the size of the market and on enterprise marketing efficiency. The bigger the market—measured by total group revenues—the bigger the table stakes. In other words, market size alone is a barrier to entry. On the other hand, the better management is at playing the game, the greater is its enterprise marketing efficiency. Greater marketing efficiency lowers the cost of entry. *Baker's* cost per point (**CPP**) is $1.20.[15]

Profit per Point. The third indicator upon which relative earnings productivity depends is gross profits per market share point. Gross profits translate into gross margin. The bigger a company's gross margin as a percent of sales revenues, the greater are profits per share point. The lower the gross margin, the lower are profits per share point compared with competitors. *Baker's* profit per point (**PPP**) is $2.00.[16]

Maximum Earnings. Earnings are maximized when the cost per point equals the profit per point. *Baker's* **m**aximum **e**arnings **m**arket **s**hare (**MEMS**)[17] occurs at 22.5% of group revenue.[18] The incremental cost and profit schedules behind this result appear in the next chart.

The vertical axis in Chart 1-10 is incremental (or marginal) cost and profit per share point. The horizontal axis is share of enterprise marketing expenses. At *Baker's* current 20% share of revenues, its cost per point is $1.88. Its share of marketing expenses is just 15.2%. This is another take on why *Baker* is so efficient: management captures 20% of group revenues with just 15.2% of the group's enterprise marketing expenses. This is good. But notice

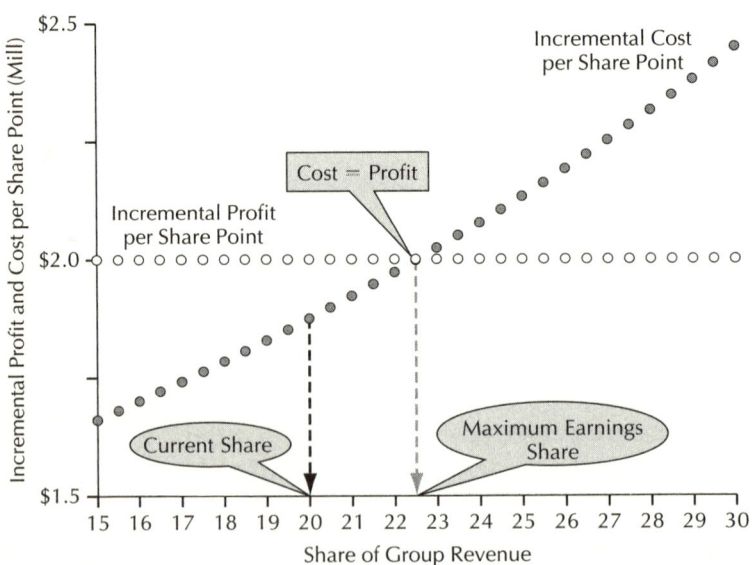

Chart 1-10 Baker's Maximum Earnings Market Share

that *Baker's* profit per point is $2.00. The company's earnings will be maximized at that share of revenues where its incremental cost equals its incremental profit per point. This occurs at a revenue share of 22.5%.

The impact on earnings of equating incremental cost and profit is documented in the next chart. The vertical axis is profits after the cost of enterprise marketing expenses. The horizontal axis is share of group revenues. *Baker's* current market share is 20% and earnings are $10. Its earnings will be maximized at $10.16 if management builds share to 22.5% of group revenues. But, beyond that point earnings fall dramatically.

It turns out that another of our hypothetical companies also is underspending, while the other two are overspending. The details appear in Table 1-2. *Able's* maximum earnings market share is 15.1%, while its current share of revenue is 10.0%.

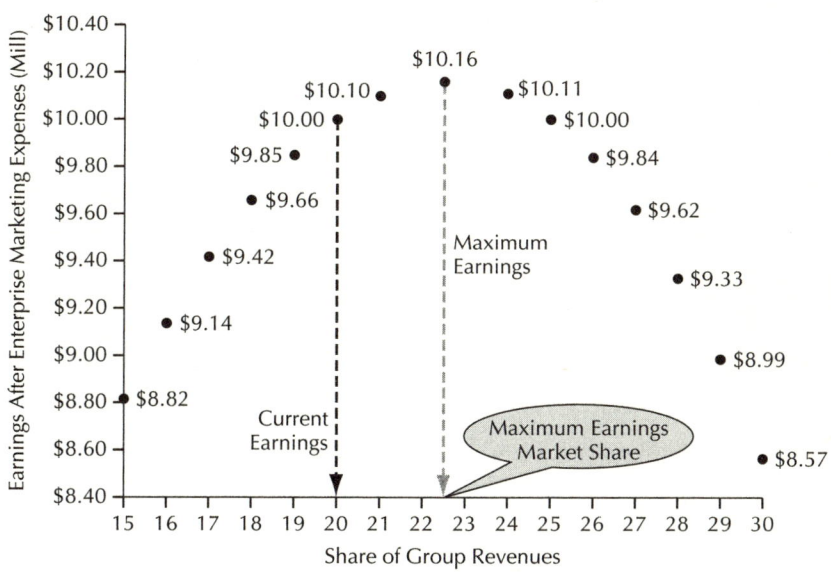

Chart 1-11   Baker's Earnings After Enterprise Marketing Costs

Table 1-2   Under- and Overspending

	MER	CPP	PPP	MEMS	SOR	U/O
Able	0.58	$1.08	$1.50	15.1	10.0	5.1
Baker	0.72	$1.20	$2.00	22.5	20.0	2.5
Charlie	1.60	$1.87	$3.33	25.2	30.0	−4.8
Delta	0.92	$1.13	$2.50	32.9	40.0	−7.1

Both *Charlie* and *Delta* companies overspent on enterprise marketing. *Charlie's* actual share of revenue is 30.0%. The company would have maximized earnings at 25.2% share of revenues. Management overspent to the tune of 4.8 share points. *Delta's* performance was even worse. The company overspent to the tune of 7.1 share points.

Recall that *Baker* created 50% of total shareholder value in this group. Table 1-2 provides some preliminary clues to *Baker's* high share of value. First, with an EMR of 0.72, it's the second-most efficient company in the group. *Baker's* efficiency keeps its cost per point $0.67 less than *Charlie's*. *Baker's* 20% gross margin is less than *Delta's* 25%, but not that much lower for a company one-half the size, so it earns a very respectable profit per point. Finally, *Baker* is closer to maximum earnings market share than any competitors.

Now we're able to fill in that important piece missing from this puzzle—relative earnings productivity. This is a new, more sophisticated measure of earnings quality. The results for our four hypothetical companies appear in Table 1-3.

Here's where *Baker* takes the gold ring. *Baker* company's relative earnings productivity is just 0.01. In other words, its actual earnings were only 1% less than maximum potential earnings.

Baker Takes the Gold Ring

Baker is the clear winner in this strategic group. The company occupies the most coveted position in the Risk-Adjusted Differential/Relative Earnings chart (Chart 1-12). *Baker* is solidly in the upper right-hand corner of the grid. The company has a risk-adjusted differential of +4.5 and a relative earnings productivity ratio of −0.01. In recognition of this singular performance, investors bid *Baker's* stock up to 50% of the group's total shareholder value.

Why Doesn't Able Line Up?

All three of *Baker's* competitors have lower risk-adjusted differentials, as you would expect. *Able, Charlie,* and *Delta* all have lower earnings productivity

Table 1-3 Relative Earnings Productivity

	Maximum Earnings	Actual Earnings	Max–Act	Relative Earnings
Able	$3.44	$3.00	$0.44	−0.13
Baker	$10.08	$10.00	$0.08	−0.01
Charlie	$21.11	$20.00	$1.11	−0.05
Delta	$27.09	$25.00	$2.09	−0.08

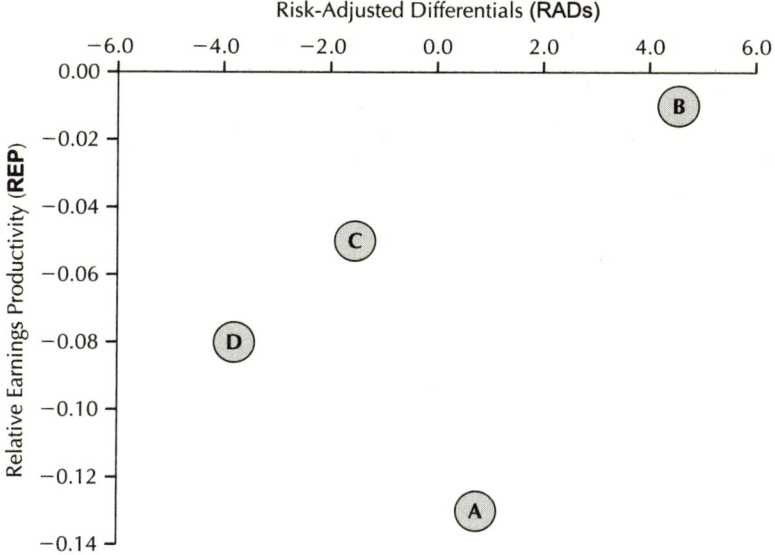

Chart 1-12 Risk-Adjusted Differentials and Relative Earnings

ratios than *Baker*, also as you would expect. But notice in Chart 1-12 that *Able* has the lowest relative earnings productivity and the second-best risk-adjusted differential. Why doesn't *Able* line up with expectations? Good question. There are many reasons. Errors in the variables are known to be among the most important and well-known ones.

Errors in the Variables

Stock valuation is a complicated and risky business. As you saw earlier in this chapter, even the most widely accepted (CAPM) model is not supported by the data. The behavior of these four hypothetical companies was set to remind you about the fact that there are errors in the variables of any model. Here are some of the sources of the errors in these variables.

Size. Errors in the variables affect small players much more than larger ones. In the case of our four hypothetical companies, *Able* is the runt of the litter. *Baker* is twice as big, *Charlie* was three times, and *Delta* four times its size.

Trend. The results shown in Chart 1-10 are based on a single period. The time trend is missing. If we had data over the 10 most recent periods, perhaps a more consistent pattern would emerge. Even so, time trends introduce their own errors. For example, seasonal effects are very important in some industries. If the data are quarterly, failure to control for seasonal effects can produce even more inconsistencies.

Risk. Every company was assumed to have the same enterprise marketing risk. It's very unlikely this would happen with real data. Volatility is a critical input.

Results. The earnings productivity results for all four companies are so similar that it would be difficult for investors to read the tea leaves. *Able,* the worst case, came within 13% of achieving maximum potential earnings.

Model. Economic models, even those based on the most widely accepted and robust theory, sometimes fail to account fully for what is observed. You will find this to be true of the valuation model used in this book.

On Building That Bridge to Tomorrow

It's difficult to get marketing and finance to engage in a mutually beneficial dialogue. But it can be done with common theoretical grounding, financial accounting data, and direct links between enterprise marketing expenses and shareholder value. It is even becoming increasingly difficult to draw a line between enterprise marketing expenses and traditional marketing costs. The *American Marketing Association* recently extended the definition of marketing to further blur this line:

> *Marketing is an organizational function and set of processes for creating, communicating, and delivering value to customers and for managing customer relationships in ways that benefit the organization and its stakeholders.* (Schultz 2005, 8)

Enterprise marketing is also responsible for creating, communicating, and delivering value to **investors.** Enterprise marketing expenses contribute to (or diminish) shareholder value in ways that we will explore in detail in the next eight chapters of this book. Hold onto your hat; you're about to discover the enterprise marketing metrics you need to compete for shareholder value—and win.

References

Agres, S., S. Daiberl, W. Moult, and J. Spaeth. 2003. "Maximizing Shareholder Value by Bridging the Metrics of Finance and Marketing." In *European Society for Opinion and Marketing Research Congress and Trade Exhibition: Management, Accountability, and Research: The Quest for the Objective Truth* (September): 21.

Banham, R. 1998. "Making Your Mark: Time for Finance to Play a Role in Brand Management." *CFO: The Magazine for Senior Financial Executives* 14 (3): 34–44.

Barney, J. B. 1986. "Strategic Factor Markets: Expectations, Luck, and Business Strategy." *Management Science* 32 (October): 1231–1234.

Bergen, M., and M. Peteraf. 2002. "Competitor Identification and Competitor Analysis: A Broad-Based Managerial Approach." *Managerial and Decision Economics* 23 (June/August): 157–169.

Buzzell, Robert D., and B. T. Gale. 1987. *The PIMS Principles: Linking Strategy to Performance*. New York: The Free Press.

Cook, V. J. Jr. 1983. "Marketing Strategy and Differential Advantage." *Journal of Marketing* 47 (Spring): 68–75.

——— 1985. "The Net Present Value of Market Share." *Journal of Marketing* 49 (Summer): 49–63.

——— 2003. "Marketing's Impact on Firm Value: The Value-Sales Differential." *Marketing Science Institute Reports* 03 (2): 55–78.

Dorfman, R. T., and P. O. Steiner. 1954. "Optimal Advertising and Optimal Quality." *American Economic Review* 44 (December): 826–836.

Fama, E. F., and K. R. French. 1992. "The Cross-Section of Expected Stock Returns." *The Journal of Finance* 47 (2): 428.

Farris, P., P. Pfeifer, D. Reibstein, and E. van Nierop. 2001. "Why is Five a Crowd in the Market Share Attraction Model: The Dynamic Stability of Competition." *Darden School Foundation*: 3.

Foster, B. P., R. Fletcher, and W. D. Stout. 2003. "Valuing Intangible Assets." *The CPA Journal* 73 (October): 50–54.

Gruca, T. S., and L. L. Rego. 2005. "Customer Satisfaction, Cash Flow, and Shareholder Value." *Journal of Marketing* 69 (July): 115–130.

Gupta, S. 2004. "Marketing Metrics: Hard Numbers on Soft Science." *Hermes Columbia Business School Alumni Magazine* 2 (Fall).

Gupta, S., D. R. Lehmann, and Je. A. Stuart. 2004. "Valuing Customers." *Journal of Marketing Research* XLI (February): 7–18.

Ho, M., S. H. Chan, and K. Wang. 2002. "Identifying Value Creators." *Center for Asian Business Cases: The University of Hong Kong School of Business* HKU185 (January): 1.

Kenton, C. 2003. "Marketing's Biggest Challenge." *Business Week Online* August 27.

Ittner, C. D., and D. F. Larcker. 2003. "Coming Up Short on Nonfinancial Performance Measurement." *Harvard Business Review Online Reprint* (November): 1–10.

Peteraf, M. A., and J. B. Barney. 2003. "Unraveling the Resource-Based Tangle." *Managerial and Decision Economics* 24: 309–323.

Porter, M. E. 1998. *Competitive Strategy: Techniques for Analyzing Industries and Competitors*. New York: The Free Press.

Rao, V. R., M. K. Agarwal, and D. Dahlhoff. 2004. "How is Manifest Branding Strategy Related to the Intangible Value of a Corporation?" *Journal of Marketing* 68 (October): 126–141.

Ross, S. A. 1978. "A Simple Approach to the Valuation of Risky Streams." *The Journal of Business* 51 (July): 453–475.

Schultz, D. E. "New Definition of Marketing Reinforces Idea of Integration." *Marketing News* June 15, 2005.

Sutton, D., and T. Klein. 2003. *Enterprise Marketing Management: The New Science of Marketing.* John Wiley & Sons, Inc.

Villalogna, B. 2004. "Intangible Resources, Tobin's q, and Sustainability of Performance Differences." *Journal of Economic Behavior & Organization* 54 (June): 205–30.

Webster, F. E. Jr., A. J. Malter, and S. Ganesan. 2003. "Can Marketing Regain Its Seat at the Table?" *Marketing Science Institute Reports* 03-003: 29–47.

End Notes

[1] *Standard & Poor's COMPUSTAT* annual data item 6 and quarterly data item 44.

[2] The URL is http://www.endocardial.com/aboutus.php.

[3] The trustees of the *Marketing Science Institute* included "Managing marketing as a 'value creator' versus an expense" as a Top Tier Research Priority. See *2004–2006 Research Priorities: A Guide to MSI Research Programs and Procedures,* Marketing Science Institute, page 8.

[4] Go to a search engine on the Internet and look up ten companies of your choice. Chances are, you will find only three or four chief marketing officers among the board level executives listed on company Web sites.

[5] "Enterprise marketing expenses," are not "intangible assets" as recognized by the Financial Accounting Standards Board (FASB) in its *SFAS 142 Goodwill and Other Intangible Assets.* See Benjamin P. Foster, Robin Fletcher, and William D. Stout, "Valuing Intangible Assets," The *CPA* Journal, Vol. 73, No. 10 (October), 2003, page 50. Instead, "enterprise marketing expenses" are the costs of capabilities and competencies not treated as assets in the balance sheet. These include people-dependent resources like customer-relationship management, advertising strategy, individual functional skills, and organizational know-how. Over time, some residual of these current expenses will appear in a company's balance sheet as "intangible assets."

[6] The *COMPUSTAT* data can be accessed online anywhere on the planet with an account ID and password to *Wharton Research Data Services* at http://wrds.wharton.upenn.edu

[7] *COMPUSTAT* data files are built on company SEC filings. As a result, if a company folds EBITDA into its SG&A expenses rather than reporting them separately,

that company cannot be included in this analysis. Note that EBITDA is reported as "Operating Income Before Depreciation" in *COMPUSTAT* annual data item 13 and quarterly data item 21.

[8] Gross profits equal sales revenues minus cost of goods sold.

[9] Gross margin equals gross profits divided by sales revenues.

[10] Summarized from "Getting a Grip on Intangible Assets," *Harvard Management Update,* A Newsletter from Harvard Business School Publishing, 2001, Article Reprint No. U0102C.

[11] Baker generates sales of $200 with $30 in SG&A expenses.

[12] The three competitors combined generate $800 in sales with $167 in SG&A expense.

[13] The reason that Eating Places and Integrated Systems Design have relatively low correlations is that the costs of people are assigned to the cost of goods rather than selling, general, and administrative expenses.

[14] The enterprise marketing efficiency ratio, $x = m/(100 - m)f$, where m is current market share and f is competitive spending on SG&A expenses. See Chapter 5 for an explanation of this formula.

[15] The average cost point $k = fx/100$. See Chapter 5 for an explanation of this formula.

[16] The average profit point $p = Rg/100$, where R is group revenues and g is company gross margin. See Chapter 5 for an explanation of this formula.

[17] $0.1349 = 1 - \sqrt{\dfrac{\$71.49}{\$95.66}}$

[18] The complex problem of calculating the marginal cost and profit schedules can be reduced to a simple two-variable equation: MEMS = 1 − square root of the ratio k/p. See Appendix A for the proof.

CHAPTER 2

Y'ALL BUCKLE THAT SEAT BELT

On Friday, June 18, 1971, *Southwest Airlines* put its first scheduled flight in the air between Houston and Dallas, Texas:

> *'Y'all buckle that seat belt,' said the hostess over the public address system, 'because we're fixin' to take off right now. Soon as we get up in the air, we want you to kick off your shoes, loosen your tie, an' let* Southwest *put a little love in your life on our way to Big D from Houston.' The passengers settled back comfortably in their seats as the brightly-colored* Boeing 737 *taxied toward the takeoff point at Dallas's Love Field airport.* (Lovelock 1982, 1)

In 1971, *Southwest* spent over half a million dollars on advertising in the Dallas/Houston markets, divided about equally between pre-operation launch and operating promotions.

The company's basic value proposition was low-fare, high-frequency, on-time flights that were fun. As if that weren't enough, *Southwest* also introduced the first frequent-flyer club in aviation history. Every sixteenth flight was free if your secretary was a member of the "Sweetheart Club."

In the first quarter of 1971, *Southwest Airlines* lost $1.831 million on revenues of $887 thousand. Despite this loss, it was clear that its major competitors, *Braniff International Airways* and *Texas International Airlines,* wanted to get *Southwest* out of the air any way they could. The competition used many different tactics. First, they tried court injunctions, but that didn't work.

Next, the competitors turned to predatory price cutting to get rid of the upstart. This tactic didn't work either. The president of *Southwest,* M. Lamar Muse, responded with a three-page leaflet that led with the headline "Nobody's going to shoot Southwest Airlines out of the sky for a lousy $13." (Lovelock 1975, 4) Lamar had to use a leaflet because the local newspapers considered his strongly worded headline unacceptable for publication. By late March 1973, the airline was nearly breaking even. As they say, the rest is history. But there's a new story about *Southwest* you may not have heard.

> *Still think of* Southwest Airlines *as a folksy company whose employees dress in golf shirts and tell jokes? Don't tell its competitors.* Southwest's *victory last week in the battle for some assets of a bankrupt rival,* ATA Airlines, *revealed an aggressive new stance at the airline. Already the largest low-fare airline in the United States,*

Southwest is on a path to becoming the industry's most influential company, something its traditional competitors might never have envisioned. (Maynard December 2004, 7)

Value-Sales Principles

Domestic airline companies are a good place to illustrate value-sales principles. This is true for three reasons. First, if you're reading this book you probably buy lots of airline tickets. So, you know airline companies as a customer. Second, the financial difficulties of many of the top airlines were front-page news in recent years, so you're familiar with the problems. Third, these principles will give you a perspective on the competition for customers and capital that you've never seen before. And the results will surprise you. As with every chapter in this book, we need to begin with some numbers.

Forbes.com is a good place to look up the numbers you need. It's easy to find sales revenues, stock price, and shares outstanding for any public company in a single keystroke. Take for example the "little airline that could"—*Southwest Airlines.* Go to a search engine and enter: *Forbes Southwest Airlines Co.* The search will return **Southwest Arlns Company Information-Forbes.com** Clicking on this link will take you directly to the *Southwest Airlines* page of *Forbes.com*.

You will find a lot of information about the company as you scroll down the *Southwest Airlines* page in *Forbes.com*. The first thing that appears is the exchange on which the company's common stock is traded (NYSE) and its ticker symbol (*LUV*). Next is the closing price of the company's stock. On June 7, 2005, the company's stock closed at $14.59 per share. On that date the following background statement appeared on the screen after news and press releases:

> Southwest Airlines Company *provides short-haul, high-frequency, point-to-point, low-fare air transportation services.* LUV's 375 *aircraft provide service between 58 cities in 30 states throughout the U.S. For the three months ended 3/31/05, revenues rose 12% to $1.66B. Net income totaled $76M, up from $26M. Revenues reflect an increase in revenue passenger miles and additional aircraft. Net income also reflects lower maintenance costs.* (Forbes.com 2005)

This paragraph is packed with information. It gives a capsule summary about three of *Southwest's* 4P marketing strategies. *Southwest's* product strategy remains to this day "short-haul, high-frequency, point-to-point" air transportation provided on *Boeing 737* aircraft. Its *pricing* strategy is still "low-fare." Its *place* strategy is to serve "58 cities in 30 states throughout the U.S."

In 1970, the company bought three *Boeing 737* aircraft and had to sell one of them to turn a profit. In 1971, it served only three cities in one state—Texas. On June 18, 2004, the 3third birthday of *Southwest Airlines,* 98 select employees took delivery of the company's 400th *Boeing 737-700* in Seattle and flew it to Dallas for a birthday party. *LUV* now serves sixty airports with 417 aircraft (*Southwest.com* 2004).

At a time when the headlines were filled with air carriers facing bankruptcy and other forms of dire straights, *Southwest Airlines'* quarterly "revenues rose 12% to $1.66B." In the same period, *LUV's* "net income totaled $76M, up from $26M." An ambitious hedging program insulated the company from rising fuel costs.

Immediately following the background statement, some key financial market numbers appeared on the *Southwest* page. The company had 784.75 million shares of common stock outstanding. Its market cap was $11,449.5 million USD ($14.59 per share multiplied by 784.75 million shares outstanding).

Who Competes with *LUV*?

The next step in developing the links between market value and sales revenue is to identify *Southwest's* top domestic competitors. Here again *Forbes.com* is a valuable resource. Scrolling up to the top of the page and clicking on **Industry: Airline** (located just below the company name) brings up a new page. The table that appeared on this screen in June 2005 listed the thirty-six airline competitors considered at that time by *Forbes.com* editors to be in the "airline transportation industry."[1]

From that list the following ten domestic air carriers were selected for this example:

> AMR Corporation; Delta Air Lines, Inc.; Continental Airlines, Inc; Frontier Airlines, Inc.; JetBlue Airways Corporati; Mesa Air Group, Inc.; Northwest Airlines Corpor; Southwest Airlines Co.; UAL Corporation; US Airways Group, Inc.

Left-clicking on the links in *Forbes.com* for each of these competitors brought up a page in the same format as the *Southwest* example discussed above. These links offered the basic numbers necessary to complete this example in the same format as *Southwest Airlines*.

The Back of an Envelope

To get a first-hand look at how companies compete for customers and capital in the airline market, complete the following exercise for the last day of trading in the ten airline stocks listed above. Begin by making a twelve-row by nine-column table, like the one shown in Table 2-1. Write the company names in row one in alphabetical order. (If you don't have a sheet of paper handy, just use the back of an envelope.)

Table 2-1 Share of Value and Share of Sales Revenue

1 Company	2 Price Close 7/3/03	3 Common Shares* (Millions)	4 Market Value (Millions)	5 Sales Revenue (Millions)	6 Share of Value (Percent)	7 Share of Revenue (Percent)	8 Ticker Symbol	9 Close of Fiscal Year
American	$10.13	156.4	$1,584	$4,120	7.21	22.53	AMR	12
Continental	$14.20	65.74	$934	$2,042	4.25	11.17	CAL	12
Delta	$14.05	123.36	$1,733	$3,155	7.88	17.25	DAL	12
Frontier	$9.80	35.23	$345	$172	1.57	0.94	FRNT	3
Jet Blue	$42.76	63.89	$2,732	$217	12.43	1.19	JBLU	12
Mesa	$9.05	31.59	$286	$137	1.3	0.75	MESA	9
Northwest	$10.89	85.83	$935	$2,375	4.25	12.99	NWAC	12
Southwest	$17.14	778.9	$13,350	$1,351	60.73	7.39	LUV	12
United	$0.83	99.51	$83	$3,184	0.38	17.41	UAL	12
USAir	$0.08	25.65	$2	$1,534	0.01	8.39	USA	12
Totals		*Q1–2003	$21,984	$18,287	100	100		

33

Enter the closing price per common share and the number of shares outstanding in columns two and three. Include the quarterly reporting period (e.g., Q1 2003) for the closing price per share at the bottom of column three.

Next, multiply price per share for each company times the number of common shares outstanding and enter the result in column four. Label this column *Market Value*. The result should be approximately the same as that reported in *Forbes.com* on the company's page as "Market Cap" for that quarter. If there are differences, they are probably due to the number of shares outstanding used to calculate the reported market capitalization.

Now enter sales revenue for the most recent quarter in column five. Make a note in the table heading that the number of shares, market value, and sales revenue are in millions.

Note that market value and sales revenues are created in separate markets. Revenues (column five of Table 2-1) are generated in **product** markets. Market value (column four) is created in **stock** markets. These measures also have very different properties. Sales revenue is a flow variable. You can sum revenues and other flow variables over time and get a meaningful result. Capitalization is a stock variable. You cannot sum market cap or any other stock variable over time and get a meaningful number. However, both flow and stock variables can be summed meaningfully over companies in the same time period.

Share of Value and Share of Revenue

Add up the **market values** for all ten companies. Enter the total in the last row of column four of your table. Now calculate *company share of market value*. Divide the **market value** of each airline by the total for all ten airlines and multiply by 100. Enter the results in column six. Repeat these calculations for **company sales revenue**. Enter the results in column seven. Finally, enter the company's ticker symbol and fiscal year-end month in columns eight and nine.

Your table should look like Table 2-1. The results will, of course, differ from the ones below depending on what happened to each company between July 3, 2003, and the date on which you ran these numbers.

Now we can get quickly to the heart of this example and the first link in the marketing-finance chain of competing for customers and capital.

Is *LUV* the Market Share Leader?

Starting with *American Airlines,* compare its Share of Value (**SOV**—column six) with its Share of Revenue (**SOR**—column seven) in Table 2-1. The first thing you will notice is that *American* created only 7.21% of the value in this industry, while generating 22.53% of the sales revenue. Next, notice that *JetBlue* created 12.43% of the value on just 1.19% of the sales. Both of these results are surprising and worth looking into.

American was the share of revenue leader in this group. *AMR,* the holding company for *American Airlines,* installed the first computerized airline reservations systems (*SABRE*) in 1964.[2] *JetBlue,* on the other hand, is a newcomer in the group. It began service between New York's JFK and Ft. Lauderdale on February 11, 2000.

An even bigger surprise is that *Southwest Airlines* created a 60.73% share of the total value in this group—$13.350 billion out of $21.984 billion— while it generated only a 7.39% share of group sales— $1.351 billion out of $18.287 billion. Is *LUV* the market share leader? It depends on whether you use the company's share of value in capital markets or its share of revenues in customer markets.

Finally, compare the results in your table with those in Table 2-1. Are there any surprising differences?

More Bang per Buck

A quick division will reveal that *LUV* created 8.2 value points for every revenue point in the first quarter of 2003. This was not just a fluke. It's a trend that developed over many years.

Southwest's share of value and share of sales from the secondsecond quarter ending in June, 1994 through the secondsecond quarter of 2001 are shown in Chart 2-1. The left-hand scale in this chart is *LUV's* share of value in capital markets (the white circles). This scale ranges from zero to sixty value share points.

The company's share of value (the black circles) grew from 27.6% in June, 1994 to 49.1% in June, 2001. Remember that the secondsecond quarter ending in June, 2001 was on the books two months **before** the 9/11 attacks on the World Trade Center and the Pentagon.

The right-hand scale in Chart 2-1 is *LUV's* share of sales revenues in customer markets (the black circles) over the same period. The range in this scale is different than the left-hand side of the chart. It ranges from zero to nine revenue share points. The company's share of revenues (**SOR**) grew from 4.8% in June, 1994, to 7.8% in June, 2001. By now you might be asking yourself: How did *LUV* management do that?

The growth in share of revenues was fairly steady over the 29 quarters. But the company's **SOV** dropped by nearly half from June, 1994 through June, 1998. Then it took off suddenly, rising from 15% in June, 1998 to 49% by June, 2001.

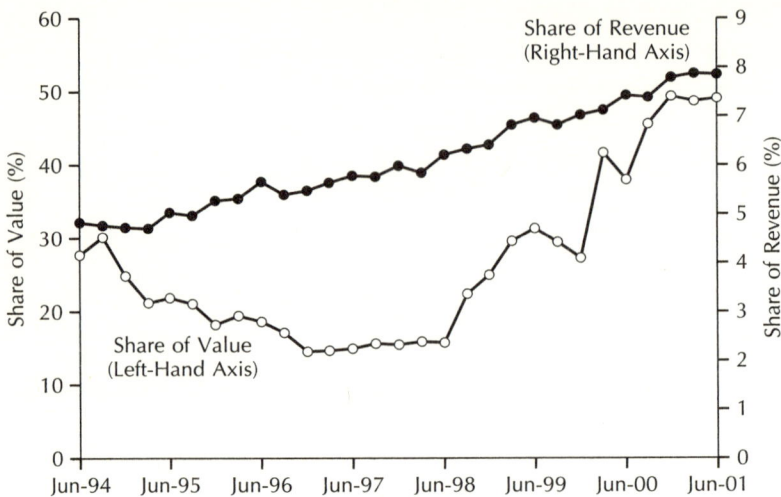

Chart 2-1 *Southwest's* Share of Value and Share of Revenue

Why did investors wait until the third quarter of 1998 to see what was going on? *Southwest* didn't change its strategy during this seven-year period. The company just went right on flying its "short-haul, high-frequency, point-to-point, low-fare air transportation service with *737 aircraft*" in more and more markets.

The Value-Sales Differential

An even more revealing number can be calculated from the market share data back in Table 2-1. That number is the difference between *Southwest's* share of value and its share of revenue (**SOV-SOR**). The company's value-sales differentials (**VSD**) from June, 1994 through June, 2001 in Chart 2-2 appear as the gap between its share of value (on the left-hand axis) and its share of revenue (on the right-hand axis).

For example, *Southwest's* value share in the second quarter ending June 2000 was $+30.5$ *points greater than its share of sales* $(+37.9 - 7.5 = +30.5)$. This *value-sales differential* gives new meaning to the term "more bang per buck." It also establishes another link between marketing and finance. *LUV* was rewarded by investors with a value share premium in every period.

Returning to Table 2-1, it is important to notice that only two other airlines in this strategic group had a positive *value-sales differential* in July, 2003. *JetBlue's* share of market value (12.5%) was $+11.3$ points greater than its share of sales revenues (1.2%). *Mesa's* value share was 0.6% greater than its revenue share. *United Airlines* took the prize for the smallest value share

Chapter 2 • Y'all Buckle That Seat Belt

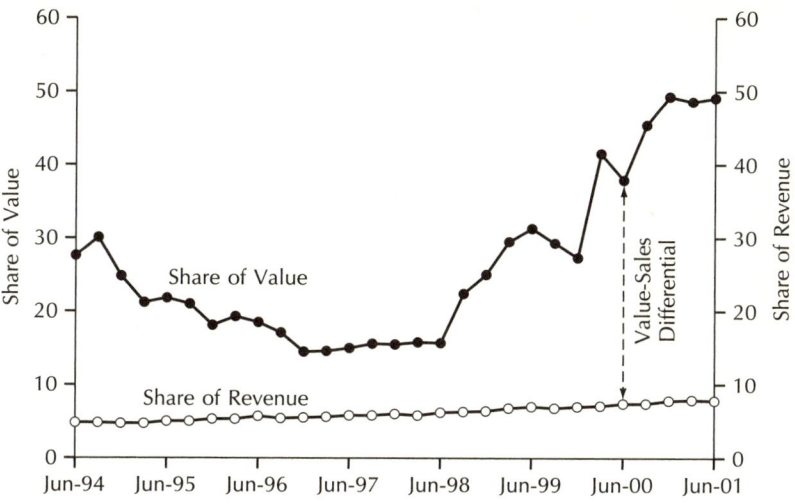

Chart 2-2 *LUV's* Value-Sales Differentials

(0.4%) compared with revenue share (17.7%). The *value-sales differential* of *UAL* was negative, at −17.3 points.

Finally, notice in Table 2-1 that the correlation between value share and revenue share appears to be very low. If you run the numbers in *Excel,* you'll find it's actually −0.1. How can these surprising facts be explained? We will explore this question in more depth later.

Will the Winner Please Stand Up?

You can identify the winners and the losers in a strategic group by their value-sales (**VSD**) differential. Take a look at Chart 2-3.

The vertical axis in this chart ranges between ±45 **VSD** points. The horizontal axis reports **VSD** for *Southwest Airlines (LUV)* and *United Airlines (UAL)* in every period from the second quarter ending in June, 1994 through the second quarter of 2001.

In all twenty-nine quarters shown in Chart 2-3, *Southwest's* **VSDs** (the triangles) were positive. In the first quarter ending in March, 1997, *Southwest's* differential was +9.0 points. It increased to over +41.5 points by the fourth quarter ending in June, 2001. In every quarter, *United's* **VSDs** (the diamonds) were negative. They ranged from a high of −2.4 points in June, 1994 to a low of −19.5 points in June, 2001.

What Does the Value-Sales Differential Mean?

You can think of the **VSD** in either one of two ways. One is technical the other is substantive.

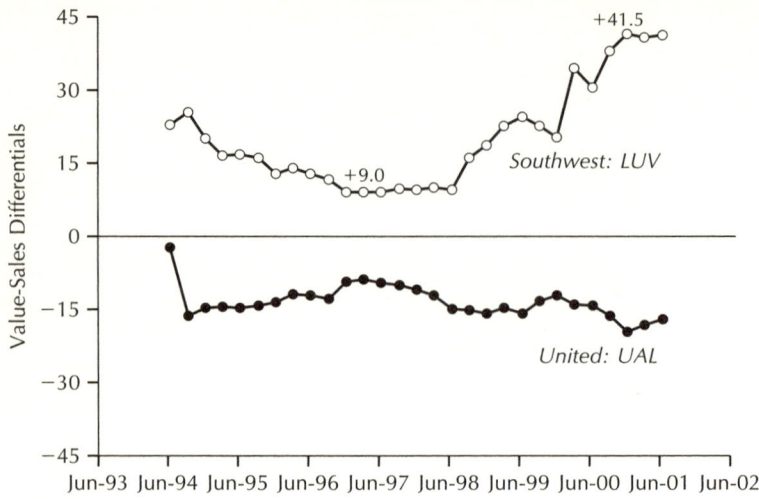

Chart 2-3 Value-Sales Differentials of *LUV* vs *UAL*

Technically, think of the value-sales differential (δ) as a new member of the class of metrics that financial managers call "Price/Earnings" ratios. The "Price/Revenue" ratio is another metric from this class. It is a close cousin of the VS differential.

The first financial ratio reported on *Southwest* in *Forbes.com* on July 3, 2003, was the company's price per share divided by its sales per share. This is the "Price/Revenue" ratio. On that date *LUV's* P/R (**T**railing **T**welve **M**onths) was 2.47.

The P/R ratio is very sensitive to the number of common shares outstanding. Look again at Table 2-1. The number of shares outstanding at the end of the first quarter 2003 ranged from a low of 25.65 million for *U.S. Airways* to a high of 776.9 million for *Southwest*. The financial custom of expressing price per share to revenue per share is appropriate for comparing stocks. If you're interested in tracking the effect of stock splits on price-to-revenue, the P/R metric is the one you want to look at.

Here's the critical distinction between the P/R ratio and the VS differential. The P/R ratio is a meaningful metric with regard to the company as a **stand-alone enterprise.** The VS differential is a meaningful metric with regard to the company as a **member of a peer group.**

You might be wondering why we use a value-sales **differential** rather than a value-sales **ratio.** We will actually use both. But the differential has several advantages. First, the value-sales differential is derived from the theory developed later in this chapter. Second, a differential is much better-behaved than a ratio. For example, the differential is bounded by upper and lower limits of

+100 and −100 points. The upper limit of a ratio is unbounded. Third, the expected value of a cross-section of value-sales differentials is exactly zero. These properties ensure that differentials are comparable across peer groups of any size. The substantive rationale behind the value-sales differential leads to a direct and powerful measure of the relative market value of a firm.

Tangible Value Intuition

Tangible assets can be cement shoes. To investigate tangible value in this airline group, let's look closely at *United Airlines*. The value-sales differential of *UAL Corp.* at the end of the first quarter 2003 was −17.3 points. Operating under Chapter 11 bankruptcy as UALAQ.OB, the company hasn't fared much better since then.

On December 31, 2003, the depreciated book value of its owned operating property and equipment was $12.9 billion. The depreciated value of its capital leases was $2.165 billion. These assets included 532 owned and leased aircraft with an average age of ten years. A total of 231 were medium- to large-capacity aircraft seating from 168 to 347 passengers. The company also owned a 93.5-acre property in Chicago with one million square feet of office space for its world headquarters. It had long-term leases on airport landing areas, gates, hanger sites, terminal buildings, and other facilities in most of the markets it served (U.S. Securities and Exchange Commission [SEC] 2004).

UAL Corp.'s asset base was built to deliver service through a "hub-and-spoke" business model.

> *The "hub-and-spoke" system, which funnels passengers from smaller cities to major ones, was embraced by most big airlines after deregulation. It may be on the endangered-species list, though, at least as the primary means or moving people around the country.* (Maynard July, 2004, 1)

Look back at Chart 2-3. Investors discounted *UAL's* market power in every period since the second quarter of 1994. That's when its value-sales differential turned sharply negative. The depth of that discount increased significantly beginning in the first quarter of 2001. By March 31, 2003 *UAL's* revenue share was 21.57%, but its share of market value was 0.44%. You can't fairly judge a company unless you compare its share of capital markets with its share of customer markets. These markets are separate but equally important is assessing competitive performance. That's a **VSD** of −21.1 points. By July, 2004 this old news was making front-page headlines in the business section of the *New York Times:*

> *Professor Michael E. Levine, a former airline executive who is now an adjunct professor of Law at Yale ... compared the traditional hub-and-spoke airline industry to an iceberg*

drifting toward the equator. 'Some of the carriers are higher up on the iceberg, and some of them are lower down,' he said. When the iceberg begins to melt as the environment changes, 'you can hope the ones down below drown before you do,' but eventually everyone will drown, he said. The Air Transportation Stabilization Board certainly turned up the heat last month, when for the third time in 18 months, it refused to guarantee loans for the industry's second biggest player, United Airlines. (Maynard July, 2004, 4)

The market value of *UAL's* assets was heavily discounted over the last ten years as evidenced by its large, continuously negative value-sales differentials. You simply cannot assess a company's performance without comparing its share in capital markets with its share in customer markets.

Intangible Value Intuition

Goodwill is both fickle and fleeting. Nelson describes this in his classic paper "The Momentum Theory of Goodwill:"

> Goodwill is about as fickle as the human nature of which it is an aspect. Some human habits are strong, but customer habit is usually not one of them. Reputations fade from memory unless the reputation is fed or replenished by new feats or reminders. Fickle or not, it is hard to build up, so the buyer of a concern will often pay a large sum of money for the goodwill. The reason is that he wants this starting "push" in his new enterprise. ...This "push" which the buyer receives for his investment in goodwill is not a continual, everlasting one, but rather is like momentum or a running start. He has to feed in new energy to keep from slowing to a standstill. (Nelson 1953, 492)

In order to understand this concept better, let's look at an example in the field of biotechnology. The common shares of the biotechnology firm, *Vasogen Inc. (VSGN)*, closed the fourth quarter of 2003 at $5.57. With 62,020 thousand shares outstanding, it had a market value of $345.5 million. A recent press report about the company stated:

> Vasogen *is a leader in the research and commercial development of immune modulation therapies targeting the chronic inflammation underlying cardiovascular disorders. Vasogen's lead product, Celacade™ is currently in phase III clinical trials for the treatment of chronic heart failure and peripheral arterial disease. Celacade™ is designed to target chronic inflammation by activating the immune system's physiological anti-inflammatory response to apoptotic cells. Celacade™ up-regulates the expression of cell surface molecules that interact with specific receptors on antigen presenting cells (APCs) to modulate the production of cytokines—potent chemical messengers that initiate and control inflammation.* (Prnewswire.com 2004)

You might think that *VSGN* is a highly profitable company in a growing peer group. Right? Wrong. In a group with four other potential competitors, *Vasogen Inc.* reported zero sales revenues in each of the five years from 1999 through 2003.

Table 2-2 Shares of Revenues in a Biotechnology Group

Company	1999	2000	2001	2002	2003
Vasogen Inc	0.0	0.0	0.0	0.0	0.0
Exegenics Inc	6.3	5.0	10.8	5.0	4.5
Sonus Pharmaceuticals	55.2	2.3	71.1	0.2	8.6
Alliance Pharmaceutical	37.8	91.8	15.1	91.6	18.3
Nymox Pharmaceutical	0.7	0.9	3.0	3.2	68.6
Peer Group Percent	100.0	100.0	100.0	100.0	100.0
Group Revenues ($US Mill)	$21.8	$17.4	$12.3	$11.3	$0.239

As shown in Table 2-2, sales leadership in this highly volatile peer group changed frequently. *Vasogen* was never one of the leaders! *Sonus Pharmaceuticals Inc.* captured 55.2% of $21.8 million in group sales in 1999, only to surrender the lead to *Alliance* in 2000, when group revenues fell to $17.4 million. By the end of 2003, *Nymox Corp* led with 68.6% of group sales.

Meanwhile, group sales declined to $12.3 million in 2001, fell to $11.3 million in 2002, and plummeted to just $239 thousand in 2003. Over the five years, revenues evaporated in this peer group.

Vasogen's successful IPO hadn't sold a nickel's worth of its patented product in five years. Furthermore, it hadn't yet received approval from the *Federal Drug Administration* to market *Celacade*. Nevertheless, its share of strategic group market value increased from 25.7% ($149.1 million) in 1999 to 70.0% at the end of 2003. At the close of business in the fourth quarter of 2004, the company's market cap was $367.76 million. *Vasogen Inc.* continued to have no sales revenue with an EBITDA of −$49.68 million. Since the company had no sales, its revenue share was zero. The company earned a significant intangible market value premium and continued to do so. In the company's last quarterly report on August 31, 2005 sales revenues were still zero!

In order to develop its treatment for peripheral arterial disease, the company spent $64.7 million on SG&A and $41.1 million on R&D expenses over the six years from 1998 through 2003. The company says this disease affects over seven million people in the United States, with related healthcare costs exceeding $10 billion annually. As a result, investors expect its lead product, *Celacade*, to generate a huge earnings stream over the remainder of the patent's life. *Vasogen* was a pure, intangible value play.

Formalizing the Intuition

To formalize our intuition, we've got to keep careful track of the variables. This means using subscripts and formal equations.

Over the last fifty years, financial analysis evolved from accounting to market-based measures of company performance. According to Megna and Klock (1993), the capitalized market value of company i in time period t (v_{it}) equals the sum of investors' expectations on the market value of a firm's tangible assets (v_{1it}) and its intangible assets (v_{2it}):

$$v_{it} = v_{1it} + v_{2it}$$

The replacement value of tangible assets like inventories, plant, property, and equipment can be used as an estimate of v_{1it}. In this way Tobin's q ratio can be estimated as:

$$q_{it} = v_{it}/v_{1it}$$

When the q ratio is greater than one, financial markets place a greater value on the firm than the replacement cost of its tangible assets. When the q ratio is less than one, the firm is valued at less than the replacement cost of its tangible assets.

The market value of intangible assets (v_{2it}) cannot be observed in the balance sheet. Villalogna (2004, 209) points out that *it can be estimated as the difference between a firm's market value and the replacement cost of its tangible assets*:

$$v_{2it} = v_{it} - v_{1it}$$

Sales revenues reflect the effects on customers' preferences of both tangible and intangible assets. The difference d_{it} between a company's market value v_{it} and sales revenue r_{it} captures the volume-weighted price premium (or discount) investors assign to firm i in period t:

$$d_{it} = v_{it} - r_{it}$$

We can easily expand this differential d_{it} to include many companies. The *multifirm differential* of company i in peer group j in time t including n firms becomes:

$$\delta_{ijt} = \left(v_{ijt} / \sum_{i=1}^{n} v_{ijt} \right) \times 100 - \left(r_{ijt} / \sum_{i=1}^{n} r_{ijt} \right) \times 100$$

This first term on the right-hand side of this formula is share of value:

$$\left(v_{ijt} / \sum_{i=1}^{n} v_{ijt} \right) \times 100$$

and the second term on the right-hand side is share of revenues:

$$\left(r_{ijt} / \sum_{i=1}^{n} r_{ijt} \right) \times 100$$

Make a note that each of these proportions are multiplied by 100 to create a whole-numbered index. This little transformation is important because it makes the results much easier to interpret.

Delta (δ_{ijt}) is thus an interval-scaled (whole number) index of a firm's tangible and intangible market value.

When:

- δ_{ijt} is zero, investors awarded neither a premium to nor a discount on the volume-weighted price of the firm's common stock, reflecting average expectations for its future product/stock market performance.
- δ_{ijt} is positive, investors added a premium to the company's volume-weighted price to reflect high expectations for its future product/stock market performance.
- δ_{ijt} is negative, investors discounted the company's volume-weighted price to reflect low expectations for its future product/stock market performance.

Is the Mean VSD Zero?

The answer to this question depends on how you take the average. If you look back at the VS differentials for each of the ten airlines in Table 2-1 you'll find the **VSDs** range from +53.4 for *Southwest* to a low of –17.3 for *United*. If you calculate the mean of these ten differentials you'll find it is zero.

The average VS differential across a sample of companies in the same time period has to be zero. That's because we're taking the difference between two percentages in sets that both sum to 100. No matter how large or small the differential is for any given company, the mean of the differences for a cross-section of companies will always be zero. This is a useful property.

Theoretically, the mean of VS differentials over time will tend toward zero. In the long run the differential will equal zero. Why? Negative VS differentials indicate that investor expectations for a firm's future performance are below its market power, while positive VS differentials must indicate that their expectations are above its market power. Since capital market expectations are derived from product market performance, theoretically the difference between the two will tend toward zero in the long run. It follows that in the long run (or in a large sample), the ratio of market value to sales revenue will move towards 1.0.

In arbitrarily short time intervals and for small samples, the mean VS differential can take on any value between +100 and −100. It also can vary a lot between periods. These possibilities suggest that company VS differentials can change dramatically from period to period. This happens to companies whose market value and/or sales revenues are highly volatile. VS differentials will vary less for companies whose market value and sales revenues are stable. Wide swings suggest the need for a "risk adjustment" to standardize differentials over time and among firms.

Adjusting for Enterprise Marketing Risk

Financial theory made famous the concept of a "risk-adjusted" rate of return (R) on a portfolio of securities.

> *The risk attached to a portfolio is to be measured by the standard deviation of* R, σ_R. *The standard deviation is a measure of the dispersion of possible returns around the mean value* μR. *A high standard deviation means, speaking roughly, high probability of large deviations from* μR, *both positive and negative. A low standard deviation means low probability of large deviations from* μR; *in the extreme case, a zero standard deviation would indicate certainty of receiving the return* μR. *Thus, a high-*σ_R *portfolio offers the investor the chance of large capital gains at the price of equivalent chances of large capital losses. A low-*σ_R *portfolio protects the investor from capital loss, and likewise gives him little prospect of unusual gains.* (Tobin 1958, 72)

The classic risk-adjusted rate of return in finance is calculated in two steps (Mastrapasqua and Bolten 1973). First, the risk-free rate of interest is subtracted from the returns on a given portfolio over time. Each of these returns then is divided by their standard deviation.

We adjust the VS differential for **enterprise marketing risk** with a simple variation on this theme. Dividing each differential by the standard deviation of a company's series of VS differentials creates risk-adjusted value (ρ):

$$\rho_{ijt} = \delta_{ijt}/\sigma(\delta_{ij})$$

The **r**isk-**a**djusted **d**ifferential will be referred to as Rho (or **RAD**) throughout this book.

Look again at *Southwest's* observed VS differentials in Chart 2-3. The unadjusted values ranged from a low of +9.0 in the first quarter of 1997 to a high of +41.5 in the fourth quarter of 2000. The standard deviation in *LUV's* unadjusted differentials over the twenty-nine quarters from June, 1994 through June, 2001 was 10.53. Dividing *LUV's* minimum unadjusted differential by the standard deviation in the series yields a risk-adjusted differential in the first quarter 1997 of +0.86 [+9.0/10.53]. Dividing the company's maximum unadjusted differential by the standard deviation in the series yields a risk-adjusted differential of +3.9 [+41.5/10.53]. When each of *LUV's* differentials is risk-adjusted in the same way, the mean of the series becomes +1.65 with a standard deviation of 1.00.

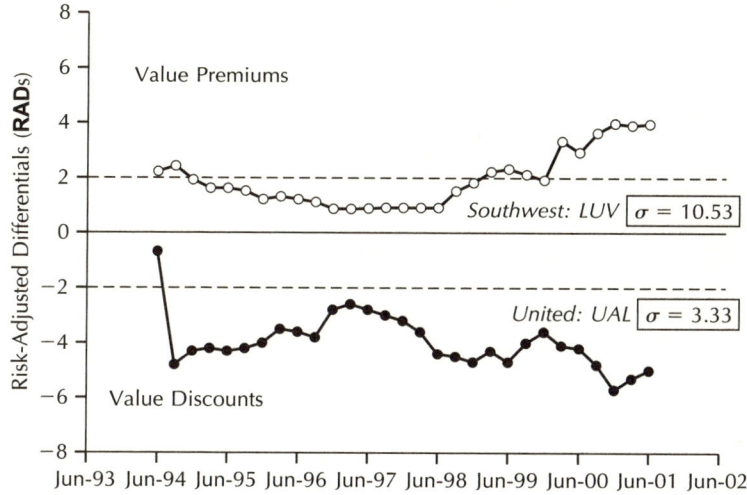

Chart 2-4 *LUV* and *UAL* Risk-Adjusted Differentials Q1'94–Q1'03

Another Useful Property

It's always true that the standard deviation in a series of company risk-adjusted differentials is exactly 1.0. This is another useful property of **RAD** because it means we can make direct comparisons between large and small companies in different peer groups. In addition, you will find this property makes it easy to place confidence intervals around stock price predictions in the competitive stock valuation model in Chapter 9.

Quarterly risk-adjusted differentials for *Southwest* and *United* for the thirty-six quarters from June, 1994 through March, 2003 appear in Chart 2-4.

Investors awarded *Southwest Airlines* a substantial value premium relative to its low product market power in every quarter over the entire period. At the same time investors heavily discounted *United Airline's* value relative to its strong product market power. Beginning with the second quarter of 1994, investors were signaling *UAL* management that the assets on its balance sheet dedicated to its "hub and spoke" business model had become *relatively* unproductive.

Interpreting Risk-Adjusted Differentials

The interpretation of risk-adjusted differentials is based on three factors: the size of the differential, its arithmetic sign, and enterprise marketing risk. A portfolio of these possible outcomes is summarized in Table 2-3.

The interpretation of marketing risk adjustment is somewhat different than that for financial risk. Value premiums are associated with two different

Table 2-3 Risk-Adjusted Differential Portfolio

Possible Outcomes	Low Risk ($\delta_{ij} < 6.6$)	High Risk ($\delta_{ij} > 6.6$)
Value Premiums ($\rho > +2.0$)	Stable Winners	Volatile Winners
Expected Values ($-2.0 \leq \rho \leq +2.0$)	Stable Expected Values	Volatile Expected Values
Value Discounts ($\rho < -2.0$)	Stable Losers	Volatile Losers

levels of enterprise marketing risk. In the case of the "Stable Winners," the standard deviation in the company's differentials is relatively small. "Small" is defined as less than 6.6, the standard deviation of VSDs in a sample of 337 companies over ten years. The closer a company's observed sigma is to zero, the lower its enterprise marketing risk.

In the case of "Volatile Winners" with a standard deviation greater than 6.6, the value premium comes at the expense of an equivalent chance of suffering a value discount. The larger the standard deviation, the greater the likelihood the value premium awarded to "Volatile Winners" will change in the future.

A low enterprise marketing risk implies that investors are more or less stuck with the value premium or discount observed historically. While *LUV* enjoyed a significant value premium in June of 2001, it's more likely to change in the future due to its greater volatility. Because of its relatively low risk the significant discounting of *UAL's* market value is far less likely to change without fundamental revisions in its business model.

Properties of RAD

The properties of the risk-adjusted differential were studied in a *Marketing Science Institute* report (Cook 2003). The *MSI* sample consisted of 337 companies in 29 strategic groups over the decade from 1991 through 2000. The mean of annual risk-adjusted differentials was nearly zero with a slight tilt to the left (−0.27). The standard deviation of RAD in the entire *MSI* sample was 2.38.[3]

The distribution is shown in Chart 2-5. The horizontal axis in this chart is risk-adjusted differentials. In the *MSI* sample, ρ ranged from −9.64 to +12.73. The vertical axis is the frequency of risk-adjusted differentials in the sample of 3,370 observations. The distribution appears to be nearly normal, but actually it deviates somewhat from normal in three ways.

First, the number of values at the center of the distribution (zero) is greater than normal (800 actual observations compared with just over

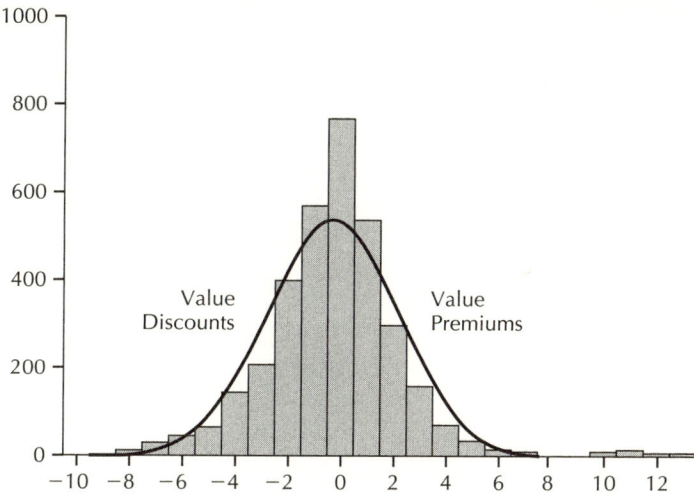

Chart 2-5 Distribution of Risk-Adjusted VS Differentials

500 observations in the theoretical *Gaussian* distribution). Second, the tails are thicker than the normal distribution. The right-hand tail extends to 12 and the left-hand tail extends to -10 standard deviations. Third, there is a negative tilt. This can be seen in the height of the negative compared with the positive bars for the same values of ρ.[4]

Even though the distribution of **RAD** departs from normal, it is approximately symmetrical with a mean near zero and a standard deviation just over two. Though high-peaked and thicker in the tails, the distribution remains relatively well-behaved statistically. These basic properties make it possible to sort companies in any strategic group into the three types of performers pictured in Chart 2-6: High-Flyers, Average-Joes, and Bottom-Feeders.

High-Flyers

High-Flyers are truly exceptional companies. Investors award such a company a value premium far in excess of its product market power. In Chapter 8, we investigate how these companies manage to pull off such unexpected premiums and whether or not they can be sustained.

- Do High-Flyers spend more (or less) on enterprise marketing assets?
- Are their gross margins bigger?
- Are they market share leaders?
- Do they have a different capital structure?
- Are their premiums a result of cost efficiencies?
- Are they more likely to maximize earnings?

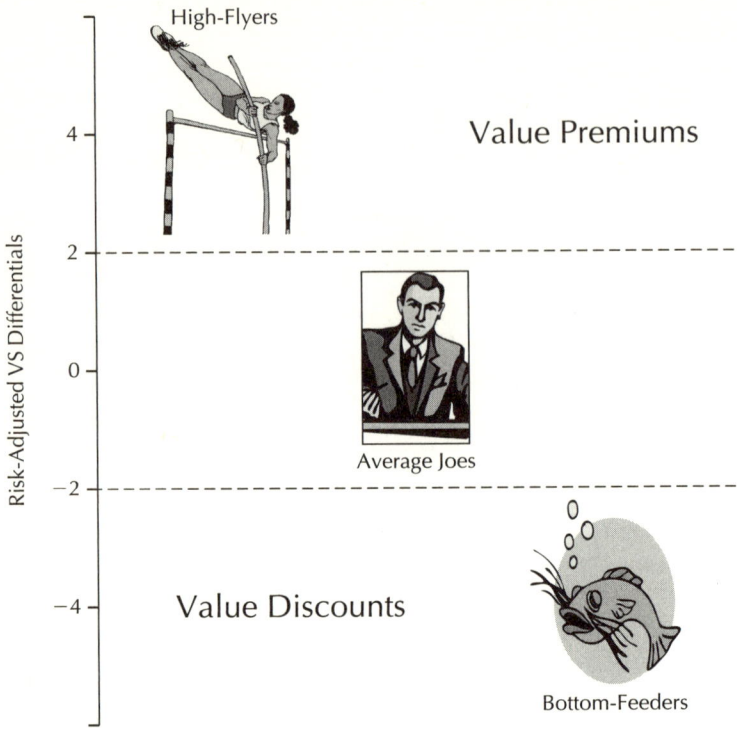

Chart 2-6 Types of Performers

Average Joes

Average Joes are companies with risk-adjusted differentials that bounce around between ±2.0 for long periods of time. These companies are doing just fine. They don't receive huge value premiums, but their market value isn't significantly discounted either. By definition, we expect most companies will be in this category. The trends in **RAD** over time within the ±2.0 range are, however, very important indicators of gains and losses in market value or sales.

Bottom-Feeders

A Bottom-Feeder is what you don't want your company to be. It means the risk-adjusted differential has been less than −2.0 for a long time. In other words, investors have punished the company with sustained and significant discounts in its market value. We also want to discover why these companies can't get off the bottom.

- Has the replacement value of their tangible assets declined?
- Is customer demand shifting from products to services?

- Has the product-service mix shifted due to acquisitions or mergers?
- Are they threatened by the development of a radical innovation?
- Has their business model become obsolete?

Burning the Candle at Both Ends?

Chart 2-7 summarizes risk-adjusted differentials for airlines in a candlestick chart. This chart packs the information from June, 1994 through March, 2003 for all eight airlines into a compact space. The values of **RAD** appear on the vertical axis, ranging between ±6. The body of each "candlestick" defines the opening and closing values of **RAD**. The "wicks" above and below each candlestick point to the company's highest and lowest **RAD**. If the opening (or closing) values were the same as the highest (or lowest) values, the candle is "wickless" on one (or both) ends.

Companies that experienced an increase in **RAD** during the period are shown as white candlesticks, whereas those that experienced a decline appear as gray candlesticks. The opening (second quarter of 1994) and closing (first quarter of 2003) values of risk-adjusted differentials mark the top and bottom of each white candlestick and the bottom and top of each

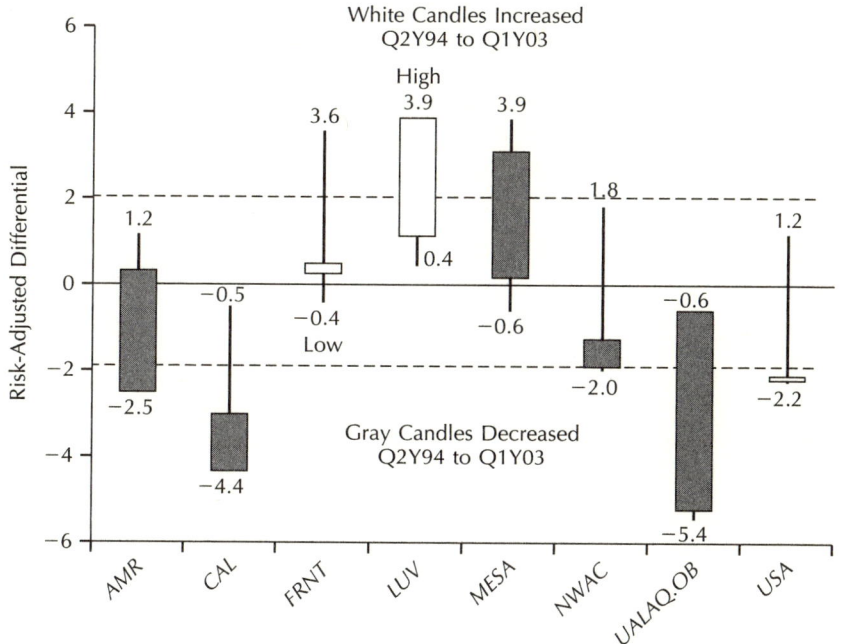

Chart 2-7 RAD Candlestick Chart for Domestic Airlines 1994–2003

striped candlestick, respectively. Finally, the eight companies are arranged in alphabetical order by their ticker symbols across the horizontal axis.

For example, *AMR* opened the second quarter of 1994 with a **RAD** of +0.3. The company's closing differential in the first quarter of 2003 was also its lowest (**RAD** = −2.5). *AMR's* highest **RAD** was +1.2. Alternatively, *LUV's* closing **RAD** in the first quarter of 2003 was also its highest (+3.9). The company's lowest **RAD** (+0.4) occurred in March, 1997. *UAL's* opening value of **RAD** was also its highest (−0.6) and occurred in the second quarter of 1994. *UAL* closed at −5.2, which was also its lowest **RAD**. The company maintained a relatively low enterprise marketing risk of 4.0. *MESA* was burning the candle at both ends. It opened with a **RAD** of +3.10 and closed at +0.15, reaching a maximum of +3.85 in the fourth quarter of 1994 and a minimum of −0.61 in the fourth quarter of 1997.

The Bottom Line

Product and stock markets interact in complex and often subtle ways. The value-sales principles developed in this chapter reveal much of that interaction. Risk-adjusted differentials are one of the two variables drive the competitive stock valuation model developed in Chapter 9.

References

Cook, V. J. Jr. 2003. "Marketing's Impact on Firm Value: The Value-Sales Differential." *Marketing Science Institute Reports* 03 (2): 55–78.

Forbes.com. 2005. "Company Details: Southwest Airlines Co." [Online information; retrieved 6/7/2005]: http://www.forbes.com/finance/mktguideapps/compinfo/CompanyTearsheet.jhtml?tkr=luv

Lovelock, Christopher H. 1975. "Southwest Airlines (B)." Harvard Business School Publishing 9-575-061: 1–7.

Lovelock, Christopher H. 1982. "Southwest Airlines (C)." Harvard Business School Publishing 575-118 (May): 1–18.

Mandlebrot, B., and R. L. Hudson. 2004. *The (Mis)Behavior of Markets*. New York: Basic Books.

Maynard, M. "Get Out the Glue for a New Business Model." *New York Times*, July 11, 2004.

———. "From Aw-Shucks to Cutthroat: Southwest's Ascent." *New York Times*, December 26, 2004, Section 3, 7.

Mastrapasqua, F., and S. Bolten. 1973. "A Note on Financial Analyst Evaluation." *The Journal of Finance* 28 (June): 707–12.

Megna, P., and M. Klock. 1993. "The Impact of Intangible Capital on Tobin's q in the Semiconductor Industry." *The American Economic Review* 83 (May): 265–269.

Nelson, R. H. 1953. "The Momentum Theory of Goodwill." *The Accounting Review* 28 (October): 491–499.

Prnewswire.com. 2004. "Vasogen's Phase II Heart Failure Results Accepted for Publication in the Journal of the American College of Cardiology." [Online article; retrieved 6/22/04]: http:// www.prnewswire.com

Southwest.com. 2005. "Southwest Airlines: History." [Online information; retrieved 8/1/05]: http://www.southwest.com/swa_people/040708_swa_people.html

Tobin, J. 1958. "Liquidity Preferences as Behavior Toward Risk." *The Review of Economic Studies* 25 (2): 65–86.

U.S. Securities and Exchange Commission. 2004. "UAL Corp. 10-K filing for December 31, 2003." [Online information; retrieved 9/1/04]: http://www.sec.gov/edgar.shtml

Villalogna, B. 2004. "Intangible Resources, Tobin's q, and Sustainability of Performance Differences." *Journal of Economic Behavior & Organization* 54 (June): 205–230.

End Notes

[1] Industry definitions are fluid and frequently updated by financial reporting services. Fort example, by early 2006, *Forbes* editors had redefined as "Regional Airlines" the industry in which they believed *Southwest* competed.

[2] SABRE was developed jointly by *American Airlines* and *IBM* in a project that began with a conversation on a flight in 1953.

[3] The mean VSD for a cross-section of companies in the same peer group is always zero, and the standard deviation (enterprise marketing risk) in the VSD series of a single company is always 1.0. But these properties do not hold for a pooled sample of companies in different peer groups.

[4] These departures from normality can have significant implications in defining not only strategic groups, but pricing stocks as well. (See Mandlebrot and Hudson 2004.)

CHAPTER 3

WHO'S IN *My* STRATEGIC GROUP?

I have a friend who manages a $250 million portfolio for a small group of private investors. Sam is among the most successful managers in the business. On June 8, 2005, I called to ask him what stock he was trading:

He said: "*The Home Depot.*"
I asked: "What was the closing price?"
"Thirty-nine sixty-seven."
"How many shares were traded?"
"About seven million."
"What was the low for the year?"
"Thirty two bucks."
"What's the company's P/E ratio trailing twelve months?"
"Sixteen ninety-two."
Then I asked: "Who are *Home Depot's* top three competitors?"
Sam said, "*Lowe's.*"
"Who's number two?"
"Just a minute while I look that up."
A long silence, except for keyboard clicks.
"I'm not sure who that is. What do you think?"

Sometimes even the most astute financial managers forget that performance is relative. Unfortunately, identifying competitors is not as easy as the airline "peer group" example in the last chapter suggests.

The answer to the question, "Who's in my strategic group?" depends on a lot of factors. One of those factors is *when* you ask the question.

The Shifting Competitive Landscape

Take the now-classic case of the leading new and old media companies. The merger of *America Online* and *Time Warner* was announced in early January, 2000. Management intended to redefine the boundaries of two different markets: *Internet service providers* and *home entertainment*. The basic idea was that the leading Internet service provider (*AOL*) would be the delivery vehicle for the leader in home entertainment products (*Time Warner*). Infamously, it didn't work. The merger was described as:

> ... *The world's first bioengineered mega-business—the corporate equivalent of a **geep** or **zorse**, an unnatural hybrid genetically engineered to sustain itself on a force-fed diet of synergy. Except the experiment hasn't gone as its progenitors predicted. Consider: Since the merger was announced on Jan. 10, 2000, the company's value has decreased by a mind-blowing $160 billion. Last month,* AOL Time Warner *took a $54 billion quarterly write-down—the biggest quarterly loss in U.S. history. To put that in perspective, the entire U.S. newspaper industry is **worth $55 billion**.* (Lasica 2002)

When the dust had settled, *Time Warner* management declared that the merger did not redefine the boundaries between these two markets.

> *Trapped in a troubled marriage, AOL Time Warner decided yesterday to return to its maiden name, dropping its first three letters. The company will now be called Time Warner, an attempt to erase a big reminder of the excesses of the Internet era, America Online's acquisition of Time Warner for shares priced at the peak of the boom.* (Sorkin and Kirkpatrick 2003)

Not only did management drop *"AOL"* from its name, it also changed its logo, the name of its new headquarters building, and *even its ticker symbol*. As the company's chairman and CEO said, these actions were taken for two reasons:

- The new (old) name *Time Warner Inc.* "better reflects" the company's portfolio of valuable businesses.
- Dropping *AOL* from the name and adding the new ticker symbol *TWX* will end "any confusion" among investors, partners, and the public between the corporate name and the *AOL* brand name.

In short, management boldly reaffirmed the company's old media positioning in its competition for customers and capital.

Which companies are the main competitors of the new *Time Warner*? A quick take on the answer is to enter *"Forbes Time Warner Inc"* in a search engine. On the day of the announcement that *AOL Time Warner* was no longer, *Forbes* editors had already assigned *TWX* to the *Computer Services industry* in the *Technology sector*. The list included 314 companies.

Which of these 314 companies would Richard D. Parsons say were competitors of the new *Time Warner Inc.* on the day *after* he made the announcement?

1. The online auto store *Autobytel, Inc (ticker symbol ABT)*;
2. Internet service providers *Earthlink (ELNK)* and *Navatech (NAVH)*;

3. The online wall street magazine *TheStreet.com (TSCM)*;
4. The information systems company *Unisys Corporation (UIS)*;
5. The search engine *Yahoo! Inc. (YHOO)*;
6. None of the above.

It's clear from the *Time Warner* case that the answer depends partly on when you ask the question. Mergers, acquisitions, divestitures, IPOs, and bankruptcies are major events that can reshape the competitive landscape overnight.

If you had entered *"Forbes Time Warner Inc"* in a search engine on June 26, 2004, just nine months after the announcement that *AOL* was no longer in the corporate name, the results would have been remarkably different. By then *Forbes* editors had moved the company to the *Broadcasting and Cable TV Industry* in the *Services Sector* of the economy. In this new industry, a sampling of competitors included:

1. *Adelphia Communications (ADELQ)*,
2. *British Sky Broadcasting Group (BSY)*,
3. *Cox Communications (COX)*,
4. *Fox Entertainment Group (FOX)*,
5. *Viacom (VIA)*, and
6. *Walt Disney (DIS)*.

Why are magazine publishers missing from this list? A single industry definition alone cannot capture the complex network of companies in a strategic group. Defining strategic groups requires a multidimensional perspective based on serving common customer needs and having access to equivalent resources. Only firms that have (or might acquire) a high degree of *market commonality* and *resource equivalence* should be considered direct competitors. (Bergen and Peteraf 2002)

Different Views of Competition

Financial managers and marketing managers often have entirely different competitors in mind. CFOs may think first of companies with which they compete for capital. Since capital markets are global, the CEO of *AT&T* may have included *France Telecom* in the list of competitors even though the French monopoly had few North American customers. *AT&T* and *France Telecom* only compete for capital today. Maybe they'll compete for customers tomorrow. Not likely now, since early in 2005 *AT&T* was no longer around.[1]

On the other hand, product markets tend to be bounded by geography and end use. The president of *AT&T's North American Business Services (NABS)* might have listed *WorldCom, Sprint, BellSouth,* and *Qwest* as top competitors. These companies share a large number of customers, but the *NABS* division is not a public company. It's not traded on any stock exchange so we can't assess the effectiveness of the *NABS* division in its competition for customers and capital. Perhaps in the future we can.

In either of these cases, the companies that managers think are their competitors will change from year-to-year, if not from quarter-to-quarter. Strategic groups are inherently dynamic collections of companies that compete simultaneously for customers and capital. The boundaries of a strategic group are fluid. As a footnote to example, *SBC* announced in January, 2005 it will acquire *AT&T,* its former parent, for $16 billion.

A trade-off between capital market equivalence and product market commonality is involved in the definition of any strategic group. In the broadest sense, every firm is in competition with all other firms in its search for capital; however, a limit is imposed by the requirement for some level of current (or anticipated) product market commonality. Otherwise, we lose an important dimension of the competitive effects (shared customers) embedded in a strategic group.

In the narrowest sense, there exist few pure competitors for a firm's customers since its products or services are to some extent unique. Even ignoring that brands are unique, it's impossible to match competing companies precisely on product characteristics, except for frequently purchased consumer products sold in a precisely defined local market segment.

Grocery stores in the same trading area with a similar mix of products and services compete for the same customers. However, such a narrow focus makes it impossible to conduct an analysis of the competition for customers and capital. Like *AT&T's NABS*, you can't measure the market value of a local supermarket because it's not traded on a stock exchange. As we will see in Chapter 4, such a restrictive definition of the grocery chain strategic group would exclude *Whole Foods Markets Inc.* as a competitor of *Kroger.* This omission would hide useful information from investors.

The goal is to achieve a balance between the *market commonality* and *resource equivalence* of members assigned to a strategic group. You want a definition that currently is meaningful both to financial and marketing management. In addition, you need a definition that will be meaningful in the future. Ask yourself: which companies fill this bill? If you don't have enough industry knowledge, educate yourself.

We've already looked at ways to identify competitors from free online resources; however, notice that each of these depended on our knowledge of the industry in which the firms compete.

We have lots of personal experience with airline companies, and the services provided by airlines for domestic travel are more or less equivalent. Given a fast Internet connection, the task is easy. The job of defining a strategic group is much more difficult for outsiders with no industry experience.

Unless you've bought its products, owned its stock, or worked for a company in a particular industry, you may have little knowledge of who the players are and which ones belong in a strategic group. A lack of knowledge is especially obvious in pure industrial plays and in very new technologies. Next, we consider in turn the cases of a pure industrial and new technology play in order to see how you can identify the companies with a high degree of market commonality and resource equivalence.

A Pure Industrial Play

Can you list *DuPont's* top ten competitors? Unless you work for one of the divisions of this diversified chemical manufacturer, chances are you can think of only one—*Dow Chemical.*

To identify other competitors in the chemical industry, let's use another free online data resource. Go to http://www.Yahoo.com, click the *Finance* button, select *Symbol Lookup,* and enter *DuPont.* In 2003, *Yahoo.com* returned the ticker symbol *DD* for *E. I. DuPont de Nemours & Co.* and identified the industry as *Chemicals-Plastics & Rubber.*

If you clicked on the company's ticker symbol *DD, Yahoo* would have taken you to the *DuPont* page. If you then clicked on the "Competitors" button in the left-hand navigation bar, on Thursday, July 3, 2003, the data in Table 3-1 would have appeared on the screen in *Yahoo.com.* When you compare Table 3-1 with the current version of *Yahoo Finance,* you'll notice that both the top companies and their market caps have changed.

The list of top competitors changed because, in the interim, *Yahoo's* financial page editors divided the chemical industry into two sub-industries: *Basic Manufacturing* and *Chemicals-Plastic & Rubber.* Every company on the 2003 list, except *DuPont* and *Dow,* were moved into the *basic manufacturing* sub-industry. We'll return to the question of *Yahoo's* shifting industry definitions later. The list in Table 3-1 contains "diversified chemical" manufacturers.

Take a close look at Table 3-1. First, some of the company names may surprise you. For example, you've probably never heard of *Akzo Nobel N.V.*

Table 3-1   Yahoo's Top Ten Chemical Manufacturers July, 2003

#	Ticker	Company	Mkt Cap	P/E	% Change	Volume
1.	MMM	3M Company	50.2B	25.2	−1.12	547,000
2.	DD	E. I. du Pont de Nemours and Company	41.4B	21.7	−1.54	796,300
3.	DOW	The Dow Chemical Company	28.0B	N/A	−1.67	1,006,500
4.	BF	BASF Aktiengesellschaft	24.4B	15.2	−0.70	20,700
5.	BAY	Bayer AG	16.5B	9.0	−1.31	62,300
6.	AKZOY	Akzo Nobel N.V.	14.7B	17.7	−1.42	23,863
7.	PX	Praxair, Inc.	9.8B	17.9	−0.54	212,000
8.	APD	Air Products and Chemicals, Inc.	9.5B	17.6	−0.36	306,900
9.	PPG	PPG Industries, Inc.	8.4B	N/A	−1.26	271,500
10.	SSL	Sasol Limited	6.9B	5.7	−0.44	220,400

Does this company have anything to do with the *Nobel Prize?* And what is *Bayer AG* doing here in a list of diversified chemical companies? Isn't *Bayer* just a brand of aspirin? You can bet the CEO of *DuPont* can list what he considers to be the top competitors without thinking twice. And his list may change even more often than the *Yahoo* list!

By the way, if you clicked the company *Profile* button in the left-hand navigation bar on the *DuPont* page in *Yahoo.com>finance,* you would have found that Charles O. Holliday, Jr. was the company's chairman and CEO. His salary in 2002 was $3.3 million. It dropped to $2.45 million in 2003 and increased to $3.5 million in 2004. Gary M. Pfeiffer was CFO and Senior VP. Mr. Pfeiffer made just over a million bucks in each of the years from 2002 to 2004. Richard Goodmanson was COO and executive VP. There was no chief marketing officer listed in this profile of the top five C level executives, even though *DuPont* is one of the world's most well-known brand names. Does this tell you something about where traditional marketing stands in *DuPont's* boardroom?

Table 3-2 Diversified Chemical Manufacturers

Ticker Symbol	Company	Market Value (Billions)	Sales Revenue (Billions)	Value Revenue Ratio	Value Share (Percent)	Sales Share (Percent)	VSD
DD	DuPont	$42.77	$24.52	1.74	34.6	19.3	15.3
DOW	Dow	$29.56	$27.61	1.07	23.9	21.7	2.2
BF	BASF	$25.01	$32.22	0.78	20.2	25.4	−5.1
BAY	Bayer	$13.44	$28.68	0.47	10.9	22.6	−11.7
AKZOY	Akzo Nobel	$12.75	$14.00	0.91	10.3	11.0	−0.7
3/3/2003	Group	$123.53	$127.03	0.97	100.0	100.0	0.0

Value/Revenue Ratios

Assume for the moment that Mr. Holliday was addressing a strategic question that led him to include the five companies listed in Table 3-2 as members of *DuPont's* strategic group in its competition for customers and capital. Company ticker symbols are listed in the first column, followed by the company name, market value, sales revenues, value/revenue ratio, value share, sales share, and value-sales differential on July, 3, 2005.

Notice how closely the total or composite market value of these five companies compares with total sales revenues: $123.5 to $127.0 billion. This is much like the relationship between total market value and combined sales revenues in the hypothetical strategic group in Chapter 1, which leads to an important measure of strategic performance—the value/revenue ratio. If this ratio is greater than one, it signals the strategic group (or industry) is creating a stock of shareholder value that is greater than the sales revenues it generates. Its value is greater than its turnover. If this ratio is less than one, the group's value is less than its turnover.

The value/revenue V/R ratio[2] for this strategic group on July 3, 2003, was 0.97. Each dollar of sales revenue was associated with only $0.97 in market value. Keep in mind that the value/revenue ratios vary significantly over time and among industries. The V/R ratio is a general measure of the health of strategic groups. It is also a measure of the performance of individual companies.

DuPont created $42.77 billion in shareholder value on sales revenues of $24.52 billion. Its v/r ratio was 1.74. On the other hand, *Bayer* generated $28.68 billion in sales revenues, but created $13.44 billion in shareholder value. Its ratio v/r was only 0.47. The company's relative performance is also captured in the value-sales differential in Table 3-2. *DuPont's* **VSD** was 15.3 while *Bayer's* was a negative 11.7. The v/r ratio and **VSD** are highly, but not perfectly, correlated. Both are useful measures with different properties.

How does *DuPont* get so much more bang per buck than *Bayer?* For openers, you can't look to the usual suspect—company market share of revenues. *Bayer's* share of sales revenue (22.58%) is 328 basis points greater than *DuPont's* (19.30%) revenue share. So, what does explain these differences? The answer to this complex question is explored in Chapter 8.

Limits of Free Online Services

How much has the performance of these top ten companies changed since July 3, 2003? Since *Yahoo Finance* added a download feature to its financial pages, you can recreate the same diversified chemical group by selecting and pasting companies from various revised sub-industry classifications. This is not a simple task because *Yahoo's* financial page editors made a number of other changes in the site's industry classifications over the years. For example, *BASF* was moved to the *basic materials* sub-industry and *Bayer* was moved to the *major drugs* industry. You would need to search out the data for each of the companies separately and paste them from one worksheet to another.

The free online financial services have their shortcomings when dealing with dynamic strategic groups over time. The easiest way to access a complete set of financial data that are consistent across years as well as quarters is to consult the *Wharton Research Data Services (WRDS)*[3] or *Standard & Poor's COMPUSTAT* data on which it is based.

Values Are More Volatile than Revenues

Table 3-3 presents a side-by-side comparison of the July 3, 2003, and June 25, 2004 *Yahoo.com* results for the five companies in the strategic group we assumed was defined by *DuPont's* CEO, Charles Holliday. If you look closely at the results in Table 3-3, you will see the importance of comparing each company's performance to the other members of its strategic group.

Table 3-3 Changes in the Diversified Chemical Group 7/3/03 to 6/25/04

Ticker	Market Value (Billions $US)		Sales Revenue (Billions $US)		Value Share (Percent)		Sales Share (Percent)	
	7/3/03	6/25/04	7/3/03	6/25/04	7/3/03	6/25/04	7/3/03	6/25/04
DD	$42.8	$43.8	$24.5	$28.8	34.6	28.7	19.3	18.7
DOW	$29.6	$37.8	$27.6	$33.9	23.9	24.8	21.7	22.0
BF	$25.0	$29.3	$32.2	$40.8	20.2	19.2	25.4	26.5
BAY	$13.4	$20.7	$28.7	$34.7	10.9	13.6	22.6	22.6
AKZOY	$12.7	$20.9	$14.0	$15.7	10.3	13.7	11.0	10.2
Group	$123.5	$152.4	$127.0	$153.7	100	100	100	100

In the upper left-hand columns of this table, you will find that *DuPont's* market value increased from $42.8 billion in July 3, 2003, to $43.8 billion in June 25, 2004, (about 2.3%). The company's sales revenues increased by 17.2% from $24.5 to $28.8 billion. As stand-alone numbers, these appear to be solid gains. Unfortunately, they pale by comparison with other companies in the group.

Table 3-4 Percent Changes

Ticker	Value % Change	Sales % Change
DD	2.3	17.6
DOW	27.7	22.8
BF	17.2	26.7
BAY	54.5	20.9
AKZOY	64.6	12.1
Group	23.4	21.0

If you were to run the percent changes in these market value numbers you'd find the results shown in Table 3-4.

Dow's market value increased by 27.7%; *BF increased* 17.2%, *BAY* increased 54.5%, and *AKZOY* by 64.6%. Three of its four competitors also outpaced *DuPont* with percentage gains in sales revenues. In addition, the company's value share declined 590 basis points and its sales share declined 60 basis points over the year while most of its competitors made gains in both measures. Notice too that market values of some companies are more volatile than sales revenues. You will see this frequently.

Risk-Adjusted Differentials

The raw numbers only tell part of the story about what happened to the market values of the companies in this strategic group. To see the rest of this story, you must look to each company's *risk-adjusted differentials*. To estimate enterprise marketing risk, you need multiple periods. This means you've got to get historical data.

The need for historical data would lead you to access to *Standard & Poor's COMPUSTAT* database online.[4] In order to align the *COMPUSTAT* data with the June/July dates in Table 3-3, ideally you would use ten or more annual reports ending in 2003 and 2004. At the time this chapter was written, the annual reports for 2003 were available for those companies whose fiscal year ended in 2003 and 2004. Calendar year 2004 reports were not yet

Table 3-5 Risk-Adjusted Differentials

Ticker	VSD 7/3/03	VSD 6/25/04	Enterprise Marketing Risk	RAD 7/03/03	RAD 6/25/04
DD	15.3	10.0	5.0	3.0	2.0
DOW	2.2	2.7	3.0	0.7	0.9
BF	−5.2	−7.3	1.5	−3.6	−5.0
BAY	−11.7	−9.0	4.4	−2.7	−2.0
AKZOY	−0.7	3.5	1.6	−0.4	2.3

available for all companies. Since enterprise marketing risk tends to be stable, we'll use estimates for each company based on the period 1993–2002. The results appear in Table 3-5. The value-sales differentials for each company appear in the second and third columns of Table 3-5.

DuPont opened in July, 2003 with a **VSD** of 15.3 points and closed at 10.0. Its ten-year enterprise marketing risk was 5.0, leading to a significant market value premium of +3.0 points in July, 2003. That premium dropped over the next twelve months, but remained significant at +2.0 in June, 2004.

For two companies in this strategic group, the market value relative to their market power was heavily discounted. The risk-adjusted discount in *BSAF's* market value opened at −3.6 and closed at −5.0 points. *Bayer's* discount remained between −2.7 and −2.0. Investors awarded *Dow* small premium market value in this period. AKZOY's risk-adjusted differential improved significantly over the year, from −0.4 to +2.3.

Global Industry Classification Standard

Over the twelve months, *Yahoo's* online classifications of these companies changed without explanation. Clearly some systematic rules for defining strategic groups would be helpful. The *Global Industry Classification Standard* (*GICS* pronounced like GĬCKS), combined with other data from financial statements, provides the information needed to define strategic groups based on *market commonality* and *resource equivalence*.

GICS is the most recent and comprehensive industry coding standard.[5]

> Our results show that GICS classifications are significantly better at explaining stock return co-movements, as well as cross-sectional variations in valuation multiples, forecasted and realized growth rates, research and development expenditures, and various key financial ratios. The GICS advantage is consistent from year to year and is most pronounced among large firms. (Bhojraj et al. 745)

At the highest level of aggregation, in 2003 *GICS* included ten economic **Sectors**. The sectors were numbered in groups of five digits from 10 for Energy through 55 for Utilities. Sectors were divided into twenty-four **Industry Groups**. In four cases—Energy, Materials, Telecommunication Services, and Utilities—the sector and the industry group had the same name.

In complex, multidimensional sectors like Consumer Discretionary products and services there are several industry groups. The Consumer Discretionary sector (25), for example, contained the five industry groups listed in Table 3-6.

Table 3-6 Industry Groups in the Consumer Discretionary Sector

Automobiles & Components	2510
Consumer Durables & Apparel	2520
Hotels, Restaurants & Leisure	2530
Media	2540
Retailing	2550

In 2003, there were a total of 63 **Industry** classifications and 139 **Sub-industries**:[6]

> *The GICS classifications aim to enhance the investment research and asset management process for financial professionals worldwide. It is the result of numerous discussions with asset owners, portfolio managers and investment analysts around the world and is designed to respond to the global financial community's need for an accurate, complete and standard industry definition.*

The *GICS* structure is:

Universal: The classification applies to companies globally.

Accurate: The structure accurately reflects the state of industries in the equity investment universe.

Flexible: The structure offers four levels of analysis, ranging from the most general sector to the most specialized sub-industry.

Evolving: Annual reviews are conducted by *MSCI* and *Standard & Poor's* to ensure that the structure remains fully representative of the equity investment universe.

By triangulating on the three industry classification systems reported in *Standard & Poor's COMPUSTAT* data, we can define a set of rules for measuring the *market commonality* of companies in an industry group.

Defining Strategic Groups in Volatile Markets

Let's illustrate the process of defining *market commonality* in an industry by tracing the **Information Technology sector (45)** through to a single strategic group. Table 3-7 shows that Information Technology contains three industry groups:

1. Software & Services (4510),
2. Technology Hardware & Equipment (4520), and
3. Semiconductors & Equipment (4530).

The Software & Services industry group includes three industry classifications. These are **Internet Software and Services (451010), IT Services (451020),** and **Software (451030).** The Internet Software and Services sub-industry is defined as those:

> *Companies developing and marketing internet software and/or providing internet services including online databases and interactive services, Web address registration services, database construction, and internet design services. Excludes companies classified in the Internet Retail sub-industry.* (http://www.msci.com/equity/gics.html; *GICS* Structure and Sub-Industry Definitions)

This sub-industry covers a lot of territory. Everything from "developing and marketing Internet software" to "database construction" to "Internet design services" is included.

As a general rule, *GICS* sub-industry definitions are sufficiently broad to cover all the companies that compete for capital. A considerable amount of hand-finishing work is required to sort out the ones that compete for customers as well.

Market Commonality

Internet Software and Services was the most volatile category in the last two years of the twentieth century and the first two years of the twenty-first century. As such, it's one of the most difficult industries in which to identify the members of a strategic group.

The first step is to identify the companies with a high degree of market commonality. To do this, you can "triangulate" on *common SIC, NAICS,* and *GICS* industry codes. Metaphorically it's a lot like triangulating on a radio signal. To find the location of a radio signal, you select three points that surround the origin of the signal and zero in on it. In order to identify the direct competitors in a strategic group, you surround their markets with three published industry classifications and zero in on the ones that match.

Table 3-7 GICS Sector, Industry Group, and Industry Definitions 2003

Sector		Industry Group		Industry
10	Energy	1010	Energy	
				101010 Energy Equipment & Services
				101020 Oil & Gas
15	Materials	1510	Materials	
				151010 Chemicals
				151020 Construction Materials
				151030 Containers & Packaging
				151040 Metals & Mining
				151050 Paper & Forest Products
20	Industrials	2010	Capital Goods	
				201010 Aerospace & Defense
				201020 Building Products
				201030 Construction & Engineering
				201040 Electrical Equipment
				201050 Industrial Conglomerates
				201060 Machinery
				201070 Trading Companies & Distributors
		2020	Commercial Services & Supplies	
				202010 Commercial Services & Supplies
		2030	Transportation	
				203010 Air Freight & Logistics
				203020 Airlines
				203030 Marine
				203040 Road & Rail Transportation
				203050 Infrastructure

25	Consumer Discretionary			
		2510	Automobiles & Components	
			251010	Auto Components
			251020	Automobiles
		2520	Consumer Durables & Apparel	
			251020	Automobiles
			252010	Household Durables
			252020	Leisure Equipment & Products
			252030	Textiles, Apparel & Luxury Goods
		2530	Hotels, Restaurants & Leisure	
			253010	Hotels, Restaurants & Leisure
		2540	Media	
			254010	Media
		2550	Retailing	
			255010	Distributors
			255020	Internet & Catalog Retail
			255030	Multiline Retail
			255040	Specialty Retail
30	Consumer Staples			
		3010	Food & Staples Retailing	
			301010	Food & Staples Retailing
		3020	Food, Beverage & Tobacco	
			302010	Beverages
			302020	Food Products
			302030	Tobacco
		3030	Household & Personal Products	
			303010	Household Products
			303020	Personal Products
35	**Health Care**			
		3510	Health Care Equipment & Services	
			351010	Health Care Equipment & Supplies
			351020	Health Care Providers & Services

(continued)

Table 3-7 (continued)

Sector		Industry Group		Industry
40 Financials	3520	**Pharmaceuticals & Biotech**	**352010**	**Biotechnology**
			352020	**Pharmaceuticals**
	4010	Banks	401010	Commercial Banks
			401020	Thrifts & Mortgage Finance
	4020	Diversified Financials	402010	Diversified Financial Services
			402020	Consumer Finance
			402030	Capital Markets
	4030	Insurance	403010	Insurance
	4040	Real Estate	404010	Real Estate
45 Information Technology	4510	**Software & Services**	**451010**	**Internet Software & Services**
			451020	**IT Services**
			451030	**Software**
	4520	Technology Hardware & Equip	452010	Communications Equipment
			452020	Computers & Peripherals
			452030	Electronic Equipment & Instruments
			452040	Office Electronics
	4530	**Semiconductors & Equipment**	453010	Semiconductors & Equipment
50 Telecomm Services	5010	Telecommunication Services	501010	Diversified Telecomm Services
			501020	Wireless Telecomm Services
55 Utilities	5510	Utilities	551010	Electric Utilities
			551020	Gas Utilities
			551030	Multi-Utilities & Unregulated Power
			551040	Water Utilities

If you were to set the clock back to the end of the second quarter of 1998, a total of 445 companies would have passed the *GICS* 45101010 screen in *Standard & Poor's Research Insight* software. This sub-industry contained many new companies with incomplete reporting. It was also riddled with start-ups that failed or were bought out—as well as with foreign companies listed as ADRs. In each case, the data for these companies were missing or dropped off the radar screen. The result is that only 61 companies reported all the data of interest in the second quarter of 1998. If you deleted all the penny stocks, you would end up with 49 companies (just over 10% of the original list).

But that's not all. At that time, a number of missing data codes (e.g., @CF => **C**ombined **F**igure; @NA => **N**ot **A**vailable; and @SF => **S**emiannual **F**igure) would have appeared for various quarters of the remaining companies. For this illustration, all the companies with one or more of these missing data codes were deleted, leaving twenty in the **Internet Software and Services** sub-industry. These companies are listed in Table 3-8. While all the companies in this table were in the same *GICS* sub-industry, they clearly were not in the same business. The first four numbered companies illustrate the need to triangulate on the three industry descriptions to establish some degree of market commonality.

Both the *SIC* and *NAICS* descriptions place *Synergy Brands* in the general line grocery wholesale business. What is *Synergy Brands* doing in the *GICS* 45101010 Internet Software and Services sub-industry? Good question. It turns out the company was a traditional grocery, health and beauty aids wholesaler with sales of $3.0 million in the second quarter of 1998 when this set was created. In the meantime, management shifted its wholesale business model to the Internet.

Here's the scoop on *Synergy Brands, Inc.*:

> Synergy Brands, Inc (SYBR *or the* Company) *is a holding company, which operates through three unique business segments that all utilize business logistics. The businesses include* **PHS Group** *(also known as* Dealbynet*), Grand Reserve Corporation* **(GRC),** *and* Proset Hair Systems **(Proset). PHS Group** *is a grocery logistics business used for the purchase of brand name grocery and Health and Beauty Aids (HBA) products and the resale to traditional customers utilizing the logistics and networking advantages of electronics commerce and in-time distribution.*
>
> **GRC** *manages multiple Internet domains that market directly to the retail consumer via electronic commerce.* GRC *owns multiple domains including* Cigargold.com, Netcigar.com *and* Beauty Buys.com. GRC *focuses on a mix of brand name premium cigar items and cigar-related accessories, and markets them through multiple cigar domains including* CigarGold.com *and* NetCigar.com. Beauty Buys

Table 3-8 Multiple Groups in the Internet Software Sub-Industry

	Company	TIC	SIC	SIC Description	NAICS	NAICS Description
1	Synergy Brands	SYBR	5141	Groceries, General Line-Whsl	424410	General Line Grocery Merchant Whlse
2	Track Data Corp	TRAC	6200	Security & Commodity Brokers	511140	Database and Directory Publishers
3	Centiv Inc	CNTV	7370	CMP Programming, Data Process	811212	Computer and Office Machine Repair
4	Cmgi Inc	CMGI	7370	CMP Programming, Data Process	511210	Software Publishers
1	Earthlink Inc	ELNK	7370	CMP Programming, Data Process	518111	Internet Service Providers
2	Frontline Comms	FNT	7370	CMP Programming, Data Process	518111	Internet Service Providers
3	Interland Inc	INLD	7370	CMP Programming, Data Process	518111	Internet Service Providers
4	Navtech Inc	3NAVH	7370	CMP Programming, Data Process	518111	Internet Service Providers
5	Tucows Inc	3TCOW	7370	CMP Programming, Data Process	518111	Internet Service Providers
1	Auto Graphics	3AUGR	7372	Prepackaged Software	511210	Software Publishers
2	Comshare Inc	CSRE	7372	Prepackaged Software	511210	Software Publishers
3	Doubleclick Inc	DCLK	7372	Prepackaged Software	511210	Software Publishers
4	Microlog Corp	3MLOG	7372	Prepackaged Software	511210	Software Publishers
5	Open Text Corp	OTEX	7372	Prepackaged Software	511210	Software Publishers
6	Unify Corp	UNFYE	7372	Prepackaged Software	511210	Software Publishers
1	Broadvision Inc	BVSN	7373	CMP Integrated Sys Design	541512	Computer Systems Design Services
2	Navidec Inc	NVDC	7373	CMP Integrated Sys Design	541512	Computer Systems Design Services
3	Rwd Technologies	RWDT	7373	CMP Integrated Sys Design	541512	Computer Systems Design Services
1	Innodata Corp	INOD	7374	CMP Processing, Data Prep Svc	518210	Data Processing and Hosting Services
2	Infonow Corp	INOW	8742	Management Consulting Svcs	541613	Marketing Consulting Services

markets beauty- related products to the customer on the Internet through multiple domains including store.perx.com.

Proset distributes salon hair care products to chain drug stores and supermarkets in the Northeastern part of the United States. Proset uses just-in-time technology and continuous replenishment programs to stock, track, and market-defined plan-o-grams within the store's beauty aisles. Plan-o-grams *can range from four feet to sixteen feet depending on the demographics of the store.*[7]

It's clear that the second and third companies in Table 3-8 also belong in different groups. *Track Data Corp* is described in *NAICS* as a "database and directory publisher." The *SIC* description says the company is a "security & commodity broker." *CENTIV Inc* is in the "computer and office machine repair" business according to *NAICS*. It's in the "CMP programming and data processing" business if you use the *SIC* description. These companies, of course, have different *SIC* and *NAICS* codes and descriptions.

The five companies in the second numbered set Table 3-8 show how you can define a strategic group by triangulating on those with the same *SIC, NAICS,* and *GICS* sub-industry descriptions and codes. In the last column of the table, the *NAICS* descriptions identified *Earthlink, Frontline, Interland, Navtech,* and *Tucows* as "Internet Service Providers." The *SIC* descriptions identify the companies as suppliers of "CMP programming and data processing." It's a safe bet to say these companies are members of a strategic group with a high degree of market commonality. Even so, if you were to select this strategic group for detailed study, you would need to confirm this bet by running a brief profile, like the one above for *Synergy Brands,* on each company.

The next numbered set of six companies listed in Table 3-7 all are probably in a "Prepackaged Software" group. Before you do any research to confirm this assumption, take a close look at how the companies in this group perform based on just the basic financial numbers. The competitive enterprise matrix defined by these six companies appears in Table 3-9.

Table 3-9 Prepackaged Software Group with Market Commonality

Company	TIC	Sales	COGS	Gross	SG&A	EBITDA	Value	v/r
Doubleclick	DCLK	$60.10	$10.90	$49.20	$36.60	$12.60	$1,062.00	17.7
Open Text	OTEX	$44.00	$11.80	$32.20	$24.40	$7.80	$541.30	12.3
Comshare	CSRE	$13.90	$4.40	$9.50	$10.20	($0.70)	$25.70	1.8
Unify Corp	UNFYE	$3.20	$0.30	$2.90	$2.60	$0.30	$6.10	1.9
Auto Graphics	3AUGR	$1.50	$0.60	$1.00	$0.60	$0.40	$1.80	1.2
Microlog	3MLOG	$1.30	$0.30	$0.90	$0.80	$0.20	$0.70	0.5
Strategic Group		$123.90	$28.20	$95.60	$75.10	$20.60	$1,637.70	13.2

One of the first things to get your attention in this group is the V/R multiple—it was 13.2 in the first quarter of 2003. That's a good thing. However, next you should see that this is a result of the top two companies in the group: *Doubleclick's* v/r multiple was 17.7 and *Open Text's* was 12.3. The other firms are closer to the expected value (one).

Another thing that should get your attention in Table 3-9 is that while the six players in this group have a high degree of *market commonality* they are endowed with very different resources. For example, *Doubleclick's* market value was $1,062 million. You might say that *Open Text,* with a market value of $541 million, had roughly equivalent resources based on a market value in the first quarter of 2003. The other four companies aren't even in the ball park.

Resource Equivalence Guidelines

We need to invent some workable guidelines to establish the level of resource equivalence among competitors before they can be assigned to the same strategic group. "Equivalence" is a slippery concept. It has two basic dimensions—financial/enterprise marketing clout and flexibility. The first dimension can be measured in at least four ways:

1. market value,
2. sales revenues,
3. gross profits, and
4. enterprise marketing expenses.

The second dimension, flexibility, is unobservable. But you've got to make an allowance for it in some way. For openers, apply the following four-step test. In general you can compare each company to the group leader with regard to each of the four dimensions listed above. If a company's resources are:

- At least 50% of the leader's resources on two or more of the dimensions, it's fair to assume they have the flexibility to achieve **Hi**gh **R**esource **E**quivalence (HIRE).
- At least 20%—but less than 50%—of the leader's position on two or more of the dimensions, it's fair to assume the company has the flexibility to achieve at least **Me**dium **R**esource **E**quivalence (MERE).
- Less than 20% of the leader's position, they have **Lo**w **R**esource **E**quivalence (LORE).

In Table 3-10, the four-step rule is applied to the six companies with high market commonality in the prepackaged software group.

- **Value Ratio:** the ratio of *OTEX's* market value to *DCLK's* was 0.51. This indicates a high degree of resource equivalence on market value. No other company even came close on this ratio.

Table 3-10 Indicators of Resource Equivalence

Company	TIC	Value Ratio	Revenue Ratio	Profit Ratio	Expense Ratio
Doubleclick	DCLK	1.00	1.00	1.00	1.00
Open Text	OTEX	0.51	0.73	0.65	0.67
Comshare	CSRE	0.02	0.23	0.19	0.28
Unify Corp	UNFYE	0.01	0.05	0.06	0.07
Auto Graphics	3AUGR	0.00	0.02	0.02	0.02
Microlog	3MLOG	0.00	0.02	0.02	0.02

- **Revenue Ratio:** *OTEX's* sales revenue to *DCLK's* was 0.73. This indicates a high degree of resource equivalence in revenues. With both v and r ratios greater than 0.50, *OTEX* qualifies as a member of this strategic group on these two dimensions alone.
- **Profit Ratio:** *OTEX* also had a high degree of resource equivalence in gross profits (0.65).
- **Expense Ratio:** *OTEX's* investments in enterprise marketing expenses compared with *DCLK* (0.67) also indicate a high degree of resource equivalence.

The other members of a strategic group must pass at least two of these four hurdles to be players. No other company came close.

These Are Just Guidelines

The hurdles for membership in a strategic group were applied to the most volatile sector of the economy over a twenty-quarter period, including the boom and bust in Internet stocks. This was a worst-case analysis designed to highlight the process of defining a strategic group based on market commonality and resource equivalence. But take note; these are just guidelines, not hard-and-fast rules.

We began with a list of 445 companies in the *GICS* Internet Software and Services sub-industry in the second quarter of 1998. **Only** forty-nine companies survived the market shake-out, appearing as candidates for analysis in the first quarter of 2003. Just twenty of these companies passed our missing data tests over the previous twenty quarters. Of these, six companies satisfied the demands of market commonality. Only two of these companies had high enough resource equivalence to qualify for membership in this strategic group.

So, what if you worked for *COMSHARE* and wanted to compare it with *DoubleClick* and *Open Text?* Go ahead and do it. Just make a note that the company had medium resource equivalence.

Strategic Groups in Stable Markets

Let's turn to a better-behaved industry in order to enrich the application and achieve a more harmonious outcome. There are few industries better-behaved than **Pharmaceuticals and Biotechnology** in the **Health Care sector** (GICS code 35 in Table 3-7). A total of 131 firms were listed in the GICS industry group Biotechnology and Pharmaceuticals (GICS code 3520) and reported all the data required to create a competitive resource matrix.

Market Commonality

First, the reporting firms must be sorted into the two industry classifications: **Biotechnology (GICS code 352010)** and **Pharmaceuticals (GICS code 352020).** There were fifty-seven companies in the Biotech sub-industry (GICS code 35201010) and seventy-four companies in the Pharmaceutical sub-industry (GICS code 35202010). Direct competitors in each of these two sub-industries were defined as firms that shared the same SIC and NAICS codes. If you were creating a strategic group of direct competitors in pharmaceuticals, then firms in the biotechnology sub-industry would be potential competitors.

In the **Pharmaceuticals** sub-industry, a total of sixty-nine out of the seventy-four listed firms also shared SIC code 2834, (Pharmaceutical Preparations) and NAICS code 325412 (Pharmaceutical Preparation Manufacturing). Five of the listed firms did not share these codes and their assignment to this sub-industry was inconsistent with those that did. These five are companies listed in Table 3-11. They were deleted from the set.

Deleted Firms

The reasons for deleting the five firms listed in Table 3-11 were substantive. For example, *Pure World Inc.* had different NAICS and SIC codes. This confirms that *Pure World Inc.* did not satisfy the same consumer needs as the other companies in this group. It was in the business of manufacturing spices and extracts used in beverages. One of the most famous cases in marketing is about spices and extracts used in a beverage. *Lydia E. Pinkham's Vegetable Compound,* a patent medicine launched in 1875, was the subject of a path-breaking study of the cumulative effects of advertising (Palda 1964). This confirms that *Pure World* did not satisfy the same consumer needs as the other companies in the group.

The same appeared to be true of *Alcide Corp.* and *PacificHealth. First Horizon* and *Provalis* were deleted because they were wholesalers. The seven

Chapter 3 • Who's in *My* Strategic Group? 73

Table 3-11 Firms Deleted from the Pharmaceutical Sub-Industry

Company Name	NAICS Code	Description	SIC Code	Description
Pure World Inc	311942	Spice and Extract Manufacturing	2080	Beverages
Alcide Corp	325320	Pesticide and Other Agricultural Chemical Manufacturing	2870	Agricultural Chemicals
Pacifichealth Laboratories	325411	Medicinal and Botanical Manufacturing	2833	Medicinal Chems, Botanicl Pds
First Horizon Pharmaceutical	424210	Drugs and Druggists' Sundries Merchant Wholesalers	5122	Drugs and Proprietary-Whsl
Provalis Plc - Spon Adr	424210	Drugs and Druggists' Sundries Merchant Wholesalers	5122	Drugs and Proprietary-Whsl

other firms were determined to be indirect competitors based on their *SIC* and *NAICS* descriptions.

A similar process was applied to the 57 companies in the Biotech sub-industry. Those companies that shared *SIC* and *NAICS* codes were defined as potential competitors. The outliers were deleted and/or assigned to the indirect competitor group. The result was that 117 firms were defined either as direct (69 companies), potential (25 companies), or indirect competitors (23 companies).

High Resource Equivalence

The four-step process for determining resource equivalence was applied to each of the three groups. The results for direct competitors with high resource equivalence are shown in Table 3-12.

The group leader and each of the companies that clear the 0.50 hurdle rate are listed in Table 3-12. The HIRE direct competitors are numbered in rank order in the first column. *Pfizer* (*PFE*) was the leader in 2000 on three

Table 3-12 High Resource Equivalence Among Direct Competitors

Direct Competitors	TIC	Value Ratio	TIC	Revenue Ratio	TIC	Profit Ratio	TIC	Expense Ratio
HIRE.1	PFE	1.00	MRK	1.00	PFE	1.00	PFE	1.00
HIRE.2	MRK	0.74	PFE	0.73	GSK	0.89	GSK	0.88
HIRE.3	GSK	0.60	JNJ	0.72	JNJ	0.85	JNJ	0.87
HIRE.4	JNJ	0.50	GSK	0.68	MRK	0.74	AVE	0.72
HIRE.5	BMY	0.50	NVS	0.55	NVS	0.65	NVS	0.69
HIRE.6			AVE	0.53	AVE	0.59	3RHHBY	0.60
HIRE.7					BMY	0.56	MRK	0.54
HIRE.8							AZN	0.50

of the four dimensions: value, profits, and enterprise marketing expenses. *Merck (MRK)* was the revenue leader.

Merck was closest to *Pfizer* with a value equivalence ratio of 0.74, followed by *GlaxoSmithKilne (GSK)* with 0.60, *Johnson & Johnson (JNJ)* with 0.50, and *Bristol-Myers Squibb (BMY) with* 0.50. The next closest competitor, *Novartis,* came in at 0.40 and so, strictly speaking, it did not clear the 0.50 hurdle ratio for market value equivalence. *BMY* drops out of the running on revenue equivalence, but *Novartis (NVS) with* 0.55, and *Aventis (AVE)* with 0.53, have high revenue equivalence. *BMY* reappears with a profit ratio of 0.56, bringing the total number of HIRE companies to seven. *Roche Holdings (3RHHBY)* with 0.60 and *Astrazeneca (AZN)* with 0.50, clear the enterprise marketing expense ratio hurdle, but not any other dimension. These two companies were moved to the second tier of potential competitors. The final cut revealed seven resource-equivalent direct competitors.

Medium Resource Equivalence

A similar process was applied to identify **Me**dium **R**esource **E**quivalence among direct competitors. The results are reported in Table 3-13. MERE companies are ordered by rank in the first column, followed by their ticker symbols and equivalence ratios. *Novartis* topped the list of seven MERE companies on market value, but cleared the hurdle on the three other dimensions, so it remained in the HIRE group. Since it appears three times in Table 3-13, the placement of *Roche Holding (3RHHBY)* as a medium resource competitor is confirmed.

Similarly, *Bristol-Myers Squibb's* position, near the top of MERE competitors on its revenue ratio (0.45) and leading the list of its expense ratio of (0.47), confirms its position in the HIRE strategic group. The remaining

Table 3-13 Medium Resource Equivalence Among Direct Competitors

Direct Competitors	TIC	Value Ratio	TIC	Revenue Ratio	TIC	Profit Ratio	TIC	Intangibles Ratio
MERE.1	NVS	0.40	3RHHBY	0.47	3RHHBY	0.36	BMY	0.47
MERE.2	LLY	0.36	BMY	0.45	LLY	0.36	WYE	0.42
MERE.3	AZN	0.31	AZN	0.39	ABT	0.33	LLY	0.33
MERE.4	WYE	0.29	ABT	0.34	WYE	0.26	SGP	0.30
MERE.5	SGP	0.29	WYE	0.33			ABT	0.27
MERE.6	ABT	0.26	LLY	0.27				
MERE.7	3RHHBY	0.24	SGP	0.24				

seven companies in Table 3-13 qualified for placement in the strategic group of competitors with medium resource equivalence.

Low Resource Equivalence

By definition, the other 49 companies in the direct-competitor group had resource equivalence ratios of less than 0.25 on all four dimensions. These companies were placed in the **Lo**w **R**esource **E**quivalence strategic group of direct competitors. *Shering AG,* founded in 1850, is the largest direct competitor in the LORE group. *Shering* combines "longstanding medical and pharmaceutical expertise with the latest discoveries from genomic research." (*Shering* 2005)

Ticker symbols of the seven pharmaceutical companies with high market commonality and resource equivalence are listed alphabetically in the lower right-hand corner of Table 3-14. These companies are household names. Known as "Big Pharmas," you probably can recognize them by their tickers.

Potential and Indirect Competitors

The same tests were applied to potential and indirect competitors. Among the 26 firms in the group of potential biotech competitors, *AMGN* cleared only one hurdle with a value ratio 0.23. Except for *Genentech* with a value ratio of 0.15, the other 24 competitors had equivalence ratios of less than 0.14 on every dimension. All 26 firms exhibited low resource equivalence.

The potential competitors produced a variety of biotechnology products. *Amgen,* the leading potential competitor, "pioneered the development of novel products based on advances in recombinant DNA and molecular biology and launched the biotechnology industry's first blockbuster medicines." (*Amgen* 2005) The second-largest potential competitor, *Genentech* "seeks significant returns to its stockholders based on the continuous pursuit

Table 3-14 Strategic Groups in Biotechnology and Pharmaceuticals

Market Commonality	Company Ticker Symbols:		
INDIRECT Instruments, Diagnostics, & Basic Research [30]	*IDXX* *GCOR* *CRL* +27 Others	<None>	<None>
POTENTIAL Biotechnology Preparations [25]	*AMGN* *BGEN* *CHIR* *DNA* +21 Others	<None>	<None>
DIRECT Pharmaceutical Preparations [62]	*AGN* *ELN* *ICN* *SHPGY* *SHR* *TEVA* +43 Others	*ABT* *AZN* *LLY* *SGP* *WYE* *3RHHBY*	*AVE* *BMY* *GSK* *JNJ* *MRK* *NVS* *PFE*
[117]	LOW	MEDIUM	HIGH
	Resource Equivalence		

of excellent science to develop biotherapeutics for unmet medical needs." (*Genentech* 2005)

The leading indirect competitor, *Idexx Lab's* "companion animal and equine businesses combine biotechnology with medical devices and information technology to support veterinarians' efforts in providing excellent care while building successful practices." (Internet web site of *Idexx Laboratories, Inc.* 2005) All 55 of these firms had resource equivalence ratios of less than 0.20 on two or more dimensions compared with *Merck* and *Pfizer*.

A Longer View

Having been buried for the better part of this chapter in the details of strategic group definition, it's time to take a longer view of what's going on. This view is provided by Chart 3-1, showing the distribution of resource equivalence ratios among direct competitors in the pharmaceutical industry.

Resource equivalence ratios among direct competitors appear on the vertical axis for market value (open circles), sales revenues (open triangles),

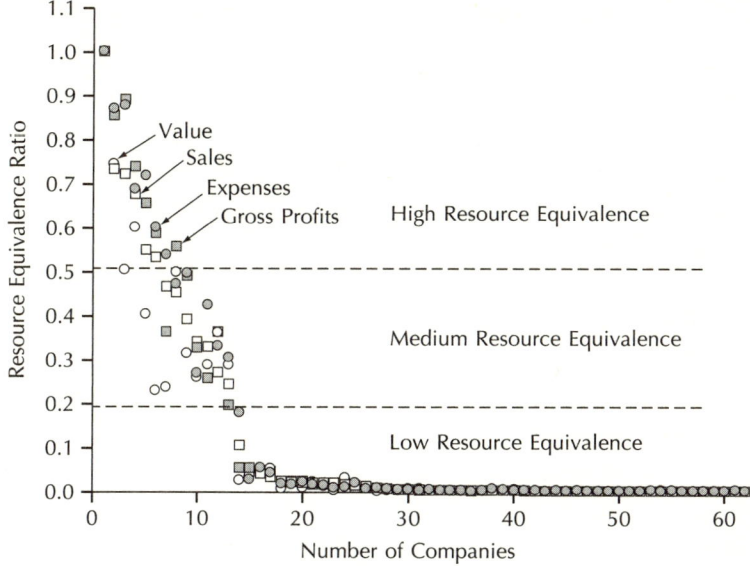

Chart 3-1 The Distribution of Resource Equivalence Ratios

enterprise marketing expenses (gray circles), and gross profits (gray squares). This is divided by the dashed lines into high, medium, and low resource equivalence. The sixty-two companies are rank-ordered by ratio across the horizontal axis.

The two leading companies with ratios of 1.0—*Merck* on market value and *Pfizer* on sales, expenses, and profits—are represented in the upper left-hand corner of the distribution. The other six companies with resource equivalence ratios of 0.5 or more on at least two dimensions are charted above the high resource equivalence dotted line. The medium and low resource equivalent companies appear below the leaders in Chart 3-1. This distribution is typical of strategic groups with a large number of direct competitors.

The dashed horizontal lines in this chart provide an intuitive rationale for selection of the break points between high, medium, and low resource equivalence.

Other Considerations

Two other considerations are useful in the formation and analysis of strategic groups. The first is the most widely used method for defining strategic groups—financial analysts' reports. The second is the question of whether or not results are robust in the number of competitors included in the group.

Financial Analysts' Reports

A shortcut to defining strategic groups is to use the "Peer Group" of companies listed in financial analysts' reports. As with any shortcut, this one carries the risk of relying on someone else's opinions, judgments, and hidden agendas. If you take this approach, then you should know the analysts and have access to the data and decisions they made in defining the peer group. You should also test these peer groups for *market commonality* and *resource equivalence*.

The *Burkenroad Reports* are produced by student financial analysts at the *Freeman School of Business* of *Tulane University*. These reports focus on companies in the Gulf South region of the U.S. Peter Ricchiuti, director of research, calls these companies "stocks under rocks" because the securities are not covered by big investment firms.

For example, consider the recent *Burkenroad Report*, "Lamar Advertising Co."[8] The analysts list three companies in the peer group: *Viacom Outdoor*, a division of *Viacom, Inc. (VIA.B)*; *Clear Channel Outdoor*, a division of *Clear Channel Communications (CCU)*; and *Lamar Advertising (LAMR)*. Quarterly and annual financial statements for *Lamar* were appended to the report, while no peer company reports were appended. The data in Table 3-15 for the three companies were taken from the *Wharton Research Data Services* for the quarter ending March 31, 2003.

While the companies in Table 3-15 are a "Peer Group," they do not belong to the same strategic group. The companies are not direct competitors since they share no common *GICS, NAICS,* or *SIC* codes. *Clear Channel* is a potential competitor, while *Lamar* is an indirect competitor of *Viacom*. Neither *Clear Channel* nor *Lamar* has high resource equivalence with

Table 3-15 An Outdoor Advertising Peer Group

Company	GICS	NAICS	SIC	Market Cap	Sales Revenue	V/R Ratio	Value Share	Revenue Share	ρ
Viacom, Inc.	25401030	515210	4833	$63,727	$6,051	10.5	72.8	75.5	−0.22
Clear Channel	25401020	515112	4832	$20,831	$1,779	11.7	23.8	22.2	0.14
Lamar Advertising	25401010	541850	7310	$2,996	$184	16.3	3.4	2.3	1.02
Peer Group				$87,555	$8,014	10.9	100.0	100.0	

Viacom; however, *Clear Channel* does have medium resource equivalence with *Viacom* on market value (0.33) and sales revenues (0.29).

The report states: "Viacom is a leading global media company, with preeminent positions in broadcast and cable television, radio, outdoor advertising, and online." The company's *GICS* sub-industry is Movies and Entertainment (25401030). Its primary *SIC* code is Television Broadcasting Stations (4833). *Viacom* dominates this peer group with 72.8% of market value and 75.5% of sales revenues. The company's risk-adjusted **VSD**, based on twenty quarters of data beginning in June, 1998, was −0.22. *Clear Channel Communications* was the second-biggest player in the space with a revenue share of 22.2% and a **RAD** of 0.14. *Lamar,* with a market value of $2,996 million and sales revenues of $184, had the highest value/revenue ratio (16.3) and an **RAD** of +1.02.

Lamar Advertising can be placed in its own strategic group using the triangulation method described earlier. A search for similar companies in the *GICS* sub-industry in the first quarter of 2003, returns a list of 257 firms, including *Time Warner Inc.* with revenues of $9,998 million. Of these, 81 companies did not report sales revenues, and nine reported less than $1,000 in sales. The remaining 167 companies ranged across a variety of *SIC* and *NAICS* codes. Three companies had the same *GICS, SIC,* and *NAICS* codes for "Display Advertising." These were *Lamar Advertising, Obie Media Corp* (*OBIE*), and *Digital Data Networks Inc.* (*3DIDA*).

Robust in Number of Competitors

Is the risk-adjusted differential robust in the number of competitors included in a strategic group? Take a long-term look at global auto companies, for example. The following table shows the share of value and share of revenue for seven companies for the ten years from 1991 through 2000.

The years are in the rows of Table 3-16 with company ticker symbols in the columns. For each year, company share of value (**SOV**) and share of revenues (**SOR**) appear in separate rows of the table. For example, in 1991 *Toyota Motors* (*TM*) created 33.0% of market value and generated 15.2% of sales revenues. *Toyota's* value-sales differential in 1991 was +17.8 points. Over the years, the company's share of value (**SOV**) gradually grew to around 40% while its share of revenue remained at about 15%.

The standard deviation in *Toyota's* value-sales differentials over the period puts its enterprise marketing risk below-average at 4.3 points. The company's **RAD** in 1991 was 4.1 points (17.8/4.3). The values of **RAD** for each company can be computed from the data in Table 3-16.

Table 3-16 Auto Share of Value (SOV) and Share of Revenue (SOR)

	TM	F	DCX	HMC	GM	NSANY	FIA	
1991	33.0	11.1	16.9	9.4	14.7	10.5	4.4	SOV
	15.2	18.8	14.0	6.5	26.0	9.0	10.5	SOR
1992	32.6	15.6	15.7	7.5	17.0	8.7	2.8	SOV
	16.4	20.2	12.6	6.7	26.4	9.7	8.1	SOR
1993	31.4	16.9	11.9	7.0	20.8	8.8	3.2	SOV
	18.4	21.0	11.1	6.9	26.2	10.3	6.1	SOR
1994	36.5	13.3	11.8	8.1	14.9	9.7	5.7	SOV
	16.2	22.3	11.7	6.5	26.5	9.8	7.0	SOR
1995	34.6	14.7	11.4	8.9	17.4	8.4	4.5	SOV
	14.6	22.0	11.6	7.1	26.5	10.5	7.6	SOR
1996	37.7	13.4	14.8	9.6	14.7	5.2	4.6	SOV
	16.3	23.7	10.0	6.5	25.8	9.2	8.5	SOR
1997	35.8	19.2	12.3	11.8	13.9	3.4	3.6	SOV
	15.5	24.1	10.8	6.7	26.4	8.4	8.1	SOR
1998	31.5	22.1	15.4	10.1	14.6	2.3	4.0	SOV
	12.7	20.8	22.3	6.5	22.8	7.2	7.7	SOR
1999	42.7	15.0	18.2	8.7	10.5	2.4	2.5	SOV
	14.1	21.7	20.1	6.9	23.3	7.2	6.7	SOR
2000	39.7	14.6	13.9	12.1	9.4	7.4	3.0	SOV
	15.1	21.4	19.2	7.2	22.8	7.1	7.1	SOR
	4.32	3.23	3.69	1.65	2.45	2.38	1.32	Sigma

How sensitive is *Toyota's* year-to-year and average **RAD** to the number of firms included in its strategic group? In other words, is **RAD** robust in the number of companies? To answer this question, companies were removed from *Toyota's* strategic group one-by-one, in order of their market cap in 2000 until there were only two companies remaining. The first to go was *Ford*, followed by *Daimler/Chrysler*, *Honda*, *General Motors*, and *Nissan Motors*. In the end, the only two remaining were *Toyota* and *Fiat*.

As you can see in Chart 3-2, the number of companies in its strategic group had little overall impact on *Toyota's* **RADs** over time. The number of firms remaining in each group is identified in the legend to Chart 3-2.

Not surprisingly, the single-biggest impact occurred when *Ford* was removed from the group in 1991. Without *Ford*, *Toyota's* **RAD** drops from 6.8 (gray circle) to 4.1 (white diamond) in that year.

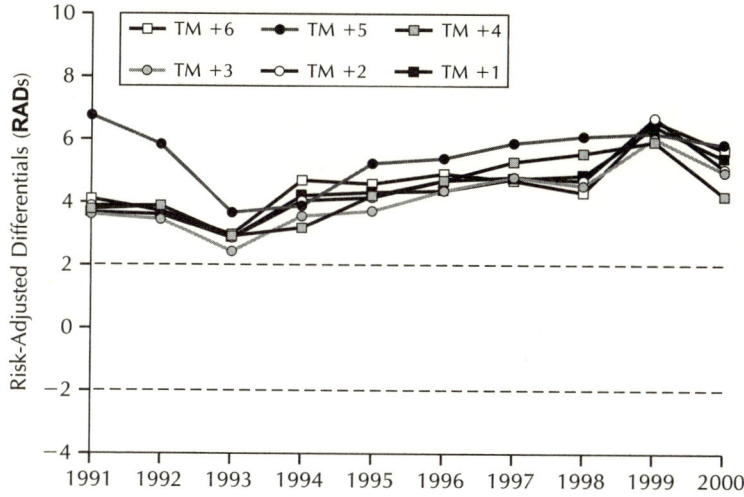

Chart 3-2 *Toyota Motor* **RADs** in Six Different Strategic Groups

The result of redefining *Toyota's* strategic group is better illustrated with an **RAD** candlestick chart. Instead of showing the high and low **RAD** for each competitor as is typical, Chart 3-2 shows *Toyota's* highest and lowest differentials over the decade for each of the ten different groups.

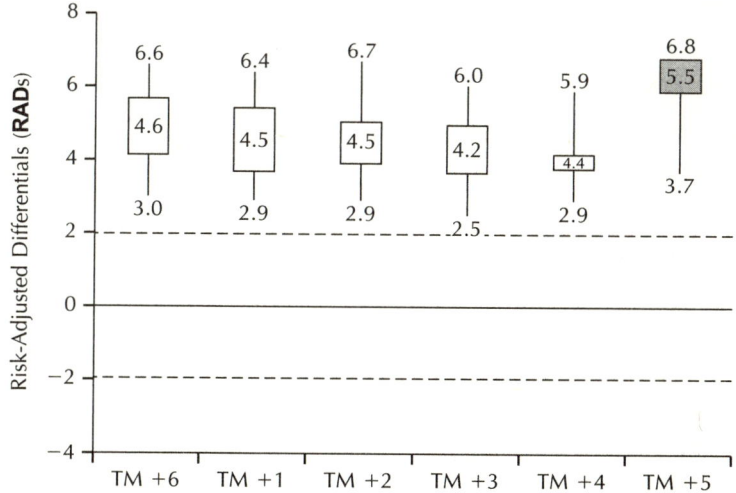

Chart 3-3 *Toyota* Candlestick Chart in Six Different Strategic Groups

In a strategic group with six other global auto companies (TM+6), the first bar in Chart 3-3, *Toyota's* highest **RAD** was +6.6 in 1999, up from 4.1 in 1991. Its lowest **RAD** was +3.0 in 1993. The average value over the ten years from 1991 through 2000 was +4.6.

When the company with the next-biggest market cap (*Ford*) was removed from the group (TM+5), *Toyota's* average **RAD** increased to +5.5 in a range that changed very little (+6.8 to +3.7).

When *Daimler-Chrysler* was removed from the group, *TM's* average **RAD** was virtually unchanged at +4.5. Its lowest value remained at +2.9, while the highest value was slightly smaller at +6.7.

Similar results are shown in Chart 3-2 for each of the different strategic groups. It's clear that **RAD** is robust in the number of companies. . . at least for *Toyota* in the global auto group.

A Final Word on Strategic Groups

If you have industry know-how, you probably can name the companies in your strategic group. However, you should check on each company's market commonality and resource equivalence before applying the rule of maximum earnings. If you lack specific industry knowledge, select the companies with high **market commonality** and **resource equivalence.** In either case, you should run current profiles on each company. If you find reasons to reject one company, try another. Keep looking until you zero in on a strategic group with four companies with complete data for ten periods.

References

Amgen. 2005. [Online article or information; retrieved 6/17/05)]: http://www.amgen.com/about/amgen.html (June 17).

Bergen, M., and M. Peteraf. 2002. "Competitor Identification and Competitor Analysis: A Broad-Based Managerial Approach." *Managerial and Decision Economics* 23 (June/August): 157–169.

Bhojraj, S., C. M. C. Lee, and D. K. Oler. 2003. "What's My Line? A Comparison of Industry Classification Schemes for Capital Market Research." *Journal of Accounting Research* 41 *(December):* 745–774.

Genentech. 2005. [Online article or information; retrieved 6/17/05)]: http://www.gene.com/gene/index.jsp (June 17).

Lasica, J. D. 2002. "AOL Time Warner: Time to Grow Up, Fast." *Online Journalism Review:* April 24. Annenberg School of Journalism, University of Southern California, http://www.ojr.org/ojr/lasica/1022201128.php

Palda, K. S. 1964. *The Measurement of Cumulative Advertising Effects.* Englewood Cliffs, NJ: Prentice-Hall.

Shering Group AG. 2005. [Online article or information; retrieved 6/17/05)]: http://www.schering.de/scripts/en/index.php.

Sorkin, A. R., and D. D. Kirkpatrick. "AOL Time Warner Drops the 'AOL'." *New York Times,* September 19, 2003, section C, 4.

End Notes

[1] *SBC* announced in January, 2005 it will acquire *AT&T*, its former parent, for 16.5 billion **USD**.

[2] It's convenient to use uppercase letters in reference to the V/R of a strategic group or industry, while using lowercase letters in reference to the v/r ratio of individual companies.

[3] Access to *WRDS* at http://www.wrds.wharton.upenn.edu is by password only and is limited to academic users.

[4] For a free trial go to http://www.support.compustat.com/support/index.htm

[5] The Global Industry Classification Standard is collaboration between *Standard & Poor's* and *Morgan Stanley Capital International*. This standard was established to streamline and rationalize investment information for financial market participants globally. For a complete description go to http://www.msci.com/equity/gics.html

[6] For updates and pending changes on the *GICS,* go to http://www.msci.com/equity/GICS map2004.xls

[7] http://www.synergybrands.com/corporate.htm

[8] Analysts: Leslie Delcambre, Randy Deroche, and Fred Michaels; Investment Research Manager: Rebecca Keithley, "Continuing Coverage: Time to Sign Up," *Burkenroad Reports,* 19 pages, January 9, 2003.

CHAPTER 4

ENTERPRISE MARKETING EXPENSES

Jeffrey Pfeffer asks a seemingly simple question in his book *Competitive Advantage Through People*. "Suppose that in 1972, someone asked you to pick the five companies that would provide the greatest return to stockholders over the next twenty years." (Pfeffer 1994, 3) If you followed conventional wisdom, you would pick market share leaders in industries with both high barriers to entry and patented technology. It turns out you would be wrong. The five firms in 1972 that created the greatest return to shareholders over the next twenty years were in highly competitive industries with low entry barriers and without patented technology. These industries were publishing, retailing, poultry processing, and airline travel. Yes, *Southwest Airlines* was one of the five top performers.

Who Creates Shareholder Value?

If you think of enterprise marketing as the act of marketing the man behind the curtain—the corporate parent as opposed to the individual products—what comes to mind? Your first thought might be that the related expenses are associated with the corporate brand (*Pfizer, Ford*) and its connotations—which are distinct from those of an individual product. You're right. The brand and its connotations are behind the first curtain. But enterprise marketing expenses are more than that. What else is on the stage? Behind the next curtain are the other expenses that contribute in one way or another to shareholder value. These are listed in Table 4-1.

***Intangibles*,**[1] like client lists, patents, copyrights, distribution rights, goodwill, licenses, and trademarks, don't just appear magically on the balance sheet. They are created by people. The current costs of the people who create technology-based "assets" (R&D expenses), customer-based "assets" (sales operation expenses), market-based "assets" (advertising and promotion expenses), talent-based organizational "assets" (employee compensation), and contract-based statutory "assets" (legal expenses) provide a flow measure of how enterprise marketing expenses create intangible value. Each of these expenses affects the way customers and investors feel, think, and act toward the firm. Conceptually, the management of these intangible "assets" is the domain of enterprise marketing.

Table 4-1 Getting a Grip on Intangible Assets (Harvard Management Update 2001)

1. **Technology-based assets:**
   - Research and development
   - Information systems
   - Internet domain names/portals
   - Secret formulas, procedure manuals
   - Technical drawings
   - Software programs
2. **Customer-based intangibles**
   - Customer base
   - Lists of subscribers and members
   - Customer records
   - Customer routes
   - Customer service capabilities
3. **Market-based assets**
   - Brand names
   - Newspaper mastheads
   - Delivery systems
   - Distribution channels
   - Advertising programs
   - Retail shelf space
   - Presence in geographic markets
4. **Workforce-based assets**
   - Technical expertise
   - Trained staff
   - Proven managers
   - Star talent
   - Ongoing recruiting
   - Training and retention programs
5. **Organization-based assets**
   - Company business model
   - Business methods
   - Financial policies
   - Financial practices
   - Government favor
   - Credit ratings
6. **Contract-based assets**
   - Consulting and licensing agreements
   - Royalty arrangement
   - Customer or vendor contracts
   - Non-compete covenants
   - Rights to other resources
7. **Statutory-based assets**
   - Patents
   - Copyrights
   - Media franchises
   - Trade names

Ongoing Costs

An inclusive measure of enterprise marketing expenses appears on the income statement of most public companies. By accounting convention these costs are called **S**elling, **G**eneral, and **A**dministrative (SG&A) expenses. What's more, this measure is taken far enough up in the earnings stream to include most of the factors that have an impact on customer behavior and perceptions. In short, almost everything a company spends on the competition for customers and capital appears in this account. These costs were sandwiched between gross profits and EBITDA as SG&A costs in the Competitive Enterprise Matrix in Chapter 1.

Reporting of SG&A expenses often follows different conventions in company income statements for different types of businesses. For example,

R&D expenses may be reported separately or combined with other expenses in a manufacturer's income statement. In pure service businesses like restaurants, operating expenses often are included in the COGS. In these instances, operating costs, which include the people costs that play a vital role in shaping customers' perceptions, must be moved into the SG&A category. The same is true for banks, which typically report in COGS the cost of operations. The true "cost of the goods sold" in financial institutions is the interest they pay for money.

Accounting for Enterprise Marketing Expenses

"Enterprise marketing expenses" include the cost of anyone (or anything) that is advantageous in the competition for customers and capital. SG&A expenses are the current and ongoing costs of enterprise marketing. They don't include the "intangible assets" recognized by the Financial Accounting Standards Board (FASB) in its *SFAS 142 Goodwill and Other Intangible Assets*. In other words, enterprise marketing expenses are not assets on a company's balance sheet:

> The balance sheet undoubtedly has significant limitations in terms of reporting an entity's true value. Internally developed intangible assets, even those for which a fair value may be determinable, are not recognized in financial statements. Other intangible assets, such as political clout and regulatory expertise, are generally net even discussed in company reports. Investors and creditors recognize these limitations, and presumably perform independent research and analysis in their investment and credit decisions. (Foster, Fletcher, and Stout 2003, 50)

As someone once said, "our most important assets walk out the door every night." Sometimes it's difficult to make the connection between the costs of people and the value of the intangible assets they create. Consider, for example, the role of accountants and financial managers in creating organization-based assets.

Are Accounting Costs Enterprise Marketing Expenses?

Before you say the accounting function isn't an enterprise marketing expense, stop and think about the impact accounting practices have on your perceptions of an organization. Take billing errors, for example. When Accounts Receivable won't let your son or daughter register on time for a course he or she wants because of an overdue library book, what does that make you think of the university? Even worse, take that overdue book to the next level: you can't get the error corrected, so your kids can't even move into the dorm after driving all the way to New Orleans from New York City.

Alternatively, think about the effect of an overly aggressive payment penalty on your perception of a credit card company. The company dings you forty-five dollars if your payment isn't received within thirty days, but sends the statement late so you have only three days to pay it. After several months of this, you find yourself not using that card as often. Eventually, you drop it from your retail credit portfolio.

Is Financial Management an Enterprise Marketing Expense?

So you say, "OK, maybe accounting practices do have some effect on customer perceptions, but what about finance?" Take financial policy as an example. Suppose the price of stock you own has been falling and you find out the company has done a big PIPE deal (**P**rivate **I**nvestment in **P**ublic **E**quity). "In a PIPE, investors buy new unregistered shares at a discount. These become public shares after a few months. Existing shareholders dislike PIPEs because they dilute the value of their shares." (Barret and Licking 2002) What does that do to your perception of the company? And by the way, the salaries and perks of financial managers show up as an SG&A expense. So may the sales commissions on the PIPES they sell show up in this account.

Financial managers engage in a lot of other activities that affect market value. Consider, as another example, the monitoring and certification services provided by underwriting syndicates in raising capital (Hansen and Torregrosa 1992). Called "flotation costs," these expenses include searching the primary market for potential investors and sales commission to agents. Some of these costs find their way into a company's selling, general, and administrative expenses.

Another role financial managers play in enterprise marketing is found in the credit rating of a company—and this rating in turn directly influences shareholder value. Remember, enterprise marketing expenses are the key to competing both for customers and for capital.

Where Does Traditional Marketing Fit?

Companies in some industries report the major components of selling, general, and administrative expenses in their financial statements. One of these is the pharmaceutical industry. Not all pharmaceutical companies report the numbers required for showing where traditional marketing fits in the picture. But in 2003, three companies did report all the numbers: *GlaxoSmithKline (GSK), Johnson & Johnson (JNJ),* and *Novartis (NVS).*

Table 4-2 Where Traditional Marketing Fits in Pharmaceuticals

2003	Sales*	Gross	SG&A	Breakdown of SG&A Expenses			
				L&R	A&P	R&D	Sum
GSK	$38,389	$32,451	$19,214	$9,024	$1,097	$4,942	$15,063****
		85%**	50%**	47%***	6%***	26%***	78%***
JNJ	$41,862	$31,555	$18,815	$10,005	$1,700	$5,602	$17,307
		75%	45%	53%	9%	30%	92%
NVS	$24,864	$20,106	$13,081	$6,252	$967	$3,756	$10,975
		81%	53%	48%	7%	29%	84%

*$values are mill US **% Sales ***% SG&A ****L&R+A&P+R&D

Table 4-2 shows what these three big pharmaceuticals spent on selling, general, and administrative expenses. It also breaks down what each one spent on the three major components of SG&A. These components are labor and related (L&R) expenses,[2] advertising and promotion (A&P) expenses,[3] and research and development (R&D) expenses.[4] The percentage of each expense category to company totals is shown immediately below the dollar amount (in millions).

There's a lot of information packed into this little table, so you need to take a close look to figure out just where traditional marketing fits. Start with *GlaxoSmithKline*. Its sales in 2003 were $38.4 billion. Gross profits in that year were $32.5 billion. These two numbers should get your attention right away. *GSK's* gross profits were 85% of sales. Fat margins are typical of big pharmaceutical companies. *JNJ's* gross margin was 75% and *NVS's* was 81%. **Make a note: gross margin *rules* in enterprise marketing.**

Meanwhile, *GlaxoSmithKline's* SG&A expenses were $19.2 billion. This is the second number that should get your attention. SG&A expenses accounted for 50% of *GSK's* sales revenues in 2003. The next three columns report the dollar amounts and percentage of SG&A expenses dedicated to L&R (47%), A&P (6%), and R&D (26%). The last column reports the sum of L&R, A&P, and R&D.

Taken together, these numbers give you the information you need to answer the question "How important are traditional marketing expenses in enterprise marketing?" Of course, the answer depends on how you define "marketing." If you subscribe to the traditional view of marketing as advertising and promotion expenses, it's a relative drop in the bucket. *A&P* was only 6% of *GSK's* total spending on selling, general, and administrative expenses in calendar year 2003, and just 9% and 7% of SG&A expenses for *JNJ* and *NVS,* respectively. Even though *GSK* and *NVS* spent around one billion U.S. dollars on A&P, and *JNJ* spent almost two billion, these costs are a small percentage of enterprise marketing expenses.

On the other hand, all three big pharmas spent around 50% of SG&A dollars on people. This may be why Jeffrey Pfeffer traces advances in shareholder value to people. L&R spending swamps even R&D expenditures in an industry famous for its heavy R&D spending. If a company's investments in people are effective, and if the talent this money buys is productive, it will have a huge positive impact on earnings and shareholder value. By implication the opposite also is true.

Take another look at Table 4-1 and the seven components of enterprise marketing expenses. Look at the details the editor's of the Harvard Management Update included for each component and you will begin to understand the complexity of the enterprise marketing puzzle illustrated in Figure 4-1 and why all the pieces—taken together—have such a far-reaching impact on the competition for customers and capital. The sum of all the ongoing costs required for supporting the people who serve in each of these areas is the cost of enterprise marketing.

Let's review the bidding so far. In the narrow, conventional sense, "marketing" doesn't matter much in pharmaceuticals. Even R&D is relatively

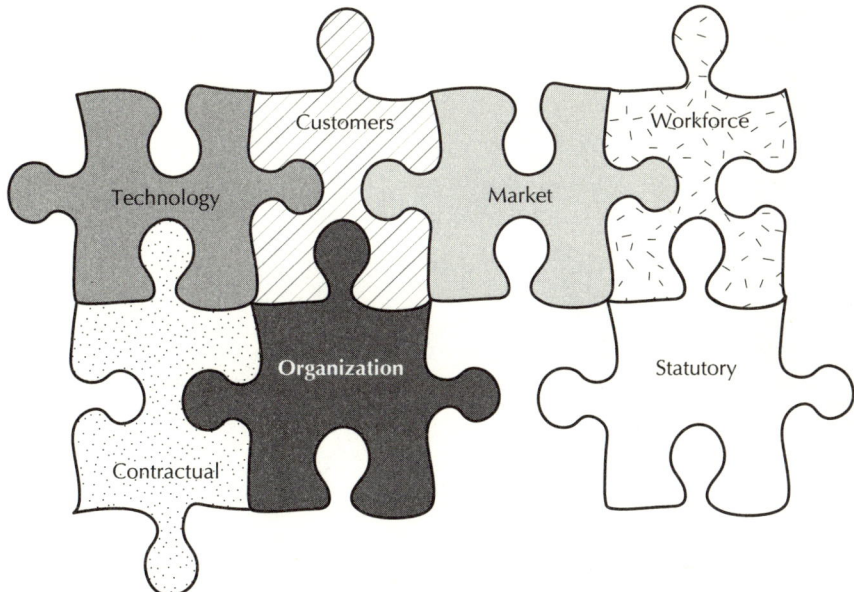

Figure 4-1 The Enterprise Marketing Puzzle

unimportant compared with the salaries, perks, pensions, benefits, and wages paid to talented people. And make no mistake; it's the people who create the intangible values that eventually show up on the balance sheet. But the balance sheet is terribly insensitive to the creation of intangible value. So we track the process by measuring the inputs, the people, promotional, and development dollars that may (or may not) eventually show up as intangibles on the balance sheet. Our focus is on how much and how efficiently a company spends money in the management of all these enterprise marketing expenses. We hope this will shed a bright light on the creation of shareholder value.

Enterprise Marketing Expenses in Autos

Reporting practices for selling, general, and administrative expenses vary widely from one sector of the economy to another. For example, the line items heavy manufacturing companies included in SG&A expenses are very different from those in pharmaceuticals. But the big picture remains about the same.

Let's look closely at the mother of all manufacturing industries—automobiles. In 2002–2003, the global automobile marketplace included seven major players. Only two of these were domestic manufacturers. These major players were:

- DCX (*Daimler-Chrysler* ADR),
- FIA (*Fiat S.p.A.* ADR),
- F (*Ford Motor Company*),
- GM (*General Motors Corporation*),
- HMC (*Honda Motors* ADR),
- NSANY (*Nissan Motors* ADR), and
- TM (*Toyota Motor Company* ADR).

Table 4-3 lists these companies in order of their ticker symbols. The numbers in this table are similar to those for the domestic airline strategic group in Chapter 2, with three important differences.

First, the stocks of five of the seven global auto companies are traded on U.S. security exchanges as ADRs. ***American Depository Receipts*** are:

> *A negotiable U.S. certificate representing ownership of shares in a non-U.S. corporation. ADRs are quoted and traded in U.S. dollars in the U.S. securities market; the associated dividends are paid to investors in U.S. dollars as well. ADRs were specifically designed to facilitate the purchase, holding, and sale of non-U.S. securities by U.S. investors as well as to provide a corporate finance vehicle for non-U.S. issuers.* (Exitexchange.com)

Table 4-3 Global Auto Group

Ticker	Price per Share (7/3/03)	Number of Shares	Market Cap (Millions)	Sales Revenues (Millions)	Sales Revenues (Mill Y02)	Value Share (Points)	Revenue Share (Points)
DCX	$35.67	1,012.8	$36,127	€ 149,583	$157,107	13.8	20.2
FIA	$ 7.50	616.4	$ 4,623	€ 58,092	$ 61,014	1.8	7.8
F	$10.87	1,830.3	$19,896	$163,420	$163,420	7.6	21.0
GM	$35.78	560.6	$20,059	$186,763	$186,763	7.7	24.0
HMC	$19.90	1,941.9	$38,643	Y7,362,438	$ 55,253	14.8	7.1
NSANY	$20.00	2,258.4	$45,169	Y6,196,241	$ 46,588	17.3	6.0
TM	$54.37	1,774	$96,345	Y14,316,874	$107,443	36.9	13.8
Totals			$260,862	NM	$777,588	100.0	100.0

Second, sales revenues for two of these companies (*DCX* and *FIA*) are reported in Euros (€), while sales revenues for three of the companies (*HMC, NSANY,* and *TM*) are reported in Japanese Yen (¥).

Finally, like the airline data in Chapter 2, the market cap for each company in this table was calculated using the closing price per share on July 3, 2003. Sales revenues in Table 4-3 were taken from *Standard & Poor's COMPUSTAT* database for the calendar year ending December 31, 2002.

Foreign companies filing ADRs with the SEC are required to submit only annual income statements. So quarterly sales data often are not available. The annual 2002 period was the closest alignment to July 2003 for the five offshore companies in this table. Stocks are, literally, a "stock variable" measured at one point in time, while sales are a "flow variable" measured over time. For this reason, it's possible to mix and match the data within proximate time periods.

Some Cautionary Notes

When you estimate market caps from ADRs, you should check to be sure that the current ADR ratio is used. The ADR ratio is the number of shares in the company's home exchange to which an ADR certificate may be converted. Management can change this ratio long before it is reported in the company's annual balance sheet. Using the wrong ADR ratio can produce wildly incorrect estimates of market value. Unknown changes in the ADR ratio can artificially inflate or deflate market cap.

Out-of-date ADR ratios sometimes appear in databases that repackage the annual financial statements of offshore companies. Periodically the *COMPUSTAT* data are updated with current ADR ratios. Sometimes the updates take place long after the ratios have changed. The only way to be sure you have the current ADR ratio is to go to the company's current annual financial statements.

To estimate foreign sales revenues, you need to be sure the exchange rates from Yen and Euros to U.S. dollars are taken on the same date for all of the companies. Differences in exchange rates also can have a significant effect on sales revenues converted to dollars. In turn, these can have a huge impact on a company's risk-adjusted VS differentials.

When foreign companies are included in a strategic group, it's a good idea to verify that currency conversions were made using exchange rates for the same date.

From Storefront to Superstar

In the summer of 1957, *Toyota Motor Sales USA* opened in an old *Nash Rambler* dealership in Hollywood, California.

> *But back in 1957 those first* Toyotas *didn't exactly fly off the ships and into the hands of eagerly waiting buyers. During its first 14 months in the United States,* Toyota *sold a grand total of 288 vehicles—287* Toyota Toyopets *and one* Land Cruiser. *The* Toyopet *was* Toyota's *staple in Japan. But it had problems here. For one thing, it was slow. And worse, at $2300, it suffered from a serious price disadvantage compared to its most serious competitor, the* Volkswagen. (Chaikin 2003)

Forty-six years later, at the end of the first quarter of 2003, *Toyota Motors* was one of the "Big 4" global auto companies.

For several years running, the *Toyota Camry* has been the top-selling car in the U.S. market. Still, the company captured only 13.8% of sales revenues generated by the seven global auto companies listed in Table 4-3. But, get this—the total market value of these seven companies on July 3, 2003, was $260,862 million. *Toyota* created 36.9% of that market value.

Let's take a closer look at the margins and enterprise marketing expenses of these companies. The data on cost of goods sold, gross profits, gross margin, and selling, general, and administrative expenses appear in Table 4-4.

In this global auto marketplace, gross profits totaled $223.2 billion in calendar year 2002. This amounted to an average of 28.7% of sales. Out of these gross profits, the companies spent $129.2 billion on enterprise marketing. This meant 57.9% of gross profits were enterprise marketing expenses.

How do the individual companies compare with the strategic group averages? Well, for openers, *Toyota* did not have the highest gross margin. In fact, at 26.5%, *TM's* gross margin was significantly below the group average of 28.7%. It was second-lowest to *General Motors'* 24.8% gross margin.

Table 4-4 Enterprise Marketing Expenses in Autos

Company	Cost of Goods Sold (Millions)	Gross Profits (Millions)	Gross Profit Margin (Percent)	Enterprise Marketing Expenses (Millions)	Marketing Expenses to Profits (Percent)
Daimler-Chrysler	$113,258	$43,849	27.9	$ 25,589	58.4
Fiat S.p.A.	$ 42,693	$18,321	30.0	$ 15,990	87.3
Ford Motor Co	$109,960	$53,460	32.7	$ 28,426	53.2
General Motors	$140,406	$46,357	24.8	$ 23,624	51.0
Honda Motors	$ 36,332	$18,921	34.2	$ 12,660	66.9
Nissan Motors	$ 32,732	$13,856	29.7	$ 8,726	63.0
Toyota Motors	$ 78,977	$28,466	26.5	$ 14,181	49.8
Totals	$554,358	$223,230	28.7	$129,196	57.9

Did *Toyota* spend more on enterprise marketing than the other competitors? No. The company spent a lot—$14.2 billion—but less than any other company except *Nissan*. As a percent of gross profits, *Toyota* spent less (49.8%) than all the others.

Little *Fiat S.p.A.* was the big spender with enterprise marketing expenses running upward of 90% of its gross profits.

At least in the global auto market, the links among margins, enterprise marketing expenses, and share of market value are less than obvious. Let's look at how the numbers stack up for a large sample of public companies.

A Really Big Picture

A natural question to ask at this point is: "How important are enterprise marketing expenses in the larger scheme of things?" To answer this question, let's look again at the domains of executive action—the three parts of a company's revenue dollar. As shown in Table 4-5, these parts are the cost of goods sold (operations management); selling, general, and administrative expenses (enterprise marketing); and earnings before depreciation (corporate finance).

In calendar year 2002, the *COMPUSTAT* database contained about 10,000 companies in its active file. A sample was drawn from this universe

Table 4-5 Domains of Executive Action

COGS ≈ Operations Management	SG&A ≈ Enterprise Marketing	EBITDA ≈ Corporate Finance

that included every company that reported a closing price for its stock, the number of common shares outstanding, sales revenues, cost of goods sold, and selling, general, and administrative expenses. Many foreign and domestic companies failed to meet these criteria because they did not report SG&A expenses separately on their income statements. Instead, they were left in *gross profits* along with *earnings before depreciation*. When companies don't report SG&A separately, the analyses outlined later in this book cannot be conducted.

A total of 5,359 companies passed this screening.[5] The sample companies covered virtually all of the 122 sub-industries included in *Standard & Poor's Global Industry Classification System*. The sub-industries ranged from *Advertising Agencies* to *Wireless Telecommunications Services*.

The combined sales revenues of the sample companies in 2002 was $8,705 billion. Their combined market cap was $10,281 billion. Yes, these numbers are correct. The combined market cap was $10.3 **trillion** and revenues were $8.8 **trillion** US$. The sum of value-to-sales ratio was 1.18. The median value/revenue ratio was 0.94. By this time it should not be a surprise that in a large sample of firms, the dollar value of market cap approaches sales revenues.

Table 4-6 also shows how the revenue dollar was divided up in these sample companies. The cost of goods sold totaled $5,554 billion, leaving $3,151 billion in gross profits. Selling, general, and administrative expenses (roughly, the cost of enterprise marketing) were $1,740 billion. **Spending on enterprise marketing consumed half the gross profits of these public companies.** Earnings before interest, taxes, depreciation, and amortization were $1,411 billion. Out of an average revenue dollar, these 5,359 sample companies:

- Spent 64¢ on operations management,
- Spent 20¢ on enterprise marketing, and
- Earned 16¢ for corporate finance.

Table 4-6 How the Revenue Dollar Is Divided Up

2002	Billions $US	Ratio
Operations Management	5,554	64%
Enterprise Marketing	1,740	20%
Corporate Finance	1,411	16%
Revenue	8,705	100%
Market Cap	10,281	1.18

Overall, gross profits as a percentage of sales averaged 36%. Enterprise marketing expenses as a percentage of gross profits averaged about 55%. Earnings averaged 45% of gross profits.

Enterprise Marketing Expenses in Banking

The competitive matrix presented in Chapter 1 can now be filled with real numbers. The first example is based on the four commercial banks that passed the screen in the sample of companies reported previously. The number of banks is so small because, historically, banks did not report an SG&A expense category as a separate line item in their income statements. The fact that three of the leading banks in the U.S. did report SG&A in the first quarter of 2003 is an indication that more will likely do so in the future.

Table 4-7 Competitive Matrix in Banking Q1-2003[6]

Millions USD	Sales Revenues	−	Interest Expense	=	Gross Profits	−	Enterprise Marketing Expenses	=	EBITDA	=>	Market Value
Wells Fargo (WFC)	$7,561	−	$879	=	$6,682	−	$2,983	=	$3,699	=>	$75,355
Bank One Corp (ONE)	$5,146	−	$1,203	=	$3,943	−	$1,944	=	$1,999	=>	$39,750
U S Bancorp (USB)	$3,697	−	$ 562	=	$3,135	−	$1,134	=	$2,001	=>	$36,424
Comerica Inc. (CMA)	$ 866	−	$135	=	$731	−	$376	=	$355	=>	$6,635
Group	$17,270	−	$2,779	=	$14,491	−	$6,437	=	$7,966	=>	$158,164

Wells Fargo & Company, with revenues of $7,561 million, is the sales leader in this group. It also is one of the oldest banks in the country:

In 1852 Henry Wells and William Fargo founded Wells, Fargo & Co. *to serve the West. The new company offered banking (buying gold, and selling paper bank drafts as good as gold)—and express (rapid delivery of the gold and anything else valuable).* Wells Fargo *opened for business in the gold rush port of San Francisco, and soon* Wells Fargo's *agents opened offices in the other new cities and mining camps of the West. In the boom-and-bust economy of the 1850s,* Wells Fargo *earned a reputation of trust by dealing rapidly and responsibly with people's money. In the 1860s, it earned everlasting fame—and its corporate symbol—with the grand adventure of the overland stagecoach line.* (Wellsfargo.com)

The second-largest player in this group is an up-and-comer named *Bank One Corp.* with first-quarter 2003 revenues of $5,146 million. Currently the sixth-largest bank in the U.S., the company leaped into the top ranks by merger. This $7.8-billion event was listed as number eight in *SNL's* "Deals of the Decade":

With its January 1997 announcement that it would acquire First USA Inc., Bank One *launched itself into the top three players in the credit card industry, trailing only* Citicorp *and* MBNA Corp. *At the time of the announcement,* Bank One *Chairman and CEO John B. McCoy was criticized for abandoning his previous acquisition discipline to pay 20x forward earnings and more than 500% of book value in a dilutive deal. He also caught flak for the timing of the transaction: Critics worried that the best of the growth days for cards was over and that delinquencies were destined to climb.* (SNL.com)[7]

This turned out to be small potatoes compared with the $59-billion merger of *J.P. Morgan Chase* with *Bank One* announced on January 14, 2004.

The third-largest company in this marketplace was *U.S. Bancorp,* with first-quarter 2003 revenues of $3,697 million. *U.S. Bancorp Piper Jaffray* was founded in Minneapolis in 1895 as the *George B. Lane, Commercial Paper and Collateral Loans & Co.* With assets of $195 billion in 2002, it was the eighth-largest financial services holding company in the country.

Comerica Inc., the smallest player in this banking group with first-quarter 2003 revenues of $866 million, has a corporate history that predates even *Wells Fargo & Company.* "*Comerica* forerunner *Detroit Savings Fund Institute* was founded by Elon Farnsworth on March 5, 1849. It took in $41 in deposits on the first day of business." (Comerica.com)

Combined sales revenues of the four banks in this group were $17,270 million. There are several important things to notice in Table 4-7.

Interest Expense

First, the cost-of-goods-sold column has been replaced with "Interest Expense." In *COMPUSTAT,* this item represents the interest expense on deposits, long-term debt, and all other borrowings of financial services companies. While these four banks reported "cost of goods sold" as a line item in their income statement, operating costs were assigned to this account over and above the cost of money in ways that are not revealed. For example, *WFC* reported $1,290 million COGS, though its total interest expenses were $879 million. The other $411 million must have been other operating expenses. For each of these banks, the difference between reported COGS and interest expense was added to the reported SG&A expenses and placed in the column labeled "Enterprise Marketing Expenses." In the case of *Wells Fargo,* the total cost of enterprise marketing was increased $411 million—from $2,572 to $2,983 million.

Large Value/Revenue Ratio

A second important fact to notice in Table 4-7 is that the $158.2 billion in value created by the four companies was nine times greater than the sales revenues they generated. The value/sales ratio for each of these companies was greater than the large sample V/S ratio of 1.18 reported Table 4-6. On average, a dollar of revenue in this banking group created $9.20 in market value. The v/r multiple ranged from a low of 7.7 for *Bank One Corp* to a high of 10.0 for *Wells Fargo & Company.*

Enterprise Marketing Expense Differences

A third fact to notice in Table 4-7 is that *Bank One* and *U.S. Bancorp* had almost identical earnings in the first quarter of 2003 ($1,999 million vs. $2,001 million). Yet *Bank One's* $1,944 million enterprise marketing expenses were 71% greater than *U.S. Bancorp's* $1,134 million. The $810 million difference reflects either a greater emphasis on the use of enterprise marketing to build customer relationships or lower efficiency in acquiring these resources. We would like to know which.

Also, notice that *Bank One's* sales revenue of $5,146 million was one-third greater than *U.S. Bancorp's* $3.697 million. Yet *Bank One's* market value was only 9% greater than *U.S. Bancorp's.*

How can these differences be explained? For clues, visit the company Web sites, read the annual reports, and look for news stories in the business press. Or just read the chapters that follow.

Your Banking Dollar

The division of each company's revenue dollar in this banking group is shown in Table 4-8. Some of the differences are surprising. For example, *Wells Fargo* paid only 11.6¢ out of every sales dollar on interest expense,

Table 4-8 Three Parts of a Revenue Dollar in Banking

Strategic Group	Interest Expenses	Enterprise Marketing Expenses	EBITDA	Marketing to Gross Profits
Wells Fargo	11.6%	39.5%	48.9%	44.6%
Bank One	23.4%	37.8%	38.8%	36.7%
U S Bancorp	15.2%	30.7%	54.1%	25.5%
Comerica Inc.	15.6%	43.4%	41.0%	36.9%

while *Bank One* spent 23.4¢. *U.S. Bancorp* spent 30.7¢ of each revenue dollar on enterprise marketing compared with the 39.5¢ spent by *Wells Fargo* and 43.4¢ for *Comerica*. Further, notice that *U.S. Bancorp's* EBITDA was 15.3 percentage points greater than *Bank One's* EBITDA, even though it generated only three-quarters of the revenue.

The ratio of enterprise marketing expenses to gross profits ranged from a low of 25.5% for *U.S. Bancorp* to a high of 44.6% for *Wells Fargo*. Finally, *Comerica* spent almost the same percent of gross profits on enterprise marketing as did *Bank One* (36%) even though *Bank One's* revenues were six times bigger that *Comerica*.

Given the significant differences in how these banks spent their money, you might expect to find huge VS differentials in this strategic group. But you don't—at least in the first quarter of 2003. The results are shown in Table 4-9. *Wells Fargo's* VS differential was −3.9, while the much smaller *Bank One* posted a differential of +4.7 points. *U.S. Bancorp* realized a negative differential (−1.6) while tiny *Comerica* posted a positive differential (+0.8). Yet all four companies had large v/r multiples. The bottom line: while banks appear to produce consistently greater market value per dollar of sales revenue—within a strategic group, there are no significant differences in the way investors value their service market performance.

Table 4-9 Shareholder Value and Revenue in Commercial Banks

Strategic Group	Share of Value	Share of Revenue	VS Differential	v/r Multiples
Wells Fargo & Co	43.8%	47.6%	−3.9%	9.97
Bank One Corp	29.8%	25.1%	4.7%	7.72
U S Bancorp	21.4%	23.0%	−1.6%	9.85
Comerica Inc.	5.0%	4.2%	0.8%	7.66

Old-Line and New-Wave Supermarket Chains

Banks report a purely market-based measure of the cost of goods sold (the interest on money they borrow); so do retailers (the cost of products bought for resale). This example is based on supermarket chains. The six chains in this group were selected from a larger sample that satisfied the data-reporting requirements discussed earlier in this chapter. These six grocery chains were selected out of the sixteen that passed the screening requirements for highlighting the differences between the old-line sales leaders and a new-wave player.

Kroger, the sales leader in this group, had revenues of $16,266 million in the first quarter of 2003. The company's first store opened at 66 East Pearl Street in Cincinnati, Ohio, in 1883. The next year, Barney Kroger bought out his partner and opened a second store. In 1901, *Kroger* became the first grocery chain to operate its own bakery. With forty stores and annual revenues of $1.75 million, *The Kroger Grocery and Baking Company* was incorporated in 1902.

On the company's 25th anniversary, 200 horses and wagons were making regular store deliveries. By 1908, *Kroger* owned and operated a total of 136 stores in Cincinnati, Dayton, Columbus, and northern Kentucky. Management replaced its horse and wagon teams with seventy-five *Model T* trucks in 1913. Three years later, self-service was tried for the first time—and the food store, as we know it today, began to take shape. (*Kroger.com*)

The second-largest grocery chain in this strategic group was *Albertsons* with first-quarter 2003 revenues of $8,940 million. The following bit of history was taken from the company's Web site:

> *In 1939, our founder, Joe Albertson, opened a small grocery store in Boise, Idaho. Joe changed the rules in the grocery business by introducing unheard-of services like a scratch bakery, magazine racks, home-made ice cream, popcorn, nuts and an automatic donut machine. He based his store on high quality, good value, and excellent service. That was the beginning of what is now one of the largest retail food & drug chains in the United States.* (Albertsons.com)

A&P is the oldest of the three old-line grocery chains in this group. *The Great Atlantic & Pacific Tea Company's* "history traces to 1859, when George F. Gilman and George Huntington Hartford founded the *Great American Tea Co.* in New York City to trade in tea bought from the cargoes of the clipper ships." *(Britannica.com)*

The smallest player in this grocery group was *Whole Foods* with 2003 first-quarter sales revenues of $725 million.

Memorial Day 1981: Eight months after the very first Whole Foods Market debued, a massive Texas flood destroyed it, filling the store with eight feet of water and muck and overturning refrigerators. 'I figured we were out of business,' says chief executive John Mackey, who spent the night wallowing out in front of his organic food store with a six-pack of beer. But the next day a steady stream of customers showed up with mops and buckets to help clean up—part of the reason the store reopened a mere 30 days later. 'Customers working day and night for no reimbursement—that was a clear message that Whole Foods *would be enormously successful,' says Mark Skiles, one of Mackey's co-founders. That kind of fierce customer loyalty has built* Whole Foods *from that one store to 143 today and to $2.7 billion in sales and $85 million in profits last year.* (Overfelt 2003)

These six grocery chains are compared in the competitive matrix of Table 4-10. Total first-quarter 2003 revenues in this strategic group were $38,817 million. There are several facts worth your attention in Table 4-10.

First, look at the last row of the sales-revenue and market-value columns in this table. Sales revenues *exceeded* market value by more than $8 billion, or 22%. Compare this to the banking group. The banks created $9.2 in market value for every sales dollar; this group of supermarket chains created only 78¢ in value per sales dollar. Market value per sales dollar was greater than

Table 4-10 Grocery Chain Competitive Matrix[8]

Company	Sales Revenues	−	Cost of Goods Sold	=	Gross Profits	−	SGA Expense	=	EBITDA	=>	Market Value
KR	$16,266	−	$12,128	=	$4,138	−	$3,030	=	$1,108	=>	$9,863
ABS	$8,940	−	$6,148	=	$2,792	−	$2,185	=	$607	=>	$6,918
SWY	$7,543	−	$5,099	=	$2,444	−	$1,841	=	$604	=>	$8,354
WIN	$2,822	−	$1,993	=	$829	−	$699	=	$131	=>	$1,862
GAP	$2,520	−	$1,750	=	$770	−	$720	=	$50	=>	$166
WFMI	$725	−	$453	=	$272	−	$206	=	$66	=>	$3,308
Group	$38,816	−	$27,570	=	$11,246	−	$8,681	=	$2,566	=>	$30,471

*USD rounded to the nearest million. Note that the companies have different fiscal year ends.

one for only *Safeway* ($1.11) and *Whole Foods* ($4.56). This is a ratio you should calculate whenever you assess career potentials in various industries and companies.

Second, *A&P* and *Winn-Dixie* are in the same ballpark in terms of sales (A&P/WD = 89%), cost of goods sold (88%), gross profits (93%), and selling expenses (103%). Yet, *A&P's* earnings are only 39% of *Winn-Dixie's*. *A&P's* $166-million market value is just 9% of *Winn-Dixie's* $1,862-million market value.

Third, the group generates $4.47 in revenue for every $1.00 in SG&A expenses. Yet every company except *Kroger* with $5.37 in revenue per dollar of enterprise marketing expenses is below the group average. *WFMI* and *GAP* are the least efficient, generating only $3.50 and $3.52 in revenue, respectively, for each dollar of SG&A expenses.

Your Grocery Dollar

The next table shows the percentage allocation of revenue dollars. It also shows how much of each company's gross profit dollar was spent on enterprise marketing.

A&P had a lower cost of goods sold as a percentage of revenue than *Winn-Dixie* and it spent almost 4% more of sales on enterprise marketing. But the most telling number in Table 4-11 is the company's spending on SG&A expenses as a percent of its gross profits. *A&P* spent over 93% of its gross profits on enterprise marketing compared with *WD's* 84.2%. It sure does look a lot like inefficient spending.

The *Whole Foods Market* provides another clue to each company's relative efficiency. It spent 28.4% of sales on enterprise marketing. This was almost exactly the same as *A&P's* 28.6%. Yet *Whole Food's* spending amounted to

Table 4-11 Three Parts of the Sales Dollar in a Grocery Chains

Strategic Group	Cost of Goods Sold	Enterprise Marketing Expenses	EBITDA	Marketing to Gross Profits
Kroger	74.6%	18.6%	6.8%	73.2%
Albertsons	68.8%	24.4%	6.8%	78.3%
Safeway	67.6%	24.4%	8.0%	75.3%
Winn-Dixie	70.6%	24.8%	4.6%	84.2%
A&P	69.4%	28.6%	2.0%	93.5%
Whole Foods	62.4%	28.4%	9.2%	75.6%

just 75.6% of gross profits. Sorting out efficiency and spending level is a complex task.

These conclusions must be tempered somewhat by the fact that quarterly periods cannot be aligned exactly since *KR* and *ABS* have fiscal years that end in January; *SWY* and *GAP's* end in December; and *WIN* and *WFMI's* end in June and September. Perfect alignment of periodicity in quarterly data is impossible when one or more companies have fiscal years that end in a month other than the last one in a calendar quarter (e.g., January).

Trends in Your Grocery Dollars

The previous snapshot shows how the grocery dollar was divided up in the first quarter of 2003. Trends over the period from the second quarter of 1998 through the first quarter of 2003 reveal important differences between the companies in this strategic group in the cost of goods sold, spending on enterprise marketing, and residual earnings.

Consider first the ten-quarter trends in cost of goods sold. Most of the grocery chains in this strategic group had fairly constant operational costs over this time interval.

Chart 4-1 shows the trends for *Kroger, Winn-Dixie, A&P,* and *Whole Foods. Kroger* and *Winn-Dixie* decreased cost of goods sold by 1.8 and 0.8 percentage points, respectively. *A&P's* cost of goods sold actually increased by 0.9 points while *Whole Foods'* cost of goods sold decreased by

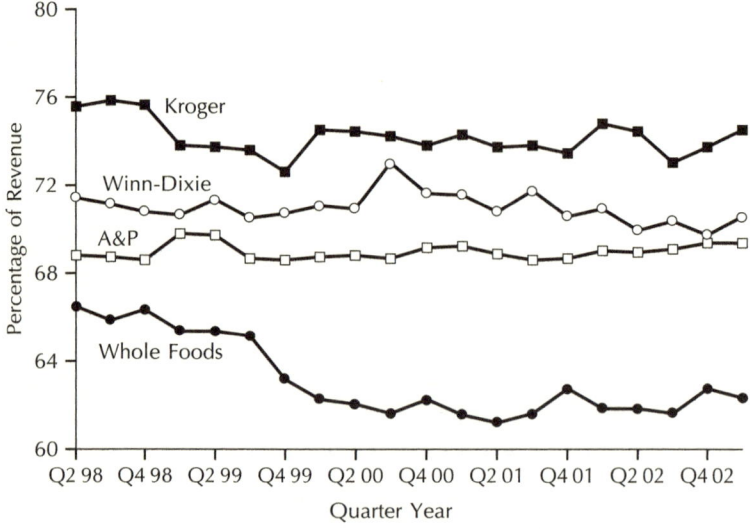

Chart 4-1 Trends in Grocery Chain Cost of Goods Sold

5.3 points. This significant reduction in cost flows directly into gross profit margins.

How does *Whole Foods* maintain a cost advantage of between seven and thirteen points over competitors and still increase that advantage over time? Two forces are possible here. One is a decrease in what the company pays for its products. The other is how much it gets when the products are resold to consumers. Both forces are probably at work here. In the large scheme of things, *WFMI* cannot have scale advantages like *Wal*Mart*. However, to the suppliers of its all-natural and organic merchandise, Whole Foods is the biggest player on the block. To its customers, it's the only player on the block.

As a direct result of its higher operating margins, *Whole Foods* is able to spend a larger percentage of sales on enterprise marketing than its competitors. Chart 4-2 shows how significant this advantage is.

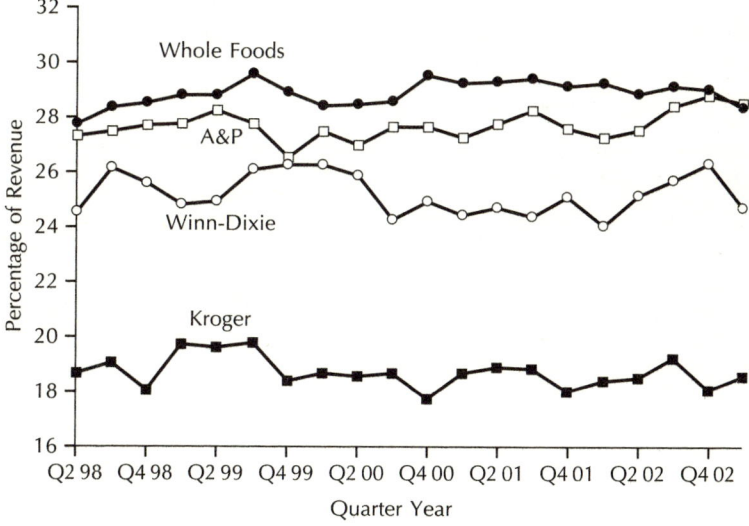

Chart 4-2 Trends in Grocery Chain Enterprise Marketing Expenses

WMFI outspent *Kroger* on enterprise marketing expenses by nine points or more in every period from Q2-1998 through Q1-2003. Those nine points weren't spent on advertising and promotion, either. For the entire year of 2002, *WMFI* spent $12.1 million on advertising and promotion (only 0.4% of sales revenues), compared with *Kroger's* $522 million (1.0% of sales). How did *WFMI* spend the additional money on enterprise marketing?

The answer to this question isn't revealed in the financial statements of *Whole Foods* or *Kroger*. You have to go the stores themselves, visit their

Web sites, and read their annual reports to find out where the additional money went. It's a fair bet that a lot of it went into store ambience (wider aisles, better lighting, and more attractive displays), employee payrolls and benefits, more generous return and allowances policies, and richer merchandise assortments.

Bottom-line comparisons among these grocery chains are even more revealing. Chart 4-3 shows EBITDA as a percentage of sales revenue for the same four chains. Over the ten quarters from 1998 through 2003, *Whole Foods'* earnings before depreciation averaged 8.0% of sales, while *Kroger's* earnings averaged 88 basis points less.

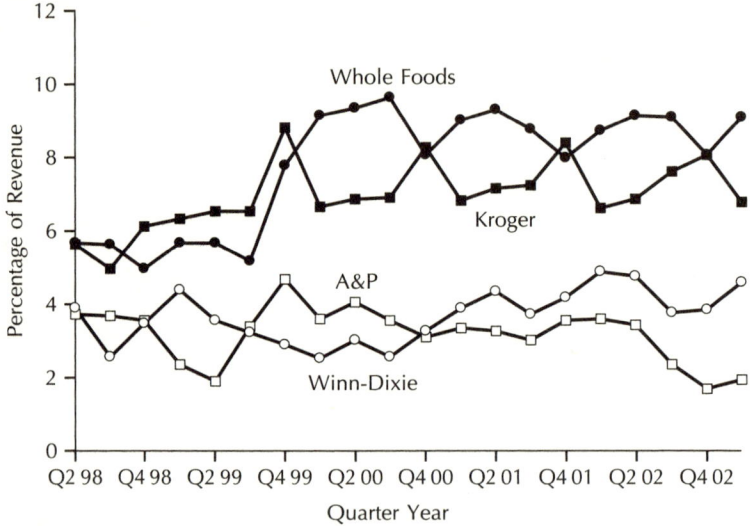

Chart 4-3   Trends in Grocery Chain EBITDA*

*Note that each company's fiscal year end is in a different month—so seasonality is not comparable.

One thing appears to be clear—to the extent that higher gross margins, more enterprise marketing expenses, and higher earnings drive shareholder value—*Whole Foods* should be the winner in this strategic group. Are these advantages reflected in the value-sales differentials? In a word, yes.

Risk-Adjusted VS Differentials in Grocery Chains

The front page news in this grocery group is found in each company's risk-adjusted VS differentials. Table 4-12 shows that *Whole Foods* created 10.9% of the capitalized value on just 1.9% of the sales revenue. *Whole Foods'* nine-point VS differential—combined with a below-average marketing risk (2.35) over the period from the second quarter of 1998 through the first quarter of

Table 4-12 Risk-Adjusted Differentials in the Grocery Group

Company	Share of Value	Share of Revenue	VS Differential	Risk-Adjusted Differential
Kroger	32.4%	41.9%	−9.5%	−1.9
Albertsons	22.7%	23.0%	−0.3%	−0.1
Safeway	27.4%	19.4%	8.0%	1.3
Winn-Dixie	6.1%	7.3%	−1.2%	−0.6
A&P	0.5%	6.5%	−5.9%	−4.0
Whole Foods	10.9%	1.9%	9.0%	3.8

2003—produced a risk-adjusted differential of +3.8. Investors rewarded WFMI a +3.8 risk-adjusted premium in market value over and above its market power. Remember, this is standard deviation greater than the expected value of RAD.

The *Great Atlantic & Pacific Tea Company* paints an entirely different picture over the same period. *A&P* created only 0.5% of the market value on 6.5% of the sales revenues in this strategic group. Its marketing risk was small ($\sigma = 1.49$). So the company's first-quarter 2003 risk-adjusted differential was −4.0 points. Investors heavily discounted *A&P's* value relative to its product market power.

Measuring Enterprise Marketing Expenses Can Be Tricky

Only about one-half of the public companies in financial databases report the line item called "selling, general, and administrative expenses" in their income statements. What accounts for all the missing companies? There are lots of reasons. For example, many of these are foreign companies traded on North American stock exchanges as ADRs. In Europe and Asia, reporting SG&A expenses is not a common practice. Many other companies operate in sectors of the economy where traditionally SG&A expenses are not reported. This is the case for most financial institutions. In capital-intensive industries, SG&A expenses are such a small part of revenues that they are just included in operating costs. In some cases, management simply prefers to be opaque in reporting SG&A expenses.

Even when SG&A expenses are reported, sorting out the full cost of enterprise marketing can be tricky. The banking group is a good example of the tendency for SG&A expenses to miss the cost of people. In banks, the convention is to report the cost of people in cost of goods sold. The same is true of restaurants. After all, consumers can't buy these services without people, so convention says they are part of the cost of goods sold; however, in these cases, convention misses the point. **Enterprise marketing expenses should include all the costs of operations that directly affect customer perceptions and behavior.** Certainly service personnel like bank tellers—as well as restaurant waiters and casino dealers—have a direct impact on both. Before you conduct the analyses that follow in the next chapters, you must understand the business enough to shift the cost of people into the enterprise marketing expense column if they are not included in selling, general, and administrative expenses.

Four Marketing Mysteries

The examples provided by autos, banks, and grocery chains lead directly to four fundamental questions:

1. *How efficient is company spending on enterprise marketing?*
   The marketing efficiency ratio is a direct measure.
2. *What should companies spend on enterprise marketing if management's objective is to maximize earnings?*
   The theory of Maximum Earnings Market Share will answer this question.
3. *Do any companies actually maximize earnings after enterprise marketing expenses?*
   Comparing a company's actual EBITDA with its theoretical maximum earnings—its relative earnings productivity—provides an answer to this question.
4. *Does maximizing earnings affect a company's stock price?*
   This mystery is the toughest one to solve. So many factors influence sales revenues and market value that investors may not be able to read the tea leaves without some help from management and investor relations.

Each of these questions is explored in depth in the following chapters.

References

Albertstons.com. 2003. [Online information; retrieved August 23, 2003]: http://www1.albertsons.com/corporate/ourcomp/oc_main.asp?cat=2&subcat=0

Barret, A., and E. Licking. 2002. "In Biotech, Private Cash is King." *Business Week Online,* February 18.

Britannica.com. 2003. [Online information; retrieved August 18, 2003]: http://www.britannica.com/eb/article?eu=38589

Chaikin, D. 2003. "Storefront to Superstar." [Online information; retrieved August 23, 2003]: http://www.popularmechanics.com

Comerica.com. 2003. [Online information; retrieved August 20, 2003]: http://www.comerica.com/cma/cda/main/0,00,3_A_767,00.html

Exitexchange.com. 2003. [Online information; retrieved August 23, 2003]: http://www.count.exitexchange.com/exit/1106661

Foster, B. P., R. Fletcher, and W. D. Stout. 2003. "Valuing Intangible Assets." *The CPA Journal* 73 (October): 50–55.

Hall, R. 1993. "A Framework Linking Intangible Resources and Capabilities to Sustainable Competitive Advantage." *Strategic Management Journal* 14: 607.

Hansen, R. S., and P. Torregrosa. 1992. "Underwriter Compensation and Corporate Monitoring." *The Journal of Finance* 47 (September): 537–555.

Harvard Management Update. 2001. "Getting a Grip on Intangible Assets." A Newsletter from Harvard Business School Publishing. Reprint No. U0102C.

Kroger.com. 2003. [Online information; retrieved August, 2003]: http://www.kroger.com/corpnewsinfo_history.htm

Overfelt, M. 2003. "The Next Big Thing: John Mackey, Whole Foods Market." *Fortune Small Business* June 4.

Pfeffer, J. 1994. *Competitive Advantage Through People: Unleashing the Power of the Work Force*. Harvard Business School Press.

Snl.com. 2003. [Online information; retrieved August 20, 2003]: http://www.snl.com/bank/manda/20000218_8.asp

Wellsfargo.com. 2003. [Online information; retrieved August 20, 2003]: http://www.wellsfargo.com/about/history/adventure/since_1852.jhtml

End Notes

[1] *COMPUSTAT* annual data item number 33. Intangibles are not reported quarterly.

[2] *COMPUSTAT* annual data item number 42: This item represents the costs of employees' wages and benefits allocated to continuing operations. This item includes incentive compensation, other benefit plans, payroll taxes, pension costs, profit sharing, salaries, and wages. This item excludes commissions. Direct labor costs in manufacturing are included in the cost of goods sold (data item 41).

[3] *COMPUSTAT* annual data item number 45: This item represents the cost of advertising media (radio, television, newspapers, and periodicals) and promotional expenses.

⁴ *COMPUSTAT* annual data item number 46: This item represents all the costs that relate to the development of new products or services. The amount reflects the company's contribution to research and development. This item includes amortization of software costs for companies that recognize software revenues, company-sponsored research and development, purchased research and development, research and development expenses, and software development expenses. This item excludes customer- or government-sponsored research and development expenses, customer-sponsored software expenses, engineering expenses, extractive industry activities, inventor royalties, market research and testing, and support expense.

⁵ A total of 319 outliers were removed from the sample: 140 had sales less than $0.5 million; 122 had market caps less than $0.5 million; 11 firms had value/sales ratios greater than 50 times (12σ from the median); and 46 had value/sales ratios less than 0.01.

⁶ Wharton Research Data Services 1/1/05.

⁷ SNL collects, standardizes, and disseminates corporate, financial, market, and M&A data—plus news and analysis—for the banking, specialized financial services, insurance, real estate, and energy sectors. http://www.snl.com/bank/manda/20000218_8.asp

⁸ Wharton Research Data Services 3/31/03.

CHAPTER 5

THE RULE OF MAXIMUM EARNINGS

Theory is a pretty blunt instrument.

In the social sciences, more often than not, a theory will fail just when you need it most. Sometimes a theory fails to predict an outcome because it's poorly formulated, like the equation: Sunshine + Umbrella = Rain. Other times the failure is just a result of a large variation in outcomes tied to a small sample. Remember that man who drowned in a river with an average depth of three feet?

Once in a while you find a theory that is robust—a theory that **works** more often than it fails, even with small samples. The principle of force is one of those theories.

Surround *IBM*

In 1983, a European computer company had about 3% of the sales revenues in the German heavy manufacturing sector. A board meeting was called to approve a strategy to increase market share. The European Director of Marketing proposed a strategy to increase the company's share to 10%. He planned to "surround *IBM*." The problem was that *IBM Germany* had one-third of the sales in this sector. After he had unveiled his surround *IBM* strategy, a lively discussion erupted in the boardroom.

Many of the company's directors were excited about this bold new strategy. A few, however, were less than enthusiastic about the need to triple the sales force from five to fifteen in order to surround *IBM*.

One of the concerned board members asked the marketing director how many salesmen (at that time there were no saleswomen in the German manufacturing sector) *IBM* had on the ground in that market. The director replied, "*IBM* have forty-five salesmen there, but our chaps are three times better!" A lot of "hear-hears" were heard around the boardroom.

The board approved the increase in-company headcount to fifteen salesmen as planned, and the strategy to surround *IBM* in Germany was implemented. Chart 5-1 illustrates graphically the challenge faced by the company.

The managing director of the company had remained silent during the discussion. He didn't want to undermine the European marketing director. But in a private conversation after the meeting he said to a small group of

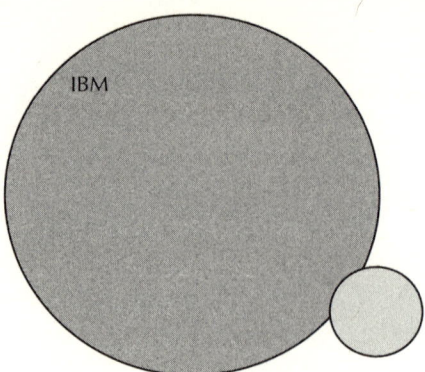

Chart 5-1 Surround *IBM*?

his direct reports: "*Surround* IBM? *This is stupid! We can't beat them at their own game; we need to change the rules.*" Which is exactly what he did. The managing director led the way for European computer manufacturers to achieve a scale influence through OSI[1] that they could not achieve through growing individual market share.

What happened to the surround *IBM* strategy? The year after it was implemented, the company's share of sales in the German heavy manufacturing sector had fallen to under 2%. The strategy was abandoned.

The Principle of Force

If the European computer company's salesmen actually were three times better than the competition, one of two things would have happened. The competition would have hired them away with more pay, or the company would have had to pay more to keep them.

> *It's easy enough to convince your own staff that better people will prevail, even against the odds. It's what they want to hear. And surely in a marketing war, quality is a factor as well as quantity. It is, but superiority of force is such an overwhelming advantage that it overcomes most quality differences. We have no doubt that the poorest team in the National Football League could consistently beat the best team in the* NFL *if it could field 12 men against the opposition's 11.* (Ries and Trout 1986, 26–27)

The rules of the game prohibit that such an inequality of force exist in football. The principle of force is also compelling in a free labor market. You pay the best people more—or you lose them.

In any event, you can't "surround" a force of forty-five *IBM* salesmen with just fifteen of your own. The European marketing director's surround *IBM* strategy was music to the ears of board members. But it was doomed to failure by the principle of force. Sun Tzu put it more eloquently: "If we are able to use many to strike few at the selected place, those we deal with will be in dire straits." (Michaelson and Michaelson 2004, 144) The marketing director was planning to do just the opposite—to strike many with few!

There are, of course, exceptions to every principle. The story of David and Goliath appears to be an exception of mythic proportions. It was, however, a battle of one-on-one. David had a vastly superior weapon and great skill at using it. In the end, force rules. "Where absolute superiority is not attainable, you must produce a relative superiority at the decisive point by making skillful use of what you have." (Michaelson and Michaelson 2004, 145).

The concept of relative superiority can be implemented with the single most widely used marketing metric in the world: market share. A survey of senior marketing managers of 697 firms in the U.S., Japan, Germany, the U.K., and France found that 79% reported using market share to measure marketing performance. The second most widely used metric was perceived product/service quality—77%, followed by customer loyalty/satisfaction—64%, profitability—64%, and relative price—63%. (Barwise and Farley 2003, 105–107)

Us Against Them?

The principle of force is not just an "us against them" game. It's worse than that. It's a game of escalating force requirements.

In the German heavy manufacturing sector, our erstwhile marketing director had five salesmen to *IBM's* forty-five. Before his surround *IBM* strategy, he had 10% of the salesmen on the ground [5/(5 + 45) = 10%]. After tripling his sales force, he had only 25% of the salesmen in this sector [15/(15 + 45) = 25%]. This is how the game works.

If he truly had wanted to surround *IBM*, what force would it require? That depends on what it would take to surround *IBM*. A ratio of two-to-one would do the job. This requires that eighty-five new salesmen be added to the original force of five.

The principle of force fits a simple formula. Let m be the number of salesforce share points you want to achieve in a market. Let f equal the combined number of people in the competitors' sales force. Then y is the number of salespeople you must field to achieve your targeted share of salespeople in that market. The total force formula[2] is:

$$y = m/(100 - m) \times f$$

Suppose the marketing director's goal had been to match *IBM* with an equal sales force rather than to surround it. To match *IBM*, the marketing director must have 50% of the salesmen in the marketplace. To achieve a 50% presence he would need forty-five salesmen. A 50% share of sales force in the German manufacturing sector required a nine-fold increase in the original sales force. The ratio:

$$m/(100 - m)$$

is the enterprise market share multiplier. This multiplier transforms the number of people in a competitive sales force f into the number of people y needed in your company's sales force to achieve market share m.

How Do We Know This Is True?

The European sales manager was also at the board meeting. When he saw this formula written on the white board in the company's headquarters, he was skeptical. He said, "How do I know that formula is true?" One of the board members replied, "How do you know that 2^3 is 8?" The sales manager, angered and embarrassed, got up and stormed out of the meeting. But there was no need to walk out. If he had stuck around a few more minutes, he would have found an explanation for his legitimate concerns.

When the *cost* per salesman is used instead of the number of salesmen, an **efficiency** adjustment must be added to the total force formula. Call this the enterprise **m**arketing **e**fficiency **r**atio x. The x ratio is calculated with this formula:

$$x = s/y$$

where s is the company's actual sales-force cost and y is the theoretical sales-force cost.

How Does x Behave?

The expected value of x is one. The markets for talent work. In the long run, the actual cost of the sales force will equal its theoretical cost. If the enterprise **m**arketing **e**fficiency **r**atio (MER) is greater than 1.0, it means the company is spending more than it needs to; its actual spending is greater than the theoretical level needed to maintain a given market share. There are three possible reasons for an MER to be greater than one. First, the company is paying more for its people than they're worth. Second, the company's people are less effective than the competition. Third, management is attempting to build market share. Theoretically, this last possibility applies only to those cases where the company's actual market share is less than its maximum earnings share.

If a company's MER is less than 1.0, it means management is spending less than it needs to maintain current market share. This could be because people are being paid less than they're worth, they're more effective than the competition, or management is harvesting market share. Theoretically, this possibility applies only to those cases where a company's actual market share is greater than its maximum earnings share.

Except for the sales-force example used here—and the number of flights used later in this chapter with *Southwest Airlines*—the value of y in this book always will be measured by the cost of enterprise marketing expenses. As a result, the marketing efficiency ratio is critical in assessing company performance.

Incremental Force

A tricky extension of the total force formula is to calculate how many people must be added to a sales force *at the margin* to achieve a desired market share. Or, more generally, how much more must a company spend to field one additional share point of enterprise marketing resources!

The question applies to the cost of sales personnel, flights between city-pairs, delivery vehicles and outlets, linear feet of shelf space, number of service staff, or any other scarce physical resource you must put into play in order to compete for customers and capital. To move from a 25% to 26% sales force in the German manufacturing segment required that one additional salesman (actually 0.82) be added to the fifteen needed to maintain a 25% revenue share.[3] This assumes the enterprise marketing efficiency ratio was exactly 1.0. The 51st share point required adding approximately two more salesmen (actually 1.87) to the forty-five required at 50%. The 61st share point meant adding three (2.96) more salesmen. If the company were more efficient with an **MER** of 0.8, incremental sales force requirements for the same share point increases would be 0.66, 1.50, and 2.37 respectively. Competition is a game of diminishing returns and escalating costs, even after adjusting for enterprise marketing efficiency.

New Orleans to West Palm Beach

Let's talk about a fixed asset that is much less fungible than a salesman. Consider the number of flights between city-pairs in the airline market. Suppose *LUV*'s management was planning to enter the MSY-PBI market segment.[4] How many flights should *LUV* schedule? One of the factors influencing the answer to this question is how many flights competitors offer in the same segment.

On July 15, 2003, *Orbitz* listed 132 round-trip flights between New Orleans and West Palm Beach.[5] Every available flight made at least one stop and most had a plane change. The lowest fare was $183 on *Delta*. It made one stop in Orlando. Flight time: four hours and forty-five minutes.

The *Delta* flight through Orlando was added in the spring of 2003. Before that all *Delta* flights between New Orleans and West Palm went through

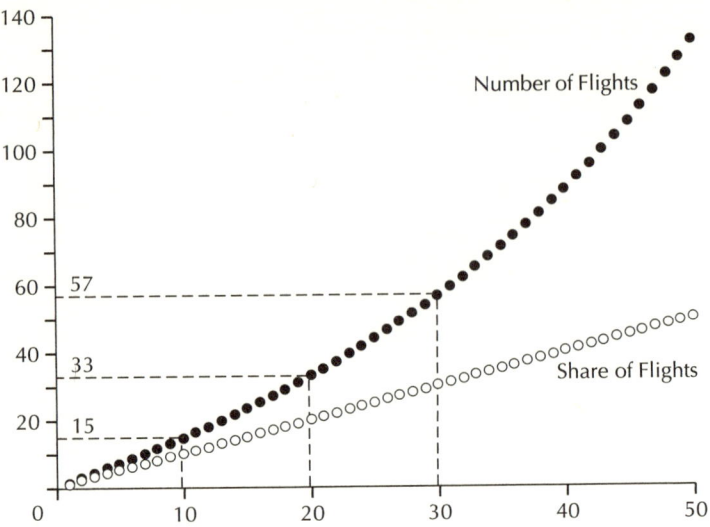

Chart 5-2 Number and Share of Flights

Atlanta. Those five-hour flights cost $588. The highest fare was $667 on *American* for a twelve-hour and fifty-eight-minute flight through Dallas/Fort Worth.

The theoretical relationship between the number of flights and share of flights is pictured in Chart 5-2. The vertical axis in this chart is the theoretical number of flights required by the principle of force if *LUV* were to achieve a given share of total flights. The horizontal axis is the target percentage of flights. The flight shares in Chart 5-2 range from 0% to 50%.

One important conclusion to draw from this chart is that the number of scheduled flights required is a continuously increasing function of the target share of scheduled flights. For *Southwest* to offer 10% of the flights in the New Orleans-West Palm Beach city-pair required the company to schedule an average of 14.7 flights a day—both ways. Suppose *Southwest's* management targeted 20% of the flights. Applying the total force formula, that's an average of 33 flights per day. A 30% share of flights requires 56.6 flights per day.

The number of flights per share point grows geometrically with the target share of flights. Matching the competition in this saturated market would require 132 round-trip flights per day!

Hubs and Spokes in a New Light

The principle of force gives a clue as to why airlines turned to the now infamous "hub-and-spoke" air networks after deregulation in 1978. Of course it was more operationally efficient. But it also shut out the competition, allowed preferential agreements between carriers and hub airports, and limited capacity expansion in non-hub airports. Here's what Alfred E. Khan, the father of airline deregulation, concluded twenty-five years after its inception:

> Most hubs will support only a single airline, and the superior efficiency of hubbing tends to insulate an airline from direct competition on short trips originating or terminating at its hub. . . . the government could actively attempt to make markets more competitive by assuming responsibilities that it has neglected. It could vigorously enforce the antitrust laws. It could also remove barriers to competition by expanding airport capacity enough to allow new competitors to operate on routes, by dissolving preferential arrangements between hub-dominating carriers and their hub airports, and above all, by allowing foreign airlines to compete for domestic traffic, either directly or by investing in American carriers. (Kahn 2002)

The principle of force works powerfully against any airline entering existing segments and motivates a carrier to expand their "hub-and-spoke" networks. That is, unless the airline can find a route less traveled. *Southwest* found many such routes.

A Route Less Traveled

In the spring of 2003, *Southwest* flew to West Palm Beach from New Orleans six times a day, both ways. Two of these flights made one stop in Tampa without a plane change. The trip took two hours and forty-five minutes. The flights were almost always on time. It cost $180 round trip with online booking. The planes were usually full because there weren't any other low-fare, frequent, point-to-point, on-time flights in this segment at that time.

Competitors couldn't easily move into this route. They didn't have the docking gates, landing times, baggage handling equipment, ticket counters, and the people necessary to serve this segment. *Delta,* for example, had all these resources at its hub in Atlanta, it's true, but they couldn't be moved to Tampa. There were two reasons. First, moving the people was problematic. They had homes, kids in school, ties to the community. You couldn't just say "Here are your bags, you're moving to Tampa." Second, there was no excess capacity in Tampa. *LUV* moved in and took an option on everything available. It was as if *Southwest* had paralyzed its competitors.

Remember: *Southwest* flew to fifty-eight cities in thirty states. New Orleans, Tampa, and West Palm Beach were just three of them. Serving only fifty-eight city-pairs—each one less populated with competing flights—meant higher load factors. Having the only flights available in the New Orleans-Tampa-West Palm segment gave *Southwest* 100% share of revenue.

Having nearly full aircraft every time one took off contributed mightily to *LUV's* market value.

Jump to the Enterprise Level

Imagine the entire *Southwest Airlines* network as a single enterprise. We saw in Chapter 2 that the company had 7.6% of the sales revenues in the domestic market. The obvious question is this: if *LUV* is so successful, why doesn't management expand from 7.6% of the domestic market to, say, a 15% share of sales revenues? The answer depends on the cost and profit of a market share point.

If the eighth market share point in the domestic airline marketplace costs less than it contributes to earnings, *LUV* should grow share. Each additional share point would contribute more to earnings than to costs. If the next share point costs more than it contributes to earnings, the company should not grow market share. Each added share point would reduce earnings. In general, management should grow share up to the point where the incremental cost equals the incremental profit of the next market share point. It's simple, once you understand the rule of maximum earnings.

Revenue per Share Point

In the first quarter of 2003, sales revenues in the domestic airline market were $17,763 million.[6] That is the sum of eight airlines' sales revenues. Divide total revenues into 100 points and you have *the revenue value of a share point* shown in Chart 5-3.

Each share point in the domestic airline marketplace was worth $177.63 million in revenues at the end of the first quarter of 2003. The *revenue per share point* is the same for the 1st, 30th, and 75th point if all competitors charge the same price.[7] The *revenue per share point* doesn't change from point to point. Which is to say that the average revenue per point equals the incremental revenue per share point so long as prices do not change with volume.

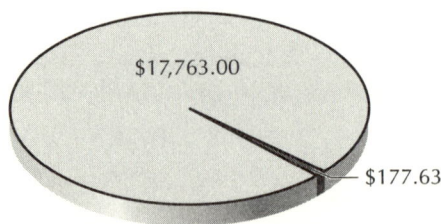

Chart 5-3 Revenue per Share Point

How much of this revenue value a company converts into gross profits depends on its cost of goods sold.

First Bite of the Revenue Dollar

The first bite of the revenue dollar goes to the "cost of goods sold." When *Southwest Airlines* puts a single *Boeing 737* in the air between two airports it's got to pay for the jet fuel and oil, aircraft maintenance, gate costs, landing fees, baggage handling and claims, insurance, and peanuts associated with each flight when it occurs. These are the **variable** factor costs of a flight. The cost of the flight crew with respect to any given flight is fixed.

The components of the cost of **services** sold and the cost of **goods** sold are quite different. Most of an airline's costs do not appear in product manufacturing organizations. Instead, the costs of production include materials, parts and components, direct labor, supervisory costs, power, machine maintenance, packing, and insurance—among other line items.

In either event, revenue minus cost of goods (or services) sold is gross profit. This measure is taken far upstream in flow of cash toward earnings.

What were the airlines' cost of services sold and spending on enterprise marketing in 2003? There are several online sites that are useful when you need to dig this deeply into a company's income statement. Among the most useful are (1) company Web sites, (2) filings with the *Securities and Exchange Commission* (SEC), (3) *Wharton Research Data Services* (*WRDS*), and (4) *Edgar Online Pro*. The first two of these sites are free.

The operating revenues, direct cost of flights, and cost of enterprise marketing for eight air carriers appear in Appendix 5-A of this chapter. These data were compiled from 10-Q reports maintained in the EDGAR SEC Filings.[8] The financial data for all eight airlines are included for comparison.[9] Two of the airlines included in the domestic strategic group in Chapter 2 (*Frontier* and *Mesa*) are excluded from this analysis because they did not report employee salaries, wages, and benefits separately in their 10-Q filings.

The cost of flights includes only the variable costs associated with moving the aircraft from point to point. The variable cost of flights differs from the accounting conventions in the airline industry. In airline financial statements, the cost of employee salaries, wages, and benefits are reported as part of the cost of services sold. Following the belief that people—as well as Selling and Marketing expenses—contribute to the intangible value of the firm, salaries, wages, and benefits were shifted to the cost of enterprise marketing for this analysis.

Southwest's president, Colleen C. Barrett, apparently agrees that people contribute mightily to the value of the company: "There hasn't been a carrier that has been able to match our people in spirit and energy and enthusiasm over the long haul." (Maynard 2004, 9)

The cost of enterprise marketing also includes *Selling and Marketing* expenses, *Food Service,* and *Agency Commissions.* The numbers that appear in bold type in Appendix 5-A of this chapter are estimates based on comparable carriers' line-item expenses as a percent of sales.

For example, *LUV* did not report selling and marketing expenses separately, so the $60 million in Appendix 5-A was estimated at 4.5% of revenues using *CAL* as the comparable, since it was also a low-fare carrier. The Selling and Marketing expenses for *AMR,* on the other hand, were estimated as 11.7% of revenues using *UAL* as the comparable, since it too was a full-service national carrier. The missing Food Service and Agency Commission numbers in Appendix 5-A were estimated in a similar fashion.

Profit per Share Point

How much profit is there in a market share point? The gross profit per share point depends on two things: total revenues in the strategic group, and company gross profit margin per dollar of sales. The results for *Southwest* appear in Chart 5-4.

Group sales revenues were $17,763 million. *LUV's* maximum potential gross profits at a gross margin of 53.85% of group revenues were $9,565.73 million. Divide potential gross profits into 100 parts and you have *LUV's* gross profit per share point of $95.66 million. Arithmetically, the theoretical profit per share point (expressed as an integer) is calculated from this formula:

$$p = (R \times \dot{g})/100$$

In this expression, p is profit per share point, R is strategic group sales revenue, $\dot{g}$ is gross margin expressed as a proportion, and 100 is the number of share points.[10]

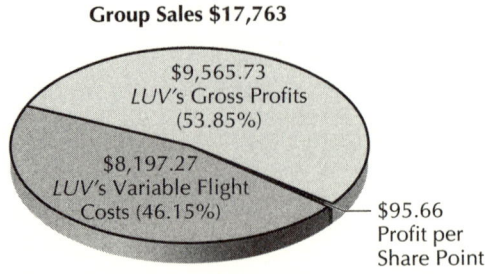

Chart 5-4   *LUV's* Profit per Share Point 2003

Think of *LUV's* management as being open to buy share points in this strategic group. Then management should be willing to pay up to $95.66 million for each one, as long as the next share point is within the company's current scale of operations.

Maximum Earnings Market Share

A company competes for customers by being open to buy market share with a known incremental cost per point. So long as the company continues to pay less for each point than it costs—at the margin—management should buy it. Actually, management should be willing to buy market share points until the profit contributed by the next one is just equal to its cost. This will maximize downstream earnings after enterprise marketing expenses[11] as well as boost company market value (all other things being equal).

The rule of maximum earnings carries a demanding stipulation, however. Either you must empirically estimate the actual incremental profit per share point or assume that **within a feasible range,** average profits equal increment profits. More about this assumption later.

Efficient Factor Markets

We know from the principle of force how many units of a physical resource a competitor must put into play in order to achieve a target share of resources. What the principle of force does not reveal is how much it costs for a given unit of force.

Financial accounting statements don't include the unit cost of a salesman, a flight, or any other physical resource. It would require detailed activity-based accounts to determine the unit, or factor cost, of a given force level. Further, those unit costs will vary with scale, efficiency, and organization.

Southwest will have **advantages** compared with its competitors on some of these costs. It may be at a **disadvantage** on others. Consider, for example, *Southwest's* cost of *Landing Fees and Other Rentals* in the first quarter of 2003. This cost appears on line 2.4 in Appendix 5-A. It was $90 million. These services were a complicated patchwork of different expenses. They varied from airport to airport and changed for each landing time throughout the day (and night), over the day of the week, and month of the year.

LUV may have had scale disadvantages here compared with *UAL*. *United* operated with a hub-and-spoke system that dominated big city airports. Historically, this may have given *United* scale advantages in the form of lower landing costs per flight as well as more favorable treatment by airport administrators in hub cities like Chicago.

Southwest, on the other hand, probably had lower unit costs for *Maintenance Materials and Repairs* (line 2.2 in Appendix 5-A), since the company flew only *Boeing 737s*. Thus, the $106 million it spent in the first quarter of 2003 probably was based on lower cost per repair and lower cost for parts than its larger competitors, who maintained multiple aircraft configurations.

The bad news is that, literally, millions of events came into play in determining *LUV's* variable cost of flights. There's also some good news. Efficient factor markets and accepted accounting standards work to ensure that financial statements provide a reliable indication of relative costs.

LUV's Enterprise Marketing Expenses

Think for a minute about the cost of people in the airline business. It takes people in many different jobs to put a flight in the air—pilots, mechanics, flight attendants, customer management personnel—to name a few. *LUV* may have had some organizational advantages here. For example, *Southwest* historically had better employee relations than many of its competitors. That put the brakes on budget-busting annual salary increases and prolonged strikes.

Every component of enterprise marketing expenses has a physical measure—such as number of messages (advertising) and number of people (sales force)—that are common to all competitors. Each measure also has a per unit factor cost that differs among companies based on scale and efficiency. Yet efficient factor markets and accepted accounting standards also lead to more or less reliable measures of relative enterprise marketing expenses. Better still, the principle of force provides a theoretical estimate of the spending levels necessary to support a given share of revenues. As you've already seen, comparing the theoretical cost of maintaining revenue share with the actual cost of enterprise marketing provides a ready-made measure of efficiency.

Table 5-1 presents a summary of the detailed data in Appendix 5-A for *Southwest* and the seven competitors in this strategic group.

Table 5-1 *LUV's* Relative Sales, Profits, and Costs

1	2	3	4	5	6	7
Quarter Ending March 31, 2003	Sales Revenues (Millions)	Market Share (Percent)	Variable Cost of Flights	Gross Profits t (Millions)	Profit Margin $\dot{g}$ (Percent)	Enterprise Marketing y (Millions)
Southwest	$ 1,350	7.6	46.15%	$ 727	53.85%	$ 588
Competitors	$16,413	92.4	50.44%	$8,134	49.56%	$10,020
Group	$17,763	100	50.12%	$8,860	49.88%	$10,608

Column 2 in this table shows *LUV's* sales revenues were $1,350 million compared with competitors' revenues of $16,413 million in the first quarter of 2003. Group revenues were $17,763 million. *LUV's* market share in that quarter (Column 3) was 7.6% compared with competitors' share of 92.4%. The company's variable cost of flights was 46.15% of sales, yielding a gross profit margin of 53.58% (Column 6). Notice *Southwest's* gross margin was 4.29 points greater than competitors' margins. This is a huge margin advantage in the airline business. Remember, in the competition for shareholder advantage, gross margin rules. *LUV's* cost of enterprise marketing was $588 million compared with competitors' costs of $10,020 million (Column 7).

This combination gave *LUV* an advantage of $7.63 million in per profit per share point over other competitors. This is illustrated in Chart 5-5.

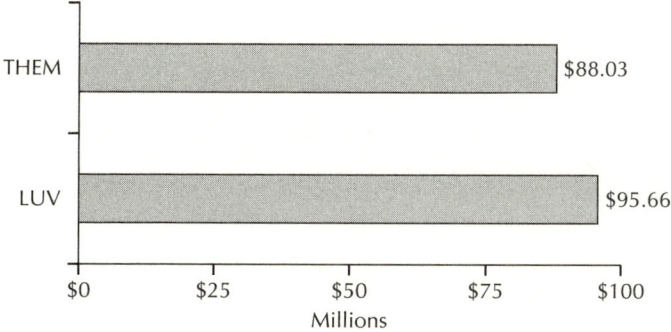

Chart 5-5 *LUV* Versus Competitors' Profit per Point

All this leads to the central question of this chapter: did *Southwest Airlines* spend the right amount of money on its enterprise marketing forces in the first quarter of 2003? In other words, did *LUV* maximize its earnings after enterprise marketing expenses?

What Should *LUV* Have Spent?

The principle of force predicts what a company should spend on enterprise marketing in order to maintain its current market share. If *Southwest* were to maintain the 7.6 point share of revenues it captured in the first quarter of 2003, the total force formula predicts it would need to spend $824 million on enterprise marketing.[12] The company actually spent $588 million—leading to an enterprise marketing efficiency ratio of 0.71.[13]

The $236 million difference between *LUV's* actual and theoretical costs of enterprise marketing represents the scale, scope, and organizational efficiencies built into the *Southwest* business model. This business model also includes loyalty incentives like the company's *Rapid Rewards* program. Customer loyalty significantly reduces the costs of customer retention[14] and increases enterprise marketing efficiency.

Here's an intuitive explanation of the enterprise marketing efficiency ratio. *LUV* spent only $0.71 for resources that cost its competitors $1.41.[15] Note that the enterprise marketing efficiency ratio is **relative** to the other companies in the peer group. This ratio may change if the group is redefined. And the ratio may change over time as well.

Intersection of Cost and Profit Schedules

The incremental cost of *LUV's* next share point in the first quarter of 2003 was $85.57 million. That was the cost of increasing its revenue share from 7.6 to 8.6 points given that competitors' enterprise marketing expenses were $10,020 million.[16] You should check the math to verify that this result is correct.

LUV's maximum earnings market share occurs when its incremental gross profit per share point $\dot{p}$ equals its incremental cost per share point $\dot{c}$. Finding this point is a bit tricky. One way to find it is to plot the incremental profit and cost per point schedules and find their intersection. But there is a simpler way to calculate maximum earnings market share.

The Ante in a Poker Game

Think of the cost of entering a market. That's the cost of the first market share point. It's just like the ante in a poker game. It's how much money you need to put on the table in order the play the game.

The cost of the first share point is a simple function: competitors' enterprise marketing expenses times your company's marketing efficiency divided by 100:

$$\dot{k} = (f \times x)/100$$

In the case of *Southwest*, in the first quarter of 2003 this was $71.49 million.[17] The cost of the first market share point was not the same as the incremental cost of the next share point. The cost of the first point was the price of entry. The cost of the next share point was the price of moving up one point. It makes life a lot simpler to calculate the price of entry, because you can use it as a direct way to estimate maximum earnings market share.

Maximum Earnings Market Share Formula

Earnings before interest, taxes, depreciation, and amortization (EBITDA) are maximized when the cost of the next share point is equal to earnings after the enterprise marketing expenses required to achieve that share point.[18]

Here is a surprisingly simple way to calculate maximum earnings market share directly from just two numbers:[19]

$$\hat{m} = 1 - \sqrt{\frac{\dot{k}}{\dot{p}}}$$

$\dot{k}$ is the cost of the first share point (the price of entry) and $\dot{p}$ is the gross profit of the next market share point.

Applying this formula to *LUV's* numbers returns 0.1355. In other words, at the close of the first quarter 2003, *Southwest's* maximum earnings market share (MEMS) after enterprise marketing expenses was 13.55 points. Now all we need to do is work forward from MEMS to EBITDA. This gets a little complicated.

Enterprise Marketing Performance

You're accustomed to calculating market share from historical sales data like we did in Table 5-2. In fact, it's safe to say you rarely have done the reverse—used market share to calculate sales revenues in a strategic group. Why? Because until now you didn't know how to estimate *future* market share. Now that you do, you can use maximum earnings market share to calculate the sales revenues that maximize earnings.

Sales revenues are the arithmetic product of maximum earnings market share (expressed as a proportion) and strategic group revenues:

$$\hat{r} = \hat{m} \times R$$

LUV's sales revenues, if the company maximized earnings, would have been $2,407 million.[20] Notice that sales revenues associated with MEMS were 77.6% greater than actual revenues in the first quarter 2003.

Next we calculate the company's variable cost of flights $(1 - \dot{g})$ at maximum earnings sales revenues—assuming it neither increases nor decreases at this higher revenue level:

$$\hat{o} = \hat{r} \times (1 - \dot{g})$$

LUV's cost of flights at maximum earnings sales revenue $\hat{o}$ were $1,111 million.[21] The company's gross profit $\hat{t}$ at the higher revenue is given by maximum earnings revenue minus cost of flights:

$$\hat{t} = \hat{r} - \hat{o}$$

At **MEMS** of 13.55%, *Southwest* would generate a gross profit of $1,296 million.[22]

Enterprise Marketing Expenses and EBITDA

Next, calculate the theoretical value of enterprise marketing expenses $\hat{y}$ necessary to achieve *LUV's* maximum earnings share of revenues:

$$\hat{y} = \hat{m}/(100 - \hat{m}) \times f \times x$$

Finally, subtracting from its theoretical gross profits the $1,115 million that *Southwest* needed to spend on enterprise marketing[23] returns its maximum EBITDA at 13.55 percent share of revenues:

$$\hat{a} = \hat{t} - \hat{y}$$

By increasing its enterprise marketing forces, *LUV* would maximize earnings at $175.57 million.[24] Actual EBITDA in the first quarter of 2003 was $139 million. Company earnings at **MEMS** represent a 26% increase in actual quarterly EBITDA. A snapshot of the change in *Southwest's* EBITDA appears in Chart 5-6.

The vertical axis in Chart 5-6 is *Southwest's* EBITDA after spending on enterprise marketing. The horizontal axis is the company's market share of revenues. *LUV's* actual EBITDA on March 31, 2003, was $139 million. Its theoretical maximum EBITDA was approximately $176 million.

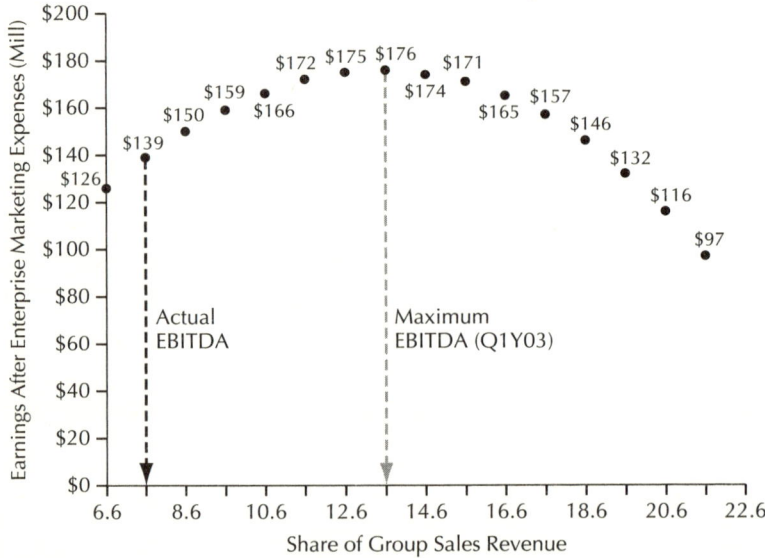

Chart 5-6 *LUV's* Actual Versus Maximum EBITDA

LUV's actual market share was 7.6% and its earnings after spending on enterprise marketing were $139 million. If the company had achieved maximum earnings, its market share would have been 13.55% and EBITDA would have been $176 million. In other words, the company theoretically could have increased its earnings in the first quarter of 2003 by about $37 million.

A Result That Makes Sense

The first thing you should note in Chart 5-6 is that the results make sense. *LUV's* maximum earnings market share is 77% greater than its current share of revenues. But it levels off at the peak of the curve. This signals a pattern of underspending in the past and an opportunity to grow profits with market share in the future, up to a point.

Also remember you can check this result for yourself. This isn't a black box. It's an empirical outcome, based on financial accounting data, derived from simple formulas verified in the Appendix to this chapter.

On the Upside of the Curve

Another thing to note about the theoretical results in Chart 5-6 is that *Southwest* is on the upside of the curve. The principle of force predicts that *LUV* could have increased EBITDA by 26% if it had grown its revenue share from 7.6% to around 14%. The target is "around 14%" because the curve gets pretty flat on top. On the upside of the curve at an 11.6% share of revenues, EBITDA is $172 million. On the downside of the curve at a 15.6% share of revenues, EBITDA drops to $171 million.

Between 11.6 and 15.6 share points *Southwest's* theoretical maximum EBITA doesn't change very much. This is a good thing. A theoretical result should not be too sensitive to inputs within the feasible range.

Dramatic Tumble on the Downside

The fourth thing to note in Chart 5-6 is that at some higher-percent share of revenues, *LUV's* profits after the cost of enterprise marketing take a dramatic tumble. Though not shown in this chart, at 25.6% share of revenues, EBITDA turns negative. So much for the idea that profits always increase with market share.

Are Incremental Cost and Profits Equal?

Let's verify that *LUV's* incremental cost equals its incremental profit at a 13.55% share of revenues. The process starts by defining a feasible range of revenue share options. From the outside looking in we can only guess what a realistic feasible range for *Southwest* might be.

For openers, let's assume that the "feasible range" is between 6.6% and 16.6% of group sales revenues. Assuming constant group revenues, *LUV's* sales at each simulated share level within this feasible range are reported in the first column of Table 5-2. The cost of flights was held constant at 46.15% percent of sales; gross margin, at 53.85% of sales. Given these assumptions, you can verify the results. The incremental cost and profit per share point ($95.66 million) are equal at 13.55 share points.

Table 5-2 *LUV's* Maximum Earnings after Enterprise Marketing Expenses

Revenue Share Points	Sales Revenues	Variable Cost of Flights	Gross Profit	Incremental Cost per Point	Incremental Profits per Point	Total Cost of Enterprise Marketing	Earnings After Enterprise Marketing
6.60	$1,172	$ 541	$ 631	$ 81.95	$95.66	$ 505	$126
7.60	**$1,350**	**$ 623**	**$ 727**	**$ 83.73**	**$95.66**	**$ 588**	**$139**
8.60	$1,528	$ 705	$ 823	$ 85.57	$95.66	$ 673	$150
9.60	$1,705	$ 787	$ 918	$ 87.48	$95.66	$ 759	$159
10.60	$1,883	$ 869	$1,014	$ 89.45	$95.66	$ 848	$166
11.60	$2,061	$ 951	$1,110	$ 91.48	$95.66	$ 938	$172
12.60	$2,238	$1,033	$1,205	$ 93.59	$95.66	$1,031	$175
13.55	**$2,407**	**$1,111**	**$1,296**	**$ 95.66**	**$95.66**	**$1,121**	**$176**
14.60	$2,593	$1,197	$1,397	$ 98.02	$95.66	$1,222	$174
15.60	$2,771	$1,279	$1,492	$100.36	$95.66	$1,321	$171
16.60	$2,949	$1,361	$1,588	$102.78	$95.66	$1,423	$165

The first bold row is *LUV's* first-quarter 2003 actual share of revenues. The next row in bold is the company's maximum earnings market share. If these assumptions are reasonable, *Southwest's* sales revenues at 13.55 share points would have been $2,407 million with maximum earnings of $176 million.

The Incremental Profit Function

Would *LUV's* variable cost of flights as a percent of sales revenues remain constant if sales increased by 77%? Maybe yes, maybe no. It depends on information we don't have. We know only that the average gross profit per share point at the current scale of operations is $95.66 million. We've got to **assume** the average profit equals the incremental profit per point. This is because, from outside the company, we can't specify what the incremental profit function looks like. More than likely, the profit from the ninth or tenth share point is the same as the eighth. And it may be true that it's the same as the fourteenth point. But at some level the company's underlying cost structure and cash flow changes so much that the assumption no longer holds.[25]

The Incremental Cost Function

We don't need to assume that **average** and **incremental cost** per share point are equal. Actually, we know they're not equal. We can apply the incremental force formula to competitors' $10,020 million spending on enterprise marketing—weighted by *LUV's* marketing efficiency ratio (0.7135)—to calculate the company's incremental share cost. Table 5-2 shows incremental costs range from $81.9 million at 6.6 revenue share points to $102.8 million at 16.6 share points. Incremental profit per share point is constant at $95.66 million so long as *Southwest's* gross profit margin and capital structure don't change.

Graph *LUV's* Incremental Profits and Costs

Now we can graphically display the rule of maximum earnings. For *Southwest*, that point occurs at a revenue share of 13.55%. As we saw in Table 5-2, at this share of revenues the incremental cost and incremental profit of a share point are equal at $95.66 million each. This result is shown graphically in the next chart.

The vertical axis in Chart 5-7 is *Southwest's* incremental profit and cost per share point. The horizontal axis is the company's share of group revenues. Maximum earnings occur at a 13.55% share of group revenues. This is the point where incremental earnings exactly equal incremental costs: both are $95.66 million per point. At any share of revenues less than 13.55%, incremental costs per point are less than incremental profits and *LUV* isn't

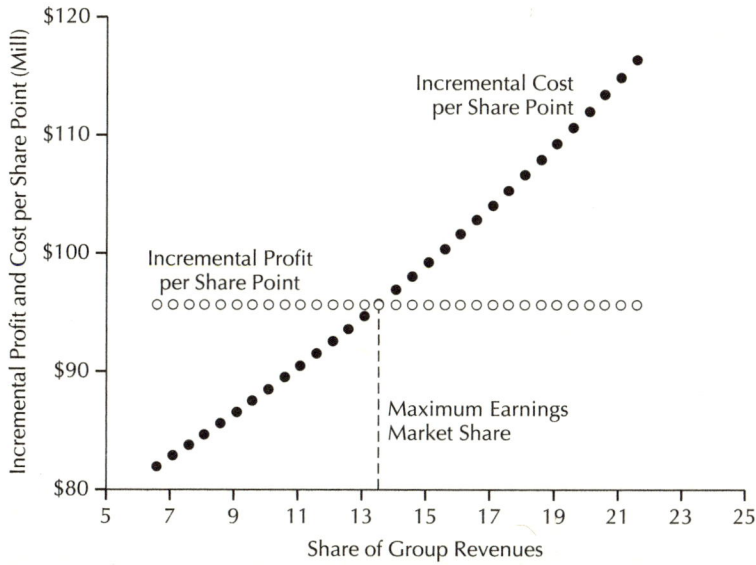

Chart 5-7   *LUV's* Maximum Earnings Market Share

spending enough on enterprise marketing. At any share of revenues greater than 13.55%, incremental costs are greater than incremental earnings and *LUV* is spending too much on enterprise marketing.

Let's review the bidding. The four factors that influence a company's maximum earnings market share of revenues are:

- Market demand—total revenue in the strategic group (R),
- Company gross profit margin ($\dot{g}$),
- Competitors' enterprise marketing expenses (f), and
- Company marketing efficiency ratio (x).

The interaction among these four factors determines a company's theoretical profit and cost per share point. But it's the real world, not the theory, that matters. Or is it?

Follow the money

Should *LUV* actually have moved to grow market share to 14%? In the 2003 market environment, management might have thought that market demand, gross profit margins, and marketing efficiency would hold at their current levels. If so, revenues in the domestic airline space would have been about $18 billion per quarter. *LUV's* gross margins would have been about 53%.

In 2003, would competitive spending on enterprise marketing hover around $10 billion? Gary C. Kelly, *Southwest's* chief financial officer at the time, thought not: "Entire divisions of airlines have been amassed to do battle with *Southwest*," he said. (Maynard op. cit., 9)

> Each of those start-ups has gone further in the frills department than JetBlue, which still does not offer meals. On Song, passengers can buy a variety of snacks, including pricey chocolates from Dylan's Candy Bar, a Manhattan shop. On Ted, there is even an official beer, Foster's Lager, and passengers can buy souvenirs like a stuffed bear named—what else?—Ted.

Will *LUV's* marketing efficiency ratio remain at 0.713? These and other questions form the background for an abbreviated scenario analysis of *LUV's* future prospects for maximizing earnings after the cost of enterprise marketing forces.[26]

Aggressive Competitive Response?

What would competitors have done if *Southwest* began aggressively to increase its share of sales with a target of 14%? Evidence that *Southwest* did just that was its service from Philadelphia, which began on May 9, 2004.

A 14% share of revenues would have given *LUV* a $1 billion revenue increase over the same quarter in 2003. Where would these sales come from if the size of the market were stable? "Both the upstart airlines flying below it and the legacy carriers cruising above are encroaching on its airspace." (Gimbel 2005, 97)

One company, *JetBlue,* was growing aggressively from a relatively small base of $217 million. *Delta* attempted to defend its $2.9 billion position with the 2003 launch of *Song* airlines. *United* launched *Ted* early in 2004 to defend its $2.5 billion revenue stake. *American* wouldn't be far behind. "The legacy carriers, meanwhile, have been driving down their costs ruthlessly, some of them using bankruptcy courts to force steep union concessions." (ibid, 97)

These competitors were weakened by labor disputes and all were saddled with inflexible hub-and-spoke networks as well as oversize aircraft in domestic routes. But they may have had the experience, people, and cash flow to maintain their customer base and return to profitability, even if they had to go into bankruptcy to do it. In short, it would have been a mistake to underestimate what the three biggest players in this peer group might do.

Without any new equipment, systems, or people, *AMR* could have joined *DAL* and *UAL* to create another formidable competitor with, say, $200 million spent on enterprise marketing for each start-up. This would raise from $10,020 to $10,620 the level of competitive enterprise marketing forces competing with *LUV* for passengers. As a result, both the incremental cost per point and the cost of the first share point would increase. If that happened, *LUV's* maximum earnings market share would fall from 13.55% to 11.1%. If, in addition, total market demand decreased by 5% to $16.875 billion, the company's maximum market share would drop to 8.6%. And if at the same time *Southwest's* variable cost of flights increased 5% as a result of its aggressive expansion plans, its maximum earnings market share would sink one full point to 6.6%.

Of course, *Southwest* faced many upside scenarios as well. On track for rapid expansion, the company added Pittsburgh to its network just after it won its bid to take over more gates at Chicago's O'Hare airport in early 2005.

> Mr. Kelly said the airline considered Pittsburgh an ideal place to start service, because it fits the criteria *Southwest* uses to figure out where to fly. "Overpriced and underserved, that's *Southwest* . . ." Adding flights in Pittsburgh will give *Southwest* a use for the 29 new *Boeing 737* jets it will acquire this year, Mr. Kelly added. (Maynard 2005, op. cit., 9)

What If *UAL* Downsized?

United Airlines was the weakest player in the group in the third quarter of 2004. What if *UAL* downsized? The impact is easy to calculate if you imagine how deep the cuts might be. Suppose *United* strikes a deal with investors to downsize by one-third both its spending on people—by cutting salaries, wages, and benefits—and its spending on Selling and Marketing in Appendix 5-A.

If *UAL* downsized to that degree, it would remove about $622 million from competitors' enterprise marketing expenses. A reduction of this magnitude would boost *LUV's* maximum earnings market share to 16.22%, yielding sales revenues of $2.88 billion and EBITDA of $251 million. Every passing day seemed to make a 14% maximum earnings market share look more and more like a realistic target for *LUV.*

It's All About People

Last year when *Southwest* closed its reservations centers in Dallas, Little Rock, and Salt Lake City "it didn't fire a single employee. In fact, the company picked up the cost of relocating them or paid for them to commute by air to jobs in other cities. This is not a fuzzy matter of morale—*Southwest's* culture has been its competitive advantage. You can't put it on the balance sheet, but it's something close to priceless." (Gimbal 2005, 98) **People** *are* **enterprise marketing assets.**

Appendix 5-A Domestic Airlines Income Statements

Consolidated Statements of Income in Millions for the Quarter Ending March 31, 2003

	LUV	AMR	CAL	DAL	JBLU	NWAC	UAL	USA
1.0 Operating Revenues:								
1.2 Passenger	1,306	3,720	1,872	2,931	209.90	1,848	2,548	1,233
1.3 Freight	22	134	170	113	7.20	167	164	35
1.4 Other	23	254	0	111		235	395	266
1.5 Total Operating Revenues	$1,350	$4,108	$2,042	$3,155	217.10	$2,250	$3,107	$1,534
2.0 Cost of Flights								
2.1 Fuel and oil	208	682	347	511	35.90	411	571	213
2.2 Maintenance materials/repairs	106	195	198	144	3.30	133	118	88
2.3 Aircraft rentals.................	45	184	223	183	13.10	118	202	109
2.4 Landing fees and other rentals.	90	639	152	218	16.30	143	239	106
2.5 Other operating expenses	174	116	255	452	35.40	296	561	368
2.6 Total Cost of Flights	$623	$1,816	$1,175	$1,508	$104	$1,101	$1,691	$884

Appendix 5-A (continued)

Consolidated Statements of Income in Millions for the Quarter Ending March 31, 2003

	LUV	AMR	CAL	DAL	JBLU	NWAC	UAL	USA
3.0 Enterprise Marketing Expenses								
3.1 Salaries, wages, and benefits	516	2,014	778	1,634	56.90	1,045	1,524	622
3.2 Selling and marketing	60	481	91	115	11.40	176	362	91
3.3 Food service	0	148	70	80	0	68	93	46
3.4 Agency commissions	12	255	36	55	19.54	45	73	31
3.5 Total Marketing Expenses	**$588**	**$2,898**	**$975**	**$1,884**	**$88**	**$1,334**	**$2,052**	**$790**
4.0 Depreciation and Amortization	93	297	116	298	10.30	142	232	67
5.0 Total Operation Expenses	$1,304	$5,011	$2,266	$3,690	$202	$2,576	$3,975	$1,741
6.0 Operating Income	$46	($903)	($224)	($535)	$15	($326)	($868)	($207)

Appendix 5-B: *LUV's* Maximum Earnings Market Share

We start with *Southwest's* theoretical profits after enterprise marketing expenses:

$$a = t - s \qquad \text{(Eq. 5-B.1)}$$

where a is EBITDA, t is total gross profits, and s is *LUV's* enterprise marketing expenses. Applying the financial numbers we derived in Table 5-1 to *LUV* in the first quarter of 2003, Eq. 5-B.1 returns (in millions of dollars):

$$a = \$139 = \$727 - \$588$$

Now, express theoretical profits after enterprise marketing expenses as an **earnings function** on market share of peer group revenues:

$$a = \dot{g} \times R \times \dot{m} - \frac{f \times x \times \dot{m}}{1 - \dot{m}}; \text{ where } 0 \leq \dot{m} \leq 1 \qquad \text{(Eq. 5-B.2)}$$

In Eq. 5-B.2, $\dot{g}$ is gross profits expressed as a proportion of *Southwest's* sales revenues; R is group sales revenues in millions; $\dot{m}$ is the company's actual market share (expressed as a proportion) of group revenues; f is the sum competitors' enterprise marketing expenses; and x is *Southwest's* enterprise marketing efficiency ratio.

Applying the financial numbers we derived previously to *LUV* in the first quarter 2003, Eq. 5-B.2 returns (in millions of dollars):

$$\$139 = 0.5385 \times \$17{,}763 \times 0.0760 - \frac{\$10{,}020 \times 0.7135 \times 0.0760}{1 - 0.0760}$$

To derive the rate of change in EBITDA after enterprise marketing expenses, take the first derivative[27] of the earnings function Eq. 5-B.2:

$$a' = \frac{\dot{g} \times R \times (1 - \dot{m})^2 - f \times x}{(1 - \dot{m})^2} \quad \text{(Eq. 5-B.3)}$$

All the variables in this equation were defined previously. Expressing the financial numbers in Eq. 5-B.3 for *LUV*, we get:

$$\$1{,}192 = \frac{0.5385 \times \$17{,}763 \times (1 - 0.0760)^2 - \$10{,}020 \times 0.7135}{(1 - 0.0760)^2}$$

LUV's incremental earnings after enterprise marketing expenses—given its **actual** market share of 7.6% in the first quarter of 2003—were $1,192 thousand. The company's **maximum** earnings after enterprise marketing expenses occur when incremental profit is exactly zero. That happens when Eq. 5-B.3 is set equal to zero:

$$0 = \frac{\dot{g} \times R \times (1 - \dot{m})^2 - f \times x}{(1 - \dot{m})^2} \quad \text{(Eq. 5-B.4)}$$

Solving Eq. 5-B.4 for maximum earnings market share of revenues,[28] the result is:

$$\hat{m} = 1 - \sqrt{\frac{f \times x}{\dot{g} \times \dot{R}}} \quad \text{(Eq. 5-B.5)}$$

Applying the *LUV* financial numbers to Eq. 5-B.5, we get the company's maximum earnings market share of revenues:

$$0.1355 = 1 - \sqrt{\frac{\$10{,}020 \times 0.7135}{0.5378 \times \$17{,}763}}$$

Equation 5-B.5 can be simplified by expressing it in terms of company incremental gross profit per share point $\dot{p}$ and the cost of the first share point $\dot{k}$. This gives us:

$$\hat{m} = 1 - \sqrt{\frac{\dot{k}}{\dot{p}}} \quad \text{(Eq. 5-B.6).}$$

Again, applying LUV's numbers to Eq. 5-B.6 returns:

$$0.1355 = 1 - \sqrt{\frac{\$71.49}{\$95.53}}$$

In other words, at the close of the first quarter 2003, *Southwest's* maximum earnings market share—after enterprise marketing expenses—was 13.55 revenue share points.

References

Barwise, P., and J. U. Farley. 2003. "Which Marketing Metrics Are Used and Where?" *Marketing Science Institute Reports* 1, No. 2: 105–107.

Cook, V. J. Jr. 1983. "Marketing Strategy and Differential Advantage." *Journal of Marketing* 47 (Spring): 68–75.

——— 1985. "The Net Present Value of Market Share." *Journal of Marketing* 49 (Summer): 49–63.

Gimbel, B. 2005. "Southwest's New Flight Plan." *Fortune* 16 (May): 93–98.

Khan, A. E. 1999–2002. "Airline Deregulation." *The Concise Encyclopedia of Economics, Liberty Fund, 1999–2002.* http://www.econlib.org/library/Enc/AirlineDeregulation.html#further

Maynard, M. "Are Peanuts No Longer Enough?" *New York Times*: Section 3, *Money and Business* March 7, 2004: 1+9

Michaelson, G. A. with S. W. Michaelson. 2004. *Sun Tzu: Strategies for Marketing (12 Essential Principles for Winning the War for Customers)*. New York: McGraw-Hill, quoted from Karl von Clausewitz *On War*.

Michaelson, G. A. with S. W. Michaelson. 2004. *Sun Tzu: Strategies for Marketing (12 Essential Principles for Winning the War for Customers)*. New York: McGraw-Hill, translation from the Chinese by Pan Jiabin, Liu Ruxian, and A. L. Sadler.

Ries, A., and J. Trout. 1986. *Marketing Warfare*. New York: McGraw-Hill Book Company.

End Notes

[1] **O**pen **S**ystems **I**ntegration.

[2] This formula was introduced as the "strategic marketing cost function" in Cook 1983, page 71. Solving the market share attraction model $m = y/(y + f)$ for y gives the total force formula $y = m/(100 - m) \times f; 0 \leq m \leq 100$.

[3] The marginal (or incremental) cost formula is

$$\dot{c} = \frac{100 \times f \times x}{(100 - m)^2}$$

where $0 \leq m \leq 100$. This formula is derived by differentiating the total force formula in (2), above. See Cook, 1985, Appendix 2.

[4] *LUV* is the ticker symbol for *Southwest Airlines*.

[5] *Southwest's* flights between New Orleans and West Palm Beach were not included in this total because the airline had not yet entered the market. *LUV* has its own

reservation system on the Web and does not allow *Orbitz* or any other reservation system to list its flight schedule.

[6] The sales revenues in this peer group are less than the $18,105 million reported in Table 2.1 primarily as a result of deleting *Frontier's* $120 million and *Mesa's* $133 million sales from first-quarter 2003 group revenues. Total revenues declined an additional $89 million due to adjustments in the 10-Q reports filed with the SEC by *AMR*, *DAL*, and *UAL*.

[7] Theoretically, the revenue value of each share point should be calculated as the total number of revenue passenger miles (RPMs) flown by all the air carriers in the peer group—multiplied by each company's average revenue-per-passenger mile (RPPM)—divided by 100 points. Because *Southwest Airlines* had lower average prices that its competitors, its revenue value per share point would be somewhat lower than that of its competitors. For example, in 2003 *LUV* flew 44,537 million passenger miles. This was 8.1% of the 527,136 million passenger miles flown in 2003 by the airlines in this group [estimated by *Frost & Sullivan* on November 6, 2003]. *Southwest's* share of sales revenues in this group was 7.6% in the first quarter of 2003. This reflects its somewhat lower average prices. The difference does not materially change the results presented here. However, if airline management were conducting this analysis, it would be necessary to work with RPM and RPPM for a higher level of precision.

[8] http://www.sec.gov/edgar.shtml **E**lectronic **D**ata **G**athering, **A**nalysis, and **R**etrieval—EDGAR.

[9] In the analysis that follows, *LUV's* seven competitors will be treated as if they were a single firm. This simplification is appropriate here, but in practice a system of equations representing each firm would be needed in order to understand fully the competitive dynamics of this strategic group.

[10] This number will differ by rounding error from that returned using a calculator. You will get the same result by dividing *LUV's* gross profits by its share of sales revenue expressed as an integer.

[11] It is a well-established principle in microeconomics that profits are maximized at the point where a firm's marginal revenue equals its marginal cost.

[12] This result is $y = 7.60/(100 - 7.60) \times \$10,020$.

[13] Calculated as *LUV's* MER = $[0.7135 = \$588/\$824]$.

[14] The author thanks Professor David Reibstein of the Wharton School for offering this insight.

[15] Competitors captured 92.4% of the market by spending $10,020 on Enterprise Marketing, so their marketing (in)efficiency ratio was $1.40 = y\star = \$10,020/(92.4/(100 - 92.4) \times \$588)$. In this formula, $y\star$ identifies combined competitors.

[16] A quick check of the math results in $\frac{100 \times \$10,020 \times 0.71345}{(100 - 8.60)^2}$.

[17] That was $\$10,020 \times 0.7135/100$.

[18] This general rule for linear profit maximization is based on Victor J. Cook, Jr., "Net Present Value of Market Share," *Journal of Marketing*, Vol. 49, (Summer) 1985, page 61.

[19] This formula is applied to *Southwest* in the appendix to this chapter. The linear assumption was tested extensively using financial accounting data in the airline, automobile, pharmaceutical, and supermarket industries over a twenty-year period—and found to hold. See Sanabria 2003.

[20] *LUV's* maximum earning sales revenues are $2,407 = 0.1355 \times \$17,763$.

[21] *LUV's* average variable cost of flights is $1,111 = \$2,407 \times 0.46154$.

[22] *LUV's* gross profits are $1,296 = \$2,407 - \$1,111$.

[23] *LUV's* maximum enterprise marketing expenses are $1,121 = 13.55/(100 - 13.55) \times \$10,020 \times 0.7135$.

[24] *LUV's* EBITDA after the enterprise marketing expenses is $175 = \$1,296 - \$1,121$.

[25] In this event, it is necessary to develop pro forma accounting statements reflecting costs at the new scale of operations. That is beyond the scope of this book.

[26] Mandelbrot distinguishes between scenario- and related-events analysis.

[27] To verify this result, go to *Quickmath.com*. In the navigation bar, select *Calculus: Differentiate*: enter equation 5-B.2 in the input window, differentiate with respect to m, and click *Differentiate*. The software will return an expression that, when simplified, will be equation 5-B.3.

[28] You can verify equation 5-B.5 by solving 5-B.4 for $\dot{m}$ in *Quickmath.com*.

Chapter 6

The Battle for Your Desktop

By now you're probably asking yourself if the *Southwest* example was just the one out of ten cases where the principle of force works. After all, the number of flights between city-pairs is a unique asset. It's duplicated only in a few other markets. A big, expensive, physical, portable asset that is central to delivering a pure service to customers.

Not only that. This is also a relatively homogeneous service business. You might say: "A seat is just a seat as long as it gets me where I want to go." And yes, the *Southwest* example was just a snapshot. It was a static glimpse into the quarterly financial statements of a troubled industry shaken largely by events beyond management's control. The unusual circumstances that put this industry in turmoil may have created a case where the idea of calculating a maximum earnings market share just happens to work.

Fair enough. Let's look more closely at a very different example.

Your Desktop

In the 1980s, computer companies began targeting your desktop. The first major player to do so was *IBM* with its new PC. Then *Hewlett Packard, Compaq,* and *Dell* joined in what was to become an epic battle for desktop supremacy. This included all the back-office equipment and services needed to support the desktop.

To test the rule of maximum earnings driven by enterprise marketing expenses, we'll first take a close look at these four players over the period 1991 through 2000. This period captures the dynamic growth in personal computer sales as well as the *Internet* boom. Using annual data makes it possible to capture the long-run strategic evolution of this market. Most of the epochal shifts that took place in this strategic group would be lost if the analysis were limited to the ten most recent quarters.

Then we'll look again at the same companies, focusing on the more recent developments from the fourth quarter of 1999 through the first quarter of 2002. These ten quarters precede the actual merger between *Hewlette Packard* and *Compaq* by just a few months. Finally, we'll review the results for a strategic group that includes *Apple* and *Gateway* from 1993 to 2002.

David and Big Blue

Remember the story of David and Goliath? David is the guy with the superior weapon and great skill in using it. Well, there are three Davids in this story: One of them—*Hewlett-Packard (HPQ)*—is a battle-tested warrior. The other two—*Compaq Computer (CPQ)*, and *Dell (DELL)*—are newcomers. Each of these Davids has had its own front-page story.

The most unexpected and controversial shock in the desktop marketplace was the September 4, 2001 announcement that *Hewlett-Packard* intended to buy *Compaq*.

> *Analysts say* HP *faces a rocky road, as it works to survive a sour PC market while combining* Compaq *business units that are quite similar to its own. Meanwhile, investors send* HP *shares lower, pushing the total value of the proposed merger below $20 billion just a day after it was announced.* (CNET News, 2001)

A comparison of the performance of these two companies during the ten years preceding the merger is revealing. It provides new insights into the reasons why so many of *HP's* stockholders were against the merger.

In contrast to this sudden turn of events in 2001 was the gradual evolution of *Dell's* extraordinary long-term business model:

> Dell *was founded in 1984 by Michael Dell, the computer industry's longest-tenured chief executive officer, on a simple concept: that by selling computer systems directly to customers,* Dell *could best understand their needs and efficiently provide the most effective computing solutions to meet those needs. This direct business model eliminates retailers that add unnecessary time and cost, or can diminish* Dell's *understanding of customer expectations. The direct model allows the company to build every system to order and offer customers powerful, richly-configured systems at competitive prices.* (http://www.dell.com)

As the stage is being set for the Davids and their battle for your desktop, let's not forget another actor: Louis Gerstner, formerly CEO of *RJR Nabisco*, president of *American Express*, partner in *Mckinsey & Company*—appointed in April 1993 as chairman of the board of *IBM*.

> *For years,* IBM *was the most interesting company in the world to watch. It was impeccable from, oh, so many standpoints—its consistent growth, its global reach, its avant-garde development of computers, its renowned policies of gentlemanly leaders, lasting jobs, quiet dress, and good manners.* IBMers *were a cult unto themselves. To be the CEO of* IBM, *well, that was the closest access to God that a mortal businessman could ask for.*
>
> *Then came the same old story.* IBM *got fat, sloppy, and bureaucratic. Brash new competitors began eating its lunch. The company lost market share, money, and its cool. The last* IBM *CEO, John Akers, lost his job. By 1993, the once-revered company was in disarray and a desperate board was looking for a new chairman and CEO who could turn the company around and save its assets and its soul.* (Lear 2005)

Table 6-1 Shares and Group Revenues in the Desktop Space

	IBM (Percent)	HPQ (Percent)	DELL (Percent)	CPQ (Percent)	Group Revenues
1991	76.612	17.138	2.381	3.868	$ 84,571
1992	73.400	18.668	3.268	4.664	$ 87,906
1993	66.933	21.683	3.709	7.675	$ 93,699
1994	60.883	23.755	5.034	10.328	$105,205
1995	57.107	25.020	6.159	11.713	$125,973
1996	52.448	26.533	8.513	12.506	$144,803
1997	47.804	26.119	11.108	14.969	$164,230
1998	44.106	25.416	13.645	16.833	$185,162
1999	43.702	21.150	15.918	19.231	$200,331
2000	41.948	23.149	14.791	20.113	$210,729

Table 6-1 shows the magnitude of the problem Lou Gerstner faced when he took over *IBM* in 1993. It also documents how the market shares of each player changed over the decade. In 1991 the four companies in this strategic group generated revenues of $84,571 million.[1]

IBM captured 76.612% of desktop revenues in 1991, or $64,792 million. But wait, why carry *IBM's* market share to three places beyond the decimal? There are two good reasons. First, when market share of group revenues is used to calculate company sales, the extra precision is needed to avoid rounding errors in the millions. For example, when *IBM's* market share—expressed as a proportion and carried to three significant places—is multiplied by group revenues, the result is actual sales revenues of $64,792 million (0.76612 × $84,571). If we rounded market share to 76%, *IBM's* sales calculated from market share would be $65,120 million, an error of $328 million! Second, in competing for customers and capital, market share drives sales revenues. Not the other way around.

By the end of 2000, *IBM's* **share of market had fallen 34.665 points** to 41.948%. But notice that its **sales revenues grew** to $88,397 million (0.41948 × $210,729) because group revenues had more than doubled over the decade.

Hewlett-Packard's market share increased 6.375 points from 17.138% in 1991 to 23.149% in 2000. *HPQ's* sales revenues grew from $14,494 million in 1991 (0.17138 × $84,571) to $48,782 million (0.23149 × $210,729) in 2000.

Dell captured only 2.381% of group revenues in 1991. This generated sales revenues of $2,014 million (0.02381 × $84,571). By 2000, *Dell's* market share had increased to 14.791%. As a result, its sales revenues grew to $31,168 million (0.14791 × $210729).

Compaq experienced even more significant growth in market share (from 3.868% to 20.113%) and sales revenues (from $3,271 to $42,383 million).

The Last Thing *IBM* Needs Is a Vision

Here's a surprising fact. In 1991 just 1/100th of *IBM's* 78th market share point had an incremental cost of $15.615 million. The earnings from that basis point[2] after enterprise marketing expenses were $4.890 million.

In other words, holding on to the last 1/100th of that 78th revenue share point in 1991 theoretically cost *IBM* $10.724 million in lost earnings after enterprise marketing expenses. In that year the company actually spent $28.0 billion on enterprise marketing. Listen to what Lou Gerstner said about this problem when he took over *IBM*:

> *At the risk of sounding pompously tutorial, a profit-making business is a relatively simple system. You need to generate revenue, which comes from selling things at an acceptable price. You have to achieve a good gross profit on those sales. And you have to manage your expenses, which are the investments you make in selling, research and development, building plants and equipment, maintaining financial control, developing and running advertising, and so on. If revenue, gross profit, and expenses are all moving in the right relationship, the net effect is growing profits and positive cash flow. Unfortunately in* IBM's *case the relationships were all wrong....*
>
> *... After months of hard work, CFO Jerry York and his team determined that* IBM's *expense-to-revenue ratio—i.e. how much expense is required to produce $1 of revenue—was wildly out of range with those of our competitors. On average, our competitors were spending 31 cents to produce $1 of revenue, while we were spending 42 cents for the same end. When we multiplied this inefficiency times the total revenue of the company, we discovered that we had a $7 billion expense problem! ...*
>
> *... the only way to save the company, at least in the short term, was to slash uncompetitive levels of expenses. So we made the decision to launch a massive program of expense reduction—$8.9 billion in total. Unfortunately, this necessitated, among other things, reducing employment by 35,000 people, in addition to the 45,000 people whom John Akers had already laid off in 1992. That meant additional pain for everyone, but this was a matter of survival, not choice.* (Gerstner 2002, 62–63)

Faced in 1993 with a business model that was wildly unprofitable, what would you have recommended that *IBM* management do? Should the company:

a. cut enterprise marketing expenses, or
b. increase profit per basis point, or
c. harvest market share, or
d. all of the above?

Apparently market mechanisms and management decisions conspired to accomplish all of the preceding. The overall result was to bring *IBM's* actual share of revenues in line with maximum earnings market share by the end of the decade.

IBM's Market Share

This front-page story is told in Chart 6-1. The vertical axis is *IBM's* year-to-year share of strategic group revenues from 1991 through 2000. Two different revenue shares are plotted in Chart 6-1.

The gray circles are *IBM's* theoretical **m**aximum **e**arnings **m**arket **s**hare (**MEMS**). These are the revenue shares management should have targeted if management's objective were to maximize earnings after marketing expenses. For example, to maximize earnings *IBM* should have captured 58.21% of strategic group revenues in 1991 and 42.85% in 2000. Or, *IBM's* target market share should have been 5,821 basis points (58.21%) in 1991 and 4,285 basis points (42.85%) in 2000.

The white circles in Chart 6-1 are *IBM's* actual market share from 1991 through 2000. *IBM's* actual market share decreased from 76.61% (7,661 basis points) in 1991 to 41.95% (4,195 basis points) in 2000. In 1991 the difference between *IBM's* actual and maximum earnings was 1,840 basis points. By 2000 *IBM's* actual and maximum earnings share were separated by only 90 basis points (4,285-4,195). These 90 basis points weren't chump change,

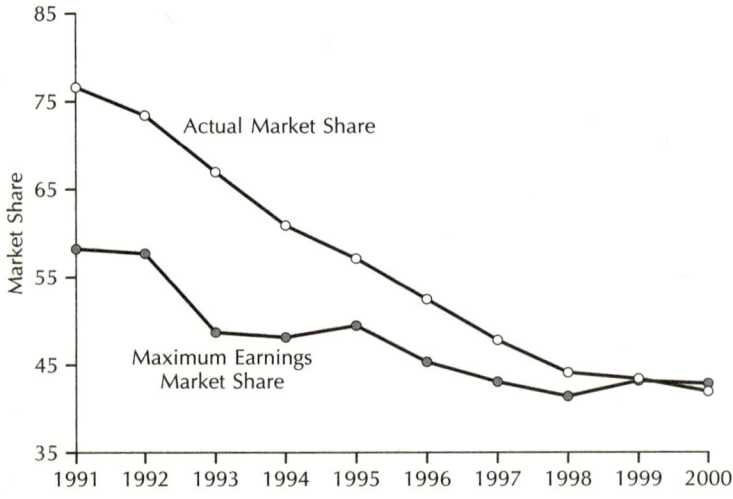

Chart 6-1 *IBM's* Actual and Maximum Earnings Market Share

but the actual and maximum earning market shares did move extraordinarily close to each other by the end of the decade.

How did this happen? Did competitive market pressure produce this outcome? Was it a result of uncanny management sensitivity to competitive market forces? Did Lou Gerstner have a sixth sense? Or was it just a result of chance?[3]

IBM's Incremental Profit and Cost per Basis Point

The subtext to this front-page story is what happened to *IBM's* incremental profit and cost per basis point over the years from 1991 through 2000. If it were true that competitive forces drove *IBM* management to seek out a position where the incremental cost of a market share point was equal to its incremental earnings, it should show up in the financial data. In Chart 6-2 you actually can see this cause-and-effect model at work.

The company's incremental cost per basis point is represented by the white circles in Chart 6-2. The cost per point fell dramatically from $15.61 million in 1991 to $8.53 million by the end of the company's fiscal year 2000. *IBM's* incremental profit per point, represented by the gray circles, rose from $4.89 million in 1991 to $8.81 million in 2000.

By 2000, *Big Blue's* incremental profit and cost per basis point were virtually equal. The company's earnings from that last 4,285th basis point were only $280 thousand more than it cost. IBM had almost achieved **MEMS!**

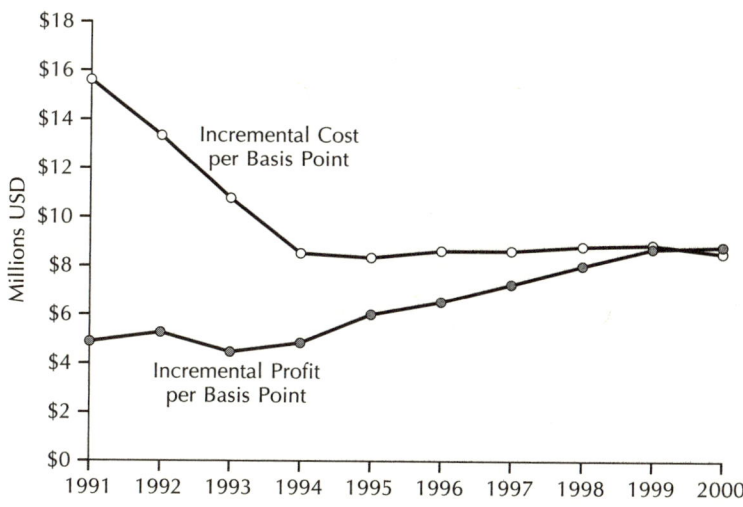

Chart 6-2 *IBM's* Profit and Cost per Basis Point

IBM's Achilles' Heel

Whatever may have been the extraordinary blend of management skills and enterprise marketing instincts that drove this remarkable march to maximum earnings market share, *IBM* suffered from a hidden weakness. Beneath the surface was the company's poor **m**arketing **e**fficiency **r**atio (MER). This is the ratio of a company's actual share to its share maintenance enterprise marketing expenses. If a company spends more on enterprise marketing in a period than it theoretically needs to maintain current market share, that spending is relatively inefficient. In *IBM's* case its MER was greater than one through the decade. If the company had spent less, it would have been relatively more efficient and earned more.

IBM's marketing (in)efficiency ratios are displayed in Chart 6-3. The expected value of this ratio is 1.0, meaning the actual and theoretical share maintenance enterprise marketing expenses are equal. Marketing efficiency ratios greater than 1.0 represent underlying inefficiencies, because actual spending exceeds theoretical spending levels. Over the period from 1991 through 2000, *IBM's* ratios ranged from a low of 1.30 in 1991 to a high of 1.51 in 1993.

Averaged over the ten years, *IBM's* (in)efficiency was 1.40. This meant the company was spending $1.40 for enterprise marketing assets that cost an average competitor in this strategic group just one dollar. And as you will see later, *Dell* was so efficient that *IBM* wasn't able to catch up.

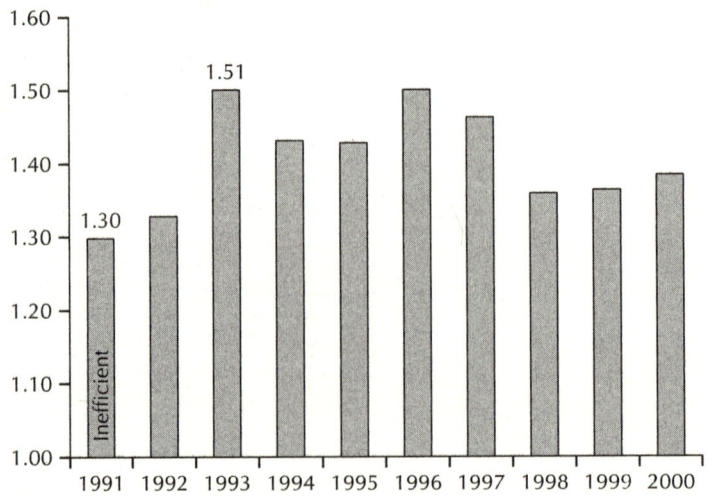

Chart 6-3 *IBM's* Marketing (In)efficiency Ratios

Chart 6-4 reveals the problem with *IBM's* marketing efficiency ratio in a more dramatic time lapse trend. Here it's expressed in the format of the

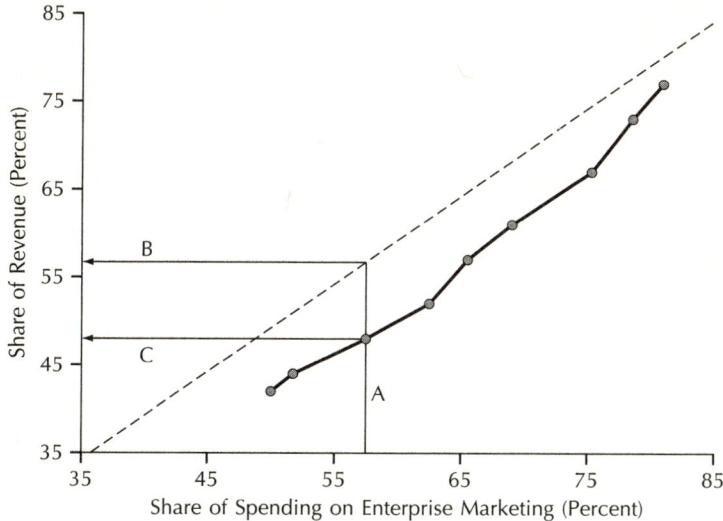

Chart 6-4 *IBM's* Achilles' Heel

classic market share attraction theorem (Bell, Keaney, and Little 1975). The horizontal axis is *IBM's* **s**hare **o**f **s**pending (SOS) on enterprise marketing. The vertical axis is its **s**hare **o**f **r**evenues (SOR) in the strategic group.

The linear market share theorem says that a company will attract customers in direct proportion to its share of enterprise marketing expenses, other things being equal. If *IBM* had attracted customers in direct proportion to its share of enterprise marketing expenses, the relationship between share of revenue and share of spending would be described by the gray dotted line in Chart 6-4. In this case its marketing efficiency ratio would have been exactly 1.

In 1997 *IBM* fielded 57% of strategic group spending on enterprise marketing forces. If the response of customers had been proportional to its efforts, *IBM* would have captured 57% of sales. This is illustrated by lines A and B, which link SOS to SOR at 57%. Instead, the company captured only the 48% of sales illustrated by lines A and C. Reading *IBM's* market share attraction from the top right-hand corner (1991) to the lower left-hand corner (2000) of Chart 6-4, you can see the systematic pattern of decline in the company's share of market. Even as management decreased its share of enterprise marketing expenses, it failed to achieve a proportional market response.

In statistical terms, a linear regression of points on the grey dotted line has an intercept of zero and a slope of one.[4] The intercept of a regression line fitted to the gray circles in Chart 6-4 has a high R^2 (0.99) and a slope greater than one (1.1), indicating that the relationship is linear but not proportional. *IBM's* Achilles' heel was its inefficient spending on enterprise marketing forces.

What a Difference 11¢ Can Make

Earlier in this chapter Lou Gerstner was quoted as saying his CFO Jerry York found that competitors were spending just 31¢ while *IBM* was spending 42¢ to produce $1 of revenue. He also said that when they multiplied this inefficiency times the total revenue of the company, they discovered they had a $7 billion expense problem. Let's see if we can reproduce Gerstner's math using enterprise marketing expenses drawn from the income statements of these four competitors.

In 1993 *IBM* had 66.933% of the $93,699 million in strategic group sales revenue. So the company's revenue was $62,716 million. Remember, sales revenue equals percent market share times group revenue [$62,716 = 0.66933 × $93,699]. With an 11¢ inefficiency per $1 revenue compared with the competition, the extra cost was $6,899 million; that was *IBM's* $7 billion expense problem referred to by Lou Gerstner earlier in this chapter.

How does Gerstner's 11¢ inefficiency relate to maximum earnings market share? He was using SG&A (enterprise marketing) expenses to estimate this and his competitors' selling cost per dollar of sales revenue. How do we know? We don't know for sure, but let's do the math using the combined spending of *DELL*, *HPQ*, and *CPQ*. The results are shown in Table 6-2.

During the two years in which these data were available preceding Gerstner's appointment as CEO, in late 1993, he would have found an 11¢ inefficiency in both years. This inefficiency actually increased to 13¢ in 1993, even though the company cut its enterprise marketing expenses. In the following years the company never did catch up with the competition.

Table 6-2 Selling, General, and Administrative Expenses per Dollar Revenue

	IBM	DELL+ HPQ+ CPQ	IBM Inefficiency (IBM−Others)
1991	43¢	32¢	11¢
1992	40¢	29¢	11¢
1993	38¢	25¢	13¢
1994	32¢	22¢	10¢
1995	28¢	19¢	9¢
1996	28¢	18¢	11¢
1997	27¢	17¢	10¢
1998	27¢	18¢	8¢
1999	25¢	17¢	8¢
2000	24¢	17¢	7¢

Was Less Really More for *IBM*?

Between 1991 and 2000, *Big Blue's* actual SG&A (enterprise marketing) expenses declined from $28.0 billion to $20.8 billion. The company's actual EBITDA rose from $9.5 to $16.2 billion. Clearly this is case where less was more.

The most surprising thing is that **even less** would have been **even more**. In 1991 *IBM's* theoretical maximum enterprise marketing expenses were $21.6 billion. Its actual expenses were $28.0 billion or 30% more than they should have been. This explains the company's poor marketing efficiency ratio. By 2000, *IBM's* enterprise marketing inefficiency had gotten worse. The company should have spent $15.0 billion on enterprise marketing, but actually spent $20.8 billion. Actual spending was 38% greater than the theoretical maximum benchmark. Gerstner's measure of company marketing efficiency, SG&A spending per dollar of revenue, provides a linear benchmark but does not account for non-linear competitive effects.

Theoretically *Big Blue's* cumulative EBITDA from 1991 through 2000 would have been $143.6 billion. Its actual cumulative EBITDA was $123.1 billion. The lost earnings opportunity was over $20 billion, or 14.2% of potential. The impact of this earnings shortfall on share price may have been significant.

Finally, by 2000 *IBM's* actual revenue share came into line with its maximum earnings market share. In that year its actual EBITDA was $16.156 billion; the theoretical earnings were $16.168 billion. Bingo! The earnings shortfall was only 0.08% of potential.

Big Blue's "less-is-more" bottom-line marketing strategy was radically different from that of its more conservative competitor *Hewlett-Packard*. Let's see how *HP* performed in the ten years before the merger with *Compaq* was announced in 2001.

Always a Bridesmaid

Maybe it's because *HPQ* had been an engineering company since its founding in 1939. It first product, built in that famous garage, was an electronic test instrument used by sound engineers.

> *Following graduation as electrical engineers from* Stanford University *in 1934, Bill Hewlett and Dave Packard go on a two-week camping and fishing trip in the Colorado mountains during which they become close friends. Bill continues graduate studies at* MIT *and* Stanford *while Dave takes a job with* General Electric. *With the encouragement of* Stanford *professor and mentor Fred Terman, the two decide to start a business 'and make a run for it' themselves.*[5]

Or, maybe it's because of *HPQ's* good fortune with the *Laser Jet*® printer series. Whatever the reasons, the company's performance over the decade

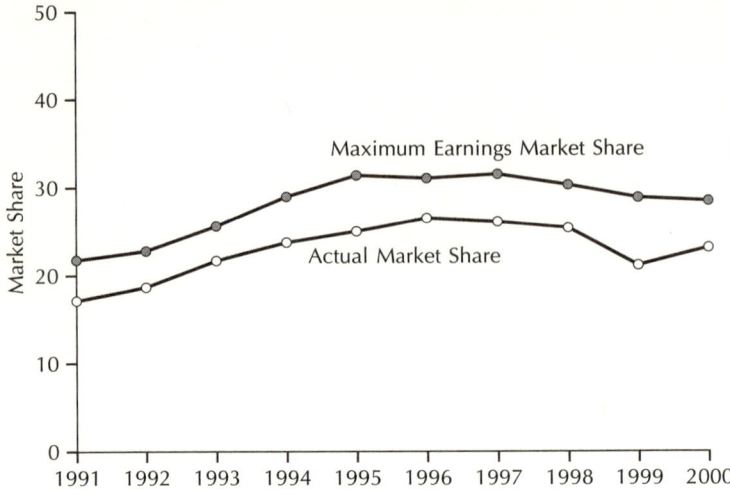

Chart 6-5 *Hewlett-Packard* Was Always a Bridesmaid

from 1991 to 2000 was surprising. Chart 6-5 displays *HPQ's* actual and maximum earnings market share. First, notice that *HPQ* underspent throughout the decade. The company's theoretical maximum earnings market share **exceeded** its actual market share in every year. Second, compared with *IBM's*, the differences were relatively small. MEMS exceeded actual market share by only 7.72 share points (772 basis points) in 1999. That was the biggest gap between the two. Third, the differences were relatively constant over the decade. The smallest gap was 4.11 share points in 1992. Yet, *HP* never closed that gap the way that *IBM* did.

Of course, these differences were driven by *HPQ's* incremental profit and cost per basis point. As shown in Chart 6-6, *Hewlett Packard's* incremental profit per basis point was always greater than its incremental cost per basis point. So the company always underspent. Its profit per basis point (the gray circles) rose from $4.23 million in 1991 to $6.51 million in 2000. The company's incremental cost per basis point (the white circles) followed a similar pattern, increasing from $3.77 million to $5.64 million over the ten years.

It turns out that *HPQ's* maximum enterprise marketing expenses were much closer to actual spending than were *IBM's*. In 1991 *HQP* actually spent $5.351 billion on enterprise marketing. Its theoretical maximum spending was $7.190 billion. In that year the company underspent by 34%. By the close of business in 2000, *HPQ* had spent $10.0 billion on enterprise marketing. The spending that would have maximized its theoretical earnings was $13.266 billion. The company underspent by 32%.

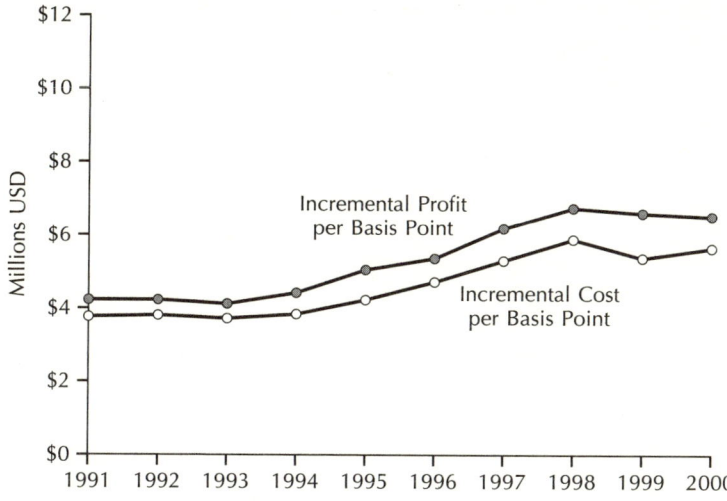

Chart 6-6   *HPQ's* Profit and Cost per Basis Point

HPQ's Bottom Line

Of course, the bottom line is what really matters. Table 6-3 documents year by year the actual and maximum EBITDA for *HPQ* from 1991 through 2000.

Table 6-3   The Proof Is in *HPQ's* Bottom Line

Millions USD	Actual EBITDA	Maximum EBITDA	Act/Max EBITDA
1991	$ 1,890	$ 1,998	0.95
1992	$ 2,106	$ 2,194	0.96
1993	$ 2,622	$ 2,703	0.97
1994	$ 3,555	$ 3,713	0.96
1995	$ 4,707	$ 4,981	0.95
1996	$ 5,023	$ 5,173	0.97
1997	$ 5,895	$ 6,140	0.96
1998	$ 5,970	$ 6,186	0.97
1999	$ 5,004	$ 5,503	0.91
2000	$ 5,044	$ 5,286	0.95
Cumulative	$41,816	$43,877	0.95

Hewlett-Packard's actual earnings after enterprise marketing expenses ranged from a low of $1,890 million in 1991 to a high of $5,044 million in 2000. Its maximum EBITDA after the cost of enterprise marketing was $1,998 in 1991 and $5,286 million in 2000. Its ten-year cumulative actual earnings were $41,816 million. The cumulative theoretical maximum earnings were $43,877 million. *HPQ's* average earnings shortfall was just 4.7%. Clearly, *HPQ* was almost on the money.

The last column of Table 6-3 shows that at no time in the decade did the ratio of actual to maximum EBITDA fall below 0.91. Compare that number with *IBM's* 18.3% and you have a new take on why some shareholders with a big stake in *HP* didn't support the merger with *Compaq*.

Hewlett-Packard Lost Its Marketing Edge

HPQ began the decade with a significant marketing edge. Its enterprise marketing efficiency ratio was 0.87. Over the next ten years the company lost this edge. *Hewlett-Packard's* **MER** fell steadily—to 1.068 in 1996. By 2000 the ratio was almost at 1.03.

Chart 6-7 shows the pattern of *HPQ's* diminished marketing edge in the format of the classic market share attraction model. In 1993, the company captured 21.9% of revenues in the desktop space with only a 20.0% share of enterprise marketing expenses. By the end of the decade, *HPQ's* share of revenues was less than its share of enterprise marketing expenses. And, like *IBM,* this seems to be a linear relationship. The drift of the points in Chart 6-7 from above to below the diagonal records the company's gradual loss of this advantage over the decade.

A close look at *Compaq's* performance adds a very different perspective to the dramatic turn of events in this strategic group.

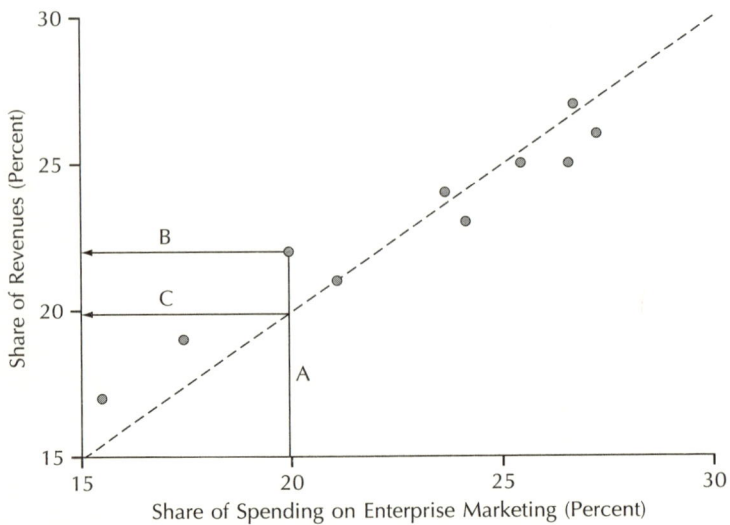

Chart 6-7   *Hewlett-Packard* Lost Its Enterprise Marketing Edge

Compaq Was Way Off the Mark

By now you know the drill. The gray circles in Chart 6-8 represent *Compaq's* maximum earnings market share. **MEMS** increased from 20.23% in 1991 to 33.32% in 1997 and then fell to 19.29 in 1998. Over the same period its actual market share rose from 3.87% to 16.83%—leaving a wide gap between the two. Then, in 1999, *Compaq's* **MEMS** increased to 20.12%, almost equaling its actual share increase of 19.23%. For a brief moment in time, the company's **MEMS** and actual market share were separated by only 89 basis points. It looked as if *Compaq* management finally had it figured out.

Chart 6-8 *Compaq* Was Off the Mark

Between 1993 and 1998, the large and growing differences between *CPQ's* actual and maximum earnings market share were significant. Of course, this was driven by comparable divergence between the company's incremental profit and cost per basis point over the same period. This is shown in Chart 6-9 on the following page.

Compaq spent less than the theoretical maximum on enterprise marketing over the entire period from 1993 through 1997. Its incremental profit per basis point was $3.59 million in 1991, at which time its incremental cost per basis point was $2.47 million. By 1997, profit per basis point rose to $4.81 million while cost per point increased to only $2.96 million. Then in 1998, the gap nearly closed. But these results do not explain the large and persistent differences between actual and maximum earnings market share.

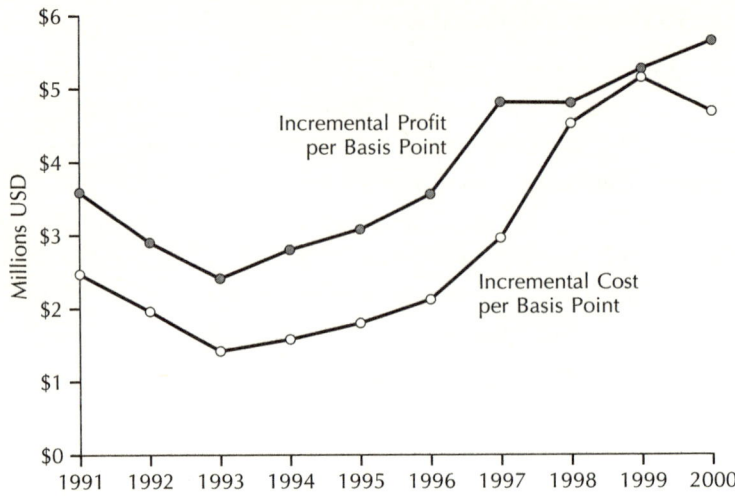

Chart 6-9 *Compaq's* Profit and Cost per Basis Point

Compaq's marketing efficiency ratios shed a light on the picture. The company's MERs appear in Chart 6-10. Beginning in 1991, *CPQ's* marketing efficiency was 0.68. Two years later it was 0.39. This meant that the company spent $0.39 for resources that cost an average competitor $1.00.

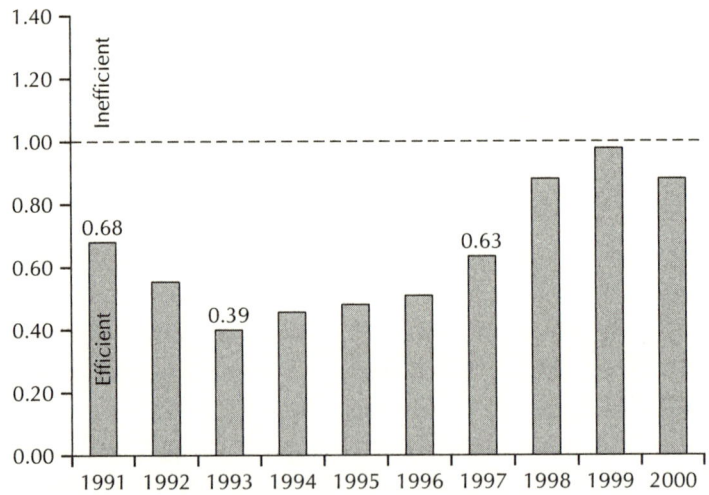

Chart 6-10 *Compaq's* Marketing Efficiency Ratios

You might speculate that there was some kind of hidden force working in the background. There was. The company's market response function was sharply non-linear.

Bow-Shaped Market Response

Chart 6-11 shows the picture of *CPQ's* enterprise marketing efficiency in the market-share attraction format. In 1991–92, the company's market response was almost proportional. The company captured about 4% of group revenues with 3% of enterprise marketing expenses. By 1997, *CPQ* was generating 15% of revenues with just 10% of the resources (lines A and B in the chart). Then, by 2000, customer response was again just about proportional. Something non-linear was definitely at work here.

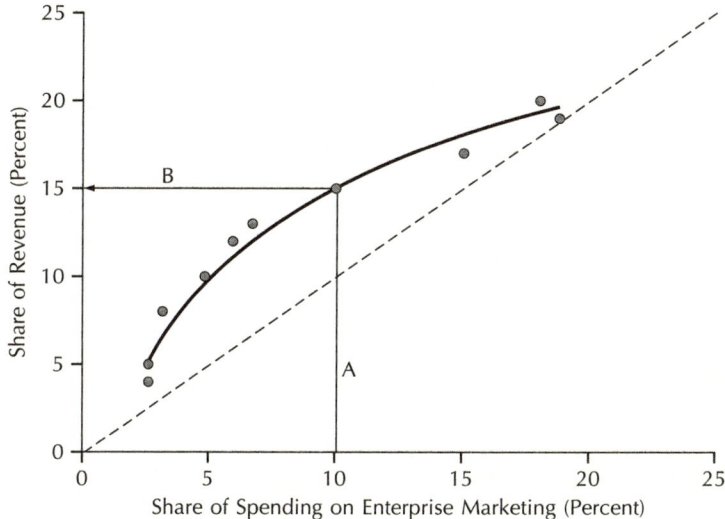

Chart 6-11 *Compaq's* Bow-Shaped Market Share Attraction

The R^2 for *Compaq's* attraction function in logs is 0.99. This establishes statistically that the divergence between actual and maximum earnings market share in the period from 1993 through 1997 was non-linear.

Unfortunately, we can't identify from financial accounting data alone the cause of this non-linear response for one company in a strategic group that otherwise appears to experience linear responses to its enterprise marketing expenses. As it happens, while under pressure in 1991 from falling market share and stock price, Ben Rosen and the board took back control of *CPQ* by telling founder and then CEO Rod Canion to take a walk. From that moment on until late 1997, Rosen ran the company. Was he responsible for the high-level of market response at *Compaq*?

Whatever the cause, *Compaq* lost a bundle of theoretical money over the decade. Over the five years from 1993 through 1997, the company actually earned $9,592 million before depreciation. If management had capitalized on its extraordinary customer response, they theoretically would have earned $17,403 million. The difference between actual and theoretical EBITDA was $7,811 million—81% of actual earnings. If these incremental earnings had been paid out in dividends, the impact on the company's share price could have been dramatic.

Finally, let's take a look at what went on in the case of the new power player on the block, *Dell*.

Hard as *Dell*

In 1991[6] *Dell* was not yet the darling of Wall Street in the desktop market. With only 2.38% of sales revenues and a radical new business model, the company was barely on the radar screen. *Compaq*, with a 3.87% share, wasn't must bigger, but it grabbed more headlines in an environment where all the big news was about the failing lights of *Big Blue*. The early part of the decade was a golden opportunity for both *Compaq* and *Dell*. And both companies significantly underspent in the desktop market.

Over the decade *Dell* emerged as a major player, crawling toward its maximum earnings market share. The situation is illustrated by Chart 6-12. In 1991, *Dell's* maximum earnings market share was 19.63%. The difference between actual share and **MEMS** in that year was 1,725 basis points (17.25 percentage points). The gap closed to 635 basis points in 1992. This decline in **MEMS** was a result of a share drop in *Dell's* operating margins from 23.29% to 18.58%. This reduced the incremental gross profit per basis point

Chart 6-12 *Dell's* Crawl Toward Maximum Earnings

and **MEMS**. By the close of the decade, *Dell* had inched closer to maximums earnings market share, but the gap remained large at 1,594 basis points.

Dell's actual compared with potential earnings, shown in Chart 6-13, reflect this large gap. In 1991 its actual EBITDA was $159 million. Its theoretical maximum EBITDA was $759 million. The company left $600 million theoretical earnings on the table. In other words, management achieved only 21% of its earnings potential. Maybe all this was a result of being a small player with a new business model in a high-growth marketplace. In any case, by 2000 *Dell's* actual market share had climbed to 14.79% of strategic group revenues. But the company's theoretical maximum earnings share of revenues also jumped—to 30.73%.

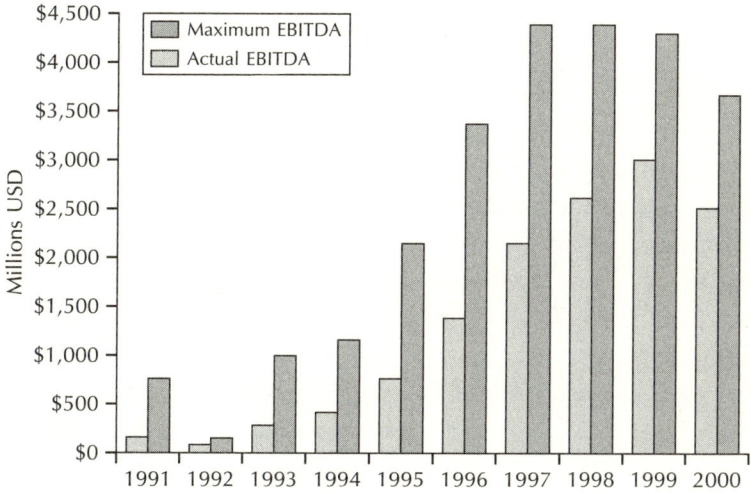

Chart 6-13 *Dell's* Actual Versus Maximum Earnings

As *Dell* crawled toward maximum earnings share, its maximum potential earnings gradually increased. The results appear in Chart 6-14. In this chart, years are listed on the horizontal axis and EBITDA in millions of dollars on the vertical axis. By 2000, *Dell's* achievement of earnings potential climbed to 68%. Nevertheless, management continued to leave a lot of theoretical money on the table. *Dell's* actual EBITDA in 2000 was $2,510 million. Its theoretical maximum EBITDA was $3,668 million. That was a $1,510 million dollar difference in a single year.

A Recent Look at *Dell*

Let's take a closer look at *Dell* by focusing in on the ten quarters from March, 2002 through June, 2004. Three major changes occurred in the strategic group for this more recent time period. (Calabrese et al. 2004)

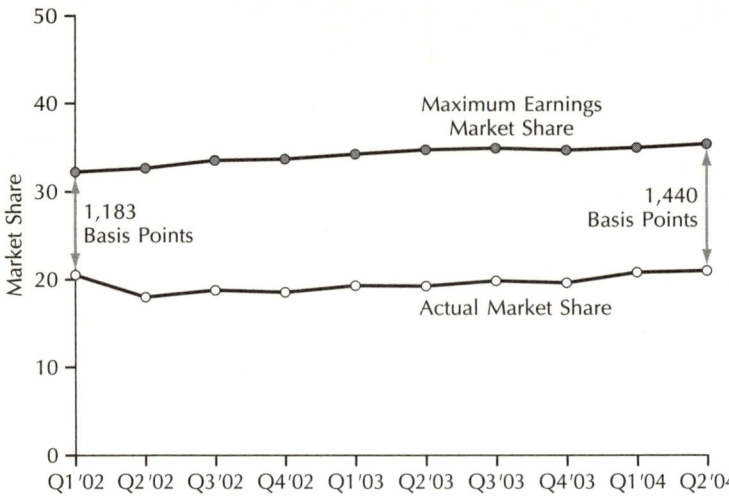

Chart 6-14 A Recent Look at *Dell* 1st Q 02 to 2nd Q 04

First, March, 2002 was the last quarter in which *Compaq* reported separate results before its merger with *Hewlett-Packard*. So nine of the ten quarters were sales of the merged companies. Second, a new company—*Sun Microsystems* (*SUNW*)—was introduced for the purpose of testing the robustness of the analysis. Finally, group revenues were changed by the shift from annual to quarterly data. Despite these changes, the picture still looks about the same for *Dell*.

Maximum earnings market share shifts upward to 32.34% of group revenues, totaling $39,325 million in the first quarter of 2002. *Dell's* actual market share was 20.51%, leaving a shortfall of 1,183 basis points. The company's **MEMS** continued to increase, reaching 35.37% by the end of the second quarter of 2004. With an actual share of 20.97%, *Dell* was 1,440 basis points short of maximum earnings share.

The bottom line is that *Dell* continued to leave a lot of theoretical money on the table right up through the second quarter of 2004. The pattern of earnings shortfalls over the ten quarters is shown in Chart 6-15. The vertical axis is EBITDA in millions. After spending on enterprise marketing forces, *Dell* earned $590 million in the first quarter of 2002. Its theoretical maximum earnings were $709 million. *Dell* had a quarterly earnings opportunity loss of $119 million. These theoretical opportunity losses increased over the next nine quarters. By the close of the second quarter of 2004, the difference between actual and maximum quarterly earnings had increased to $267 million. Annualized, this shortfall would amount to over $1 billion in earnings.

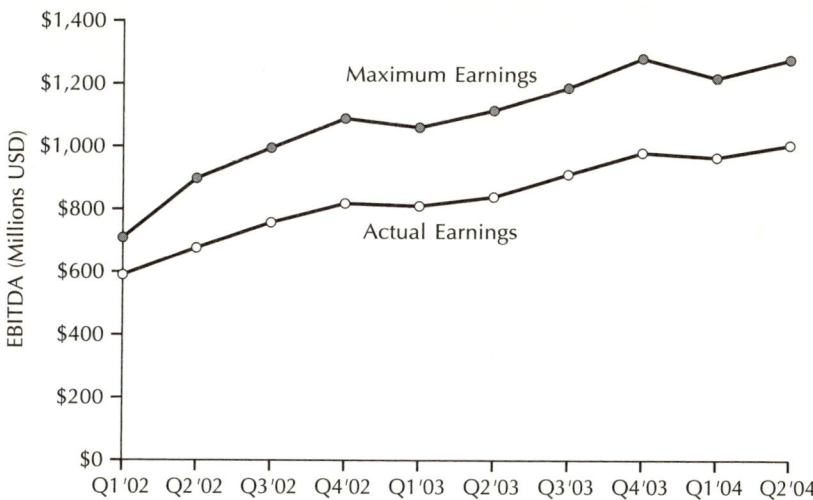

Chart 6-15 *Dell's* Earnings Shortfall 1st Q'02 Through 2nd Q'04

Why was *Dell's* failure to maximize earnings after enterprise marketing expenses so persistent? Perhaps the company's business model, for all its efficiencies, was strategically limiting. But despite all this, or perhaps because of it, *Dell* rules the world in enterprise marketing efficiency.

Dell's Incredible Marketing Machine

Dell's enterprise marketing efficiency over the decade is captured in the following market share attraction chart. In 1991, the company generated 2.4% of group revenues with just 0.9% of enterprise marketing expenses—a greater than two-to-one ratio of outputs to inputs.

By 1998, *Dell* generated nearly 13.8% of the desktop sales with less than 6.6% enterprise marketing expenses (lines A and B in the chart). The slope of *Dell's* market response function was 2.0. Put in other terms, *Dell's* enterprise marketing efficiency ratio in 2000 was 0.51. Compare that with *IBM's* 1.35, and you see why *Big Blue* never caught up with *Little Blue*.

Even as *Dell's* sales revenues and market share grew over the decade, the company maintained a two-to-one ratio of revenue share to marketing-expense share. This performance was unmatched by any other player in the desktop marketplace. In terms of bang per buck, *Dell* won the battle for your desktop, even though it didn't achieve maximum earnings market share.

Desktop Differential Performance

Looking only at its stock market performance, you would think the company couldn't do much better. *Dell's* market value grew from $607 million

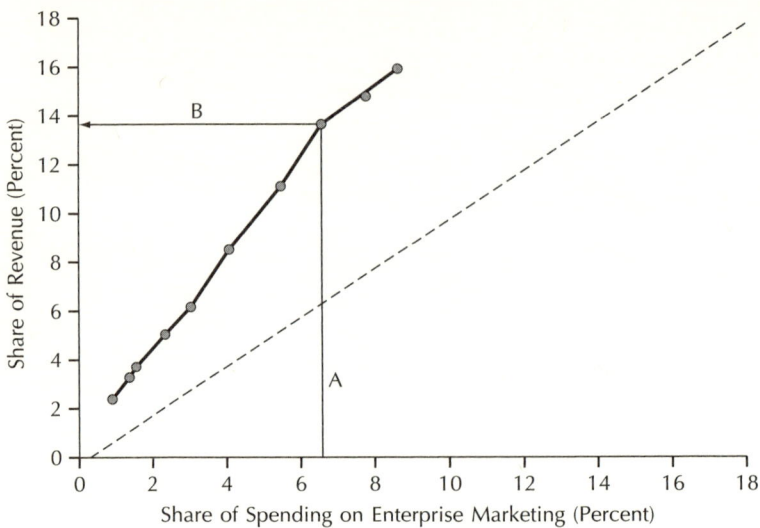

Chart 6-16 Tracking *Little Blue's* Enterprise Marketing Supremacy

in 1991 to $89,313 million in the second quarter of 2004. In this quarter *Dell* was worth more than the combined value of *Hewlett-Packard* ($63,316) and *Sun Microsystems* ($15,597). Its value equaled 60% of *IBM's* $148,057 million market cap. A picture of how these players performed is shown in this candlestick chart of risk-adjusted differentials.

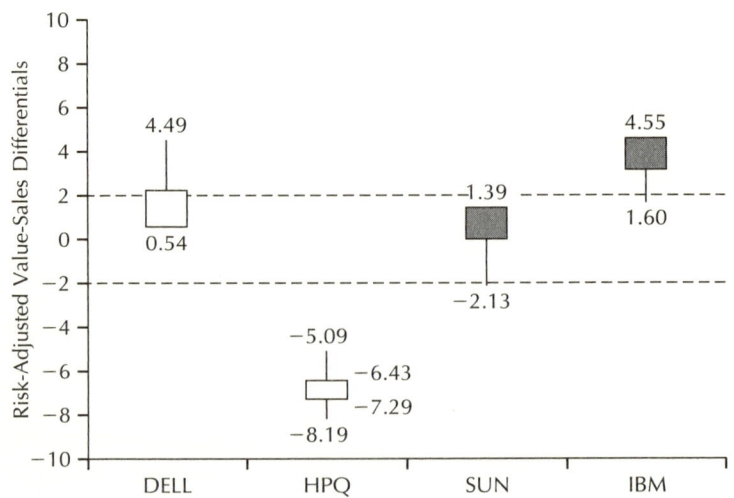

Chart 6-17 Risk-Adjusted Value-Sales Differentials 1st Q'02 to 2nd Q'04

It's clear in Chart 6-17 that *HPQ* was the weakest performer in the group. The company opened the first quarter of 2002 with a risk-adjusted differential (RAD) of −7.29. Investors didn't like the impending merger. Then *HPQ* moved upward to close at −6.43 in the second quarter of 2004. Along the way the company hit a high note of −5.09 and a low one of −8.19.

Given these numbers, it's easy to see why the board urged *HPQ's* controversial CEO Carleton S. Fiorina to resign on February 8, 2005.

> It seemed like the corporate equivalent of Clint Eastwood's *Million Dollar Baby:* In a woman-to-woman confrontation that never could have happened in the male-dominated executive world of ten years ago, Hewlett-Packard director Pattie Dunn, who in her day job is vice chairman of *Barclays Global Investors,* knocked Carly Fiorina out of her post as CEO of *HP* and took over as the nonexecutive chairman of the board. Or at least that's the way Hollywood might have told it. (Loomis 2005, 99)

What's difficult to understand is why investors didn't see the underlying strength of *HPQ's* performance during Fiorina's tenure as CEO. Her enterprise marketing performance is pictured in Chart 6-18.

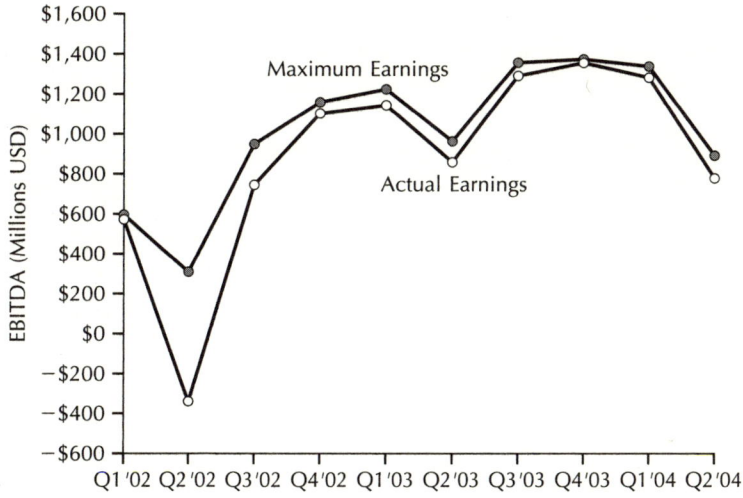

Chart 6-18 *HPQ's* Actual Versus Maximum Earnings

With the exception of the two quarters following the merger, *HPQ's* achievement of maximum earnings potential was no different than during the ten years from 1991 through 2000 before Fiorina took control. It averaged 93.8% during her tenure as CEO. Perhaps there **was** something more behind her exit than financial performance. She wasn't an engineer by training, but she engineered first-class earnings. Or perhaps investors would have taken a different view of *HP's* performance if they had seen the evidence presented here.

Dell, on the other hand, continued to underperform against potential earnings. Nevertheless, investors rewarded the company a significant premium over the ten quarters. Take another look at Chart 6-17. The company opened the first quarter of 2002 with a risk-adjusted differential of +0.54 and closed the second quarter of 2004 with a +2.47. Not bad for a company with half the sales revenue of *IBM*. But *Dell* wasn't the *Southwest* of the desktop space. Even though *IBM* slipped significantly, opening at +4.55 and closing at +2.55, it hit a low of +1.6 and remained above *Dell* in seven of the ten quarters.

Why Did *Dell* Fall Short?

You're probably saying to yourself, "Fall short? *Dell* didn't fall short! You just put the company in a strategic group where it didn't belong."

Read what the CEO Kevin Rollins told *Fortune* magazine in February 2005:

> *I'll tell you why we think we're an underdog, and that is, we have been a PC company. We've been migrating the last three or four years out of being a PC company. We've moved into servers, and storage, mobility products, services, software peripheral categories, and printers, and become a diversified IT company. If you look at those other categories, we're not the leader, we're not the biggest. So as we've built out a diversified IT portfolio, we're a small guy again, and it keeps this notion of the underdog, gotta struggle, gotta change, gotta do things for the customer.* (Serwer 2005, 74)

If the company is to transplant its fabled enterprise marketing efficiency into all the new categories, three things must change: its basic business model, its sales strategy, and its distribution system. These factors limited its ability to reach 35.37% of the desktop marketplace in the second quarter of 2004. In other words, *Dell's* direct sales model limits its potential in its new diversified IT corporate markets.

Remember *Dell's* business model? It's "selling computer systems directly to customers," which "eliminates retailers that add unnecessary time and cost." Well and good. But this model was not designed for the corporate IT customer.

It's a Different Ball Game

In large organizations there's a wide gulf between the buyer and the end user. The buyer is usually an IT specialist. The end user is usually a professional who does not have the authority to make his or her own purchasing decisions or to buy over the *Internet*. And even those users who have this authority will usually be required to buy the brand that is supported by their employer's IT infrastructure.

In *Dell's* model, the buyer and end user are the same. In the first desktop marketplace examined in this chapter, *Dell* was surrounded by three competitors who specialized in the corporate buyer. The business model worked against *Dell* in the corporate segment, because of the company's tradition of carrying little inventory and building machines to order. No doubt this is changing now, along with the company's entry into new corporate categories.

Dell must find a way to duplicate its enterprise marketing efficiency with the corporate buyer. To serve this segment, *Dell* needs either to develop its own direct sales force or negotiate a change in the purchasing behavior of corporate customers. Both of these options take time—and changing the purchasing behavior of purchasing departments in companies with high switching costs is a complex and costly process.

Tapping the Corporate Market

The motivation for switching to *Dell* has to be based on a combination of superior service, product performance and price discounts. It also requires significant investments by the corporate purchasing departments to change ordering and billing practices. Superior product performance might be achieved by allowing end users to configure their own systems within the framework of the corporate purchasing organization. But this in turn requires the design and installation of new accounting and control systems for managing end-user buying decisions. No doubt *Dell* and its major corporate customers are working on how to add many of these features to their relationship. In this regard, *Dell's* situation was a mirror image of how that company from Bentonville, Arkansas had to forge new relationships with its suppliers in order to close the arms-length operating gap between them.

Roadblocks in the Consumer Market

Dell's direct distribution also limits the company's access to the consumer market. In 2004, a majority of households still did not have the level of experience with and knowledge of personal computers that direct buying demanded. This is changing over time as college students with both experience and knowledge form households of their own. In the meantime, without retail stores, *Dell* does not have access to the inexperienced consumer.

Finally, *Dell's* direct-distribution system cannot be easily duplicated in Europe or Asia. Terms of trade in the U.S. are relatively homogeneous. Throughout Europe and Asia, the languages, laws, currencies, accounting conventions, and trade infrastructures are different. This makes the job of direct distribution much more difficult in foreign countries.

Of course, the problems with *Dell* were relative to the companies in this strategic group. If placed in a different group with companies such as *Gateway* and *Apple Computer*, would *Dell's* maximum earnings market share change? Not much.

Dell in Another Strategic Group

A *Bottom Line Marketing* analysis of *Dell*—in a strategic group with *Apple, Gateway,* and *Hewlett-Packard-Compaq* during the period from 1993 through 2002—was published in 2003 (Newton). In calendar year 2002, *Dell's* market shares against these two smaller competitors were higher of course: maximum earnings share was 41.95% compared with an actual revenue share of 34.74%. The company continued to underspend on enterprise marketing, but the gap was narrowed to 621 basis points.

Are the Markets Finally Catching Up?

In the November 16, 2005 issue of *Fortune* magazine, Andy Serwer wrote the about *Dell's* growing midlife crisis:

> The witching hour came, fittingly enough, on Halloween: *Dell* chief executive Kevin Rollins issued an early warning about the company's third-quarter financial performance. He probably wished he could hide behind a mask. Earnings and sales would both be below expectations.... How about this dirty little secret: while *Dell's* stock is down 22% over the past year, *HP's* is up more than 40%.

Review the Bidding

What's driving these very different enterprise marketing performances? The results are driven by the relationships between competitive cost and profit per basis point. And these relationships are purely theoretical. Let's review the bidding.

First, the gross profit per basis point $\bar{p}$ depends on two things: strategic group revenue (R) and the company's gross margin expressed as a proportion $\bar{g}$.

The bigger the group's revenue and the longer the time interval, the greater the profit per basis point. For example, group revenue in a quarter will be only about one-fourth the revenue for the same group in a year. The smaller the company's gross margin and the shorter the time interval, the less the gross profit per basis point. Basis point profits are standardized over companies via the division of each revenue share point into 100 basis points. We assume the average is equal to the incremental profit per basis point within a feasible range of operations.

Second, the cost of a basis point is driven by the principle of force. The enterprise marketing expenses (y) required to maintain a given share of revenues are the arithmetic product of a scaling factor $m/(100 - m)$, competitors' enterprise marketing forces (f), and enterprise marketing efficiency (x). In the scaling factor, m is the company's revenue share expressed as an integer. The greater a company's share of revenues, the more competitors spend, and the longer the time interval, the higher the cost of a basis point. The more efficient the company is in acquiring and deploying its enterprise marketing forces and the shorter the time interval, the lower the cost of a basis point.

Third, the incremental cost of a basis point is the first derivative of the total force formula. The incremental cost per basis point $\ddot{c}$ equals the arithmetic product of competitors' marketing forces f and the company's efficiency ratio x, divided by $(100 - m)^2$.

Fourth, maximum earnings market share $\hat{m}$ equals one minus the square root of the ratio of the cost of the first basis point $\ddot{k}$ divided by the incremental profit of the next basis point $\ddot{p}$.

Remember the Rule of Maximum Earnings

In this analysis of the competition for customers and capital, what you see is what you get. There's no complex regression model hiding in the wings. Yet the results are non-linear and interdependent. That's why the results for one company can be so radically different from another. Yet they are computationally manageable even when applied to the real world. You actually can make these computations with a calculator, pencil, and the back of an envelope using audited financial statements. This means you can verify the results, if not the interpretation of them.

This chapter's analyses and discussions of the decade-long (1991–2000) battle for your desktop are based on data presented in the three tables in Appendix 6-A of this chapter: sales revenues, cost of goods sold, and selling, general, and administrative expenses.[7]

Remember the rule of maximum earnings. The next time you review financial statements for competing companies, you'll be able to develop a strategic analysis of enterprise marketing that gets the attention of your peers. You'll be able to teach them something they don't know about competing for customers and capital. If you work at it, you may even be able to find ways to boost your company's shareholder value. That should even get the attention of your CEO.

Appendix 6-A: Desktop Data

Table A-1 Sales Revenues

MILL USD (Fiscal Year End)	IBM (December)	HPQ (November)	DELL (January)	CPQ (December)	Group Totals
1991	$64,792	$14,494	$ 2,014	$ 3,271	$ 84,571
1992	$64,523	$16,410	$ 2,873	$ 4,100	$ 87,906
1993	$62,716	$20,317	$ 3,475	$ 7,191	$ 93,699
1994	$64,052	$24,991	$ 5,296	$10,866	$105,205
1995	$71,940	$31,519	$ 7,759	$14,755	$125,973
1996	$75,947	$38,420	$12,327	$18,109	$144,803
1997	$78,508	$42,895	$18,243	$24,584	$164,230
1998	$81,667	$47,061	$25,265	$31,169	$185,162
1999	$87,548	$42,370	$31,888	$38,525	$200,331
2000	$88,396	$48,782	$31,168	$42,383	$210,729

Table A-2 Cost of Goods Sold

MILL USD	IBM	HPQ	DELL	CPQ	Totals
1991	$27,325	$ 7,253	$ 1,545	$ 1,883	$ 38,006
1992	$25,848	$ 8,519	$ 2,339	$ 2,746	$ 39,453
1993	$32,790	$11,380	$ 2,704	$ 5,338	$ 52,212
1994	$34,571	$14,484	$ 4,191	$ 7,971	$ 61,217
1995	$37,618	$18,875	$ 6,046	$11,153	$ 73,692
1996	$41,732	$24,202	$ 9,538	$13,651	$ 89,123
1997	$43,881	$26,763	$14,034	$17,386	$102,064
1998	$46,320	$29,943	$19,891	$23,087	$119,241
1999	$49,460	$28,404	$25,205	$28,396	$131,465
2000	$51,459	$33,709	$25,422	$31,010	$141,600

Table A-3 Selling, General, and Administrative Expenses

MILL USD	IBM	HPQ	DELL	CPQ	Totals
1991	$27,978	$ 5,351	$ 310	$ 919	$34,558
1992	$26,048	$ 5,785	$ 451	$ 872	$33,155
1993	$23,840	$ 6,315	$ 489	$1,006	$31,650
1994	$20,279	$ 6,952	$ 690	$1,461	$29,382
1995	$20,448	$ 7,937	$ 952	$1,864	$31,201
1996	$21,508	$ 9,195	$1,406	$2,319	$34,428
1997	$21,511	$10,237	$2,060	$3,764	$37,572
1998	$21,708	$11,148	$2,761	$6,331	$41,948
1999	$21,854	$ 8,962	$3,675	$8,001	$42,492
2000	$20,781	$10,029	$3,236	$7,513	$41,559

Appendix 6-B: Periodicity in the Desktop Space

Calendar	IBM*	CPQ*	HPQ*	DELL*
30-Nov-90				
31-Dec-90				
31-Jan-91				$890
28-Feb-91				
31-Mar-91				
30-Apr-91				
31-May-91				
30-Jun-91				
31-Jul-91				
31-Aug-91				
30-Sep-91				
31-Oct-91			$14,494	
30-Nov-91				
31-Dec-91	$64,792	$33,554		
31-Jan-92				$2,014
29-Feb-92				
31-Mar-92				
30-Apr-92				
31-May-92				
30-Jun-92				
31-Jul-92				
31-Aug-92				
30-Sep-92				
31-Oct-92				
30-Nov-92				
31-Dec-92				
31-Jan-93				$2,873

*Fiscal year end month and sales revenues in millions of USD

References

Bell, D., R. L. Keaney, and J. D. C. Little. 1975. "A Market Share Theorem." *Journal of Marketing Research* 12: 136–141.

Calabrese, M., S. O. Chonglerttham, M. Dodson, and J. G. Bruton. 2004. "Dell Grows Up: Advertising alone will not allow Dell to capture B2B market share and earnings. Are key acquisitions in its future?" *Bottom Line Marketing Reports*. A. B. Freeman School of Business, Tulane University, 2 (December).

CNET News.com, "Big Iron: HP to Buy Compaq." September 5, 2001.

Gerstner, L. V., Jr. 2002. *Who Says Elephants Can't Dance? Leading a Great Enterprise Through Dramatic Change.* New York: Harper Business. ". . . the last thing *IBM* needs right now is a vision" was a comment made by *IBM's* new CEO at his first press conference on July 27, 1993.

http://www.dell.com/us/en/gen/corporate/access_facts_fact_pak.htm

Lear, R. W. "IBM: Turnabout Is Good Play." www.chiefexecutive.net/depts/ceobook/150.htm

Loomis, C. J. 2005. "How the HP Board KO's Carly." *Fortune.* March 7: 99–102.

Newton, K. 2003. "The PC Market: Does it Compute?: *AAPL + DELL + GTW + HPQ* 1993–2002." *Bottom Line Marketing Reports.* A. B. Freeman School of Business, Tulane University, 1, 8 (December).

Serwer, A. 2005. "The Education of Michael Dell." *Fortune.* February 22.

———. 2005. "Dell's Midlife Crisis." *Fortune.* November 16.

End Notes

[1] See Appendix A, page 250 for the data used in this chapter.

[2] The phrase "market share *basis* points" used here always refers to 1/100th of a "market *share* point" or to 1/100th of a given "*share* of revenues."

[3] *IBM's* risk-adjusted VS differential rose from a minimum of -2.3 in 1992 to a $+1.4$ in 2000.

[4] This was found by Raul Sanabria in his dissertation research to be true most of the time for most companies.

[5] http://www.hp.com/hpinfo/abouthp/histnfacts/timeline/index.html

[6] All of the results reported in this chapter, as well as any competitive analysis of financial accounting data, require alignment of each company's fiscal year end. In finance this is called the "periodicity" problem. With a very large sample of companies the problem is easily solved by using only those firms with a fiscal year ending in December. And in some industries, either convention or regulations lead to common fiscal year ends. In computers and Internet services you often find companies with different fiscal year end months. Alignment is easy if every company's fiscal year ends in the third month of a calendar quarter. It becomes a bit more difficult when companies use off-quarter fiscal year ends. For example, in the desktop space, *HPQ's* fiscal year ends in October and *Dell's* ends in January. In these two cases, correct alignment makes a significant difference. The effect is documented in Appendix 6-B of this chapter. Notice that *Dell's* sales revenues would enter the calculations as $890 million if the 1991 calendar year were used to align its sales with the other companies. A much closer alignment is achieved by assigning *Dell's* $2,014 million in sales—reported in its fiscal year ending January 1992—to the 1991 results for *IBM* and *Compaq.*

[7] Except for the short discussion of risk-adjusted differentials on page 161, which require balance-sheet data.

CHAPTER 7

IN SEARCH OF MAXIMUM EARNINGS

Now you understand the math and you know how maximum earnings market share analysis works. So what strategic lessons can we take away from all this number crunching? To answer this question we'll apply the model to twenty-two competitors in five very different industries. From each one of these cases we'll learn an important lesson. The chapter concludes with three general lessons about maximum earnings market share analysis.

We lead off with one of the most dynamic and competitive businesses on the planet—online retailers—in a case called *I Gotta Check My Auction*. Of course, *Amazon.com* and *eBay.com* are the stars of this galaxy. The supporting players are *Yahoo.com, PriceLine.com,* and *Google.com*. The action is documented over three different time periods. The first is calendar years from 1995 through 2002. The second is data from the fourth quarter of 2000 through the first quarter of 2003. Finally, to bring the analysis more up-to-date we look at the quarterly numbers from December, 2001 through March, 2004 just before Google want public.

Next we review **The Sundown Rule,** staring *Wal*Mart*. The competitors are *Costco, K-Mart, Sears,* and *Target*. This case covers the period from the fourth quarter of 2000 through the first quarter of 2003. "Combining high quality with stunningly low prices" that appeal to upscale customers, *Costco's* CEO Jim Sinegal "just might be the shrewdest merchant since Sam Walton." (Greenhouse 2005, 8) The coming stand-off between *Costco* and *Wal*Mart* for the top gun position in mass retailing adds a surprising twist to their relative performance.

All the News That Fits is a case about the leading U.S. companies in the "dual-segment communications" business. The strategic group includes *Fox Entertainment Group, Gannett Co. Inc., New York Times Co.,* and *Tribune Co.* These companies don't make much money on newspapers and TV stations—the real money comes from selling advertising space and time. Here you get a chance to see one of the more surprising strategic directions to come out of the analysis of maximum earnings market share.

Next, we turn to the biggest, hottest, high-tech industry in the world, wireless phone services. In **Buy on the Rumor, Sell on the News** we see how

Sprint, Wireless, Nextel, and *USM* compete for customers and capital over the period from the fourth quarter of 2000 through the first quarter of 2003.

The last case is based on one of the biggest, most profitable businesses in the world—pharmaceuticals. In **The Medicine Men,** we catch an industry in the grip of dynamic change as a result of new rules of play brought about by the FDA permitting direct-to-consumer television advertising. *Bristol-Myers Squibb, GlaxoSmithKline, Johnson & Johnson, Merck,* and *Novartis* reach for the sky over the period from 1985 through 2004.

The final three lessons cover the **Sum Constraint, Demand Multiplier Effects,** and **Carryover Effects.**

I Gotta Check My Auction

Pure online retailers are a phenomenon. The competitors of consequence in this strategic group have only their distribution channel (the Internet) in common.

On the one hand, you have radically new forms of trading companies in this market, like *eBay.com,* that don't even own the goods they sell and that serve only as clearing houses for transactions between buyers and sellers. *eBay.com* was launched in September, 1995. The company's Web site says its "mission is to provide a global trading platform where practically anyone can trade practically anything."

Alternative versions of online trading companies appeared before and after *eBay.com.* Among these were *Bidz.com* "for the anxious bidders with little time to wait"; *Onsale.com, which was* launched in May, 1995 as "a premiere eCommerce company"; and *PriceLine.com,* which auctioned personal travel and financial services to consumers.

On the other hand, you have the spectacular online reinvention of traditional brick-and-mortar retailers exemplified by *Amazon.com*. That company carries massive inventories of products that are sold on credit and shipped to consumers via *Federal Express.* This makes Amazon's current business model very different than *eBay.* But both business models already are changing.

In addition, there were the pure search engines like *Google.com* that traded in free search information while it sold cost-per-click advertising on the same screen image, and hybrids like *Yahoo.com* that also gave away information, sold products for affiliated retailers, cost-per-click advertising, and offered person-to-person auctions as well.

Porous Boundaries

If ever there were an industry that personified the need for analysis of porous and dynamic strategic groups, online retailers is it. The possible combination of players and groups is nearly endless and continuously changing. Some of these companies are public; some are about to go public; most are privately held. *Amazon, eBay, Yahoo,* and *PriceLine* defined the strategic group in the following analyses.

In the summer of 2004, the public membership of this strategic group changed dramatically.

> *Amid a stock market sagging in summer doldrums,* Google *gave a bullish assessment of its worth yesterday. . . . it expected its shares to sell for $108 to $135 each. That would value the company at $29 billion to $36 billion, putting its market value just below the $38 billion value of* Yahoo, *a larger and far more mature Internet company. The most valuable Internet company,* eBay, *is worth $49 billion.* (Hansell and Rivlin 2004, 1)

Of course, when sufficient data are available *Google* should replace Price-Line in the group to assess its influence on quarterly performance. The company's annual financial statements for the year ending December 31, 1999, through the year ending 2003 were filed with the SEC on April 24, 2004.[1] These filings also included data for the first quarters of 2003 and 2004. Since *Google* remained a company without a market cap until its stock was traded, we cannot calculate its risk-adjusted differentials until at least eight quarters of trading data become available.[2]

Out of Nowhere

This strategic group seemingly developed out of nowhere. It first appeared on investors' radar screens in 1995. Before the century ended this group led the now infamous *Internet Boom.* First, we'll look at nine-year trends in the group's sales revenues, market capitalization, and share of revenues. This period documents the emergence of the players, the boom that followed, the collapse in shareholder value, and the recovery that followed.

The trend in sales revenues of this strategic group gives new meaning to the concept of dynamic growth. As shown in Chart 7-1, revenues increased from just $2 million in 1995 to $5.5 billion in 2000. This extraordinary growth was interrupted when the Internet bubble burst early that year. After a year of near-zero growth, strategic group revenue first recovered in 2002, reaching $7.1 billion, and then accelerated to $9.918 billion in 2003.[3]

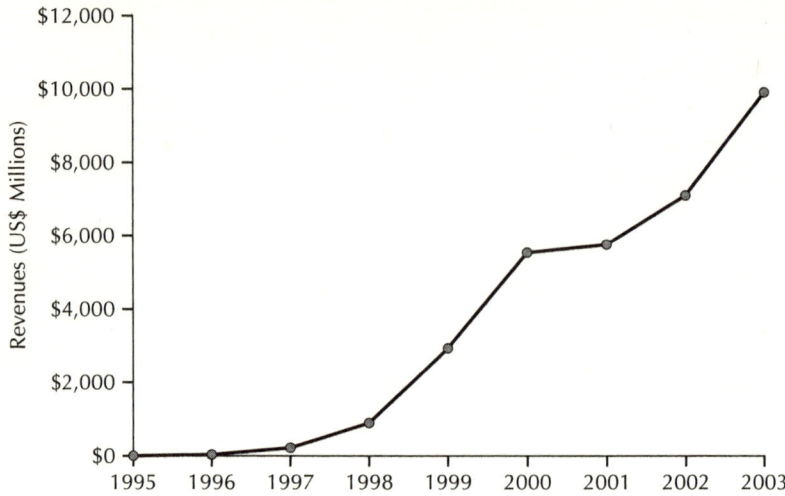

Chart 7-1 Trend in Online Retailer Revenues

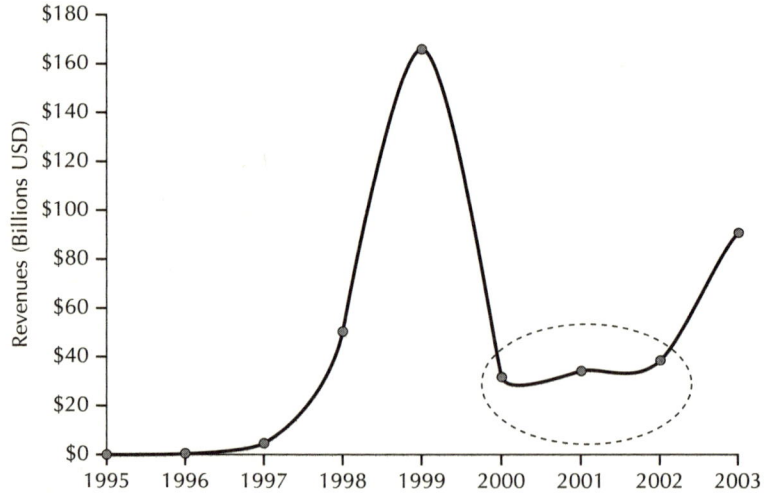

Chart 7-2 Online Retailer Shareholder Value

Chart 7-2 documents how the 2000–2001 "interruption" in sales growth devastated the group's shareholder value. The vertical axis in this chart is the combined market value of all four players. The scale ranges from $0 to $180 billion. In 1995, *Amazon* (ticker *AMZN*) and *Yahoo* (*YHOO*) were the first kids on the block. Their combined sales were $2 million. That's what kicked off the Internet play. But both these companies had yet to issue IPOs. So their combined market value was zero.

From this inauspicious beginning—in just four years—combined market value rocketed from under $0.5 billion in 1996 to $165.6 billion in 1999.

The growth in group revenue from 1999 to 2000 was 89%. The growth in strategic group market cap was 229% in 1998–1999. This growth rate plummeted to a decline of 89% in 1999–2000. This was the real "Y2K" problem faced by online retailers. It led the collapse of the equities market. A growth rate of 8% in 2000–2001 was the first sign of recovery. This was followed the next year by 13% growth, and jumped 136% to $90.6 billion in 2003.

Share of Revenues

The next step in looking beneath the surface of these remarkable numbers is to track company share of revenues over the nine years from 1995 through the close of business in 2003.

You will be surprised by what you see in Table 7-1. The shares of revenue for *Amazon, eBay, PriceLine,* and *Yahoo* are in the rows of this table. In 1995, *Amazon* and *Yahoo* split the revenue in this strategic group with shares of 27.3% and 72.7%, respectively. Remember that the group's total revenue was only $2 million in 1995? Well, these two companies spent $2.3 million on enterprise marketing that year, setting off the buzz that became the Internet boom.

eBay first reported annual data in 1996 with a revenue share of 1.1%. Its share of annual revenue was 0.0 in 1995. *PriceLine* entered the public arena by reporting sales data in 1998. Its share of annual group revenue in that year was 3.9%.

By the close of business in 2003, *Amazon* generated 53.1% of group revenue, down 230 basis points from the year before. Note that *AMZN's* market share peaked in 1998 at 68.1%. In 2003 *Yahoo* was at a 16.4% share—an increase of 300 basis points over 2002. *eBay* was up to 21.8% and *PriceLine* declined from 14.1% to 8.7% of revenues.

Table 7-1   Online Retailer Share of Revenues 1995–2003

	Amazon	*eBay*	*PriceLine*	*Yahoo*
1995	27.3	0.0	0.0	72.7
1996	44.7	1.1	0.0	54.2
1997	66.9	2.6	0.0	30.5
1998	68.1	5.3	3.9	22.7
1999	55.9	7.7	16.4	20.1
2000	49.9	7.8	22.3	20.0
2001	54.2	13.0	20.3	12.5
2002	55.4	17.1	14.1	13.4
2003	53.1	21.8	8.7	16.4

Table 7-2 Online Retailer Share of Value 1995–2003

	Amazon	*eBay*	*PriceLine*	*Yahoo*
1995	0.0	0.0	0.0	0.0
1996	0.0	0.0	0.0	100.0
1997	31.6	0.0	0.0	68.4
1998	33.9	19.3	0.0	46.8
1999	15.9	9.8	4.7	69.6
2000	17.6	28.2	0.7	53.5
2001	11.8	54.4	3.8	29.9
2002	19.0	54.8	0.9	25.2
2003	23.4	46.3	0.7	29.6
1st Monthly Close	5/30/1997	9/30/1998	3/31/1999	4/30/1996

Share of Market Value

Just as *Google* reported sales revenues before it went public, so too did the other firms in this strategic group. As a result, you will find in Table 7-2 that company shares of market value lagged in time behind their annual sales revenue.

Yahoo was the first company to report a monthly closing price. That occurred on April 30, 1996. As a result, *Yahoo* created 100% of the market value in that year. *Amazon* was the next company to report a monthly closing price. That occurred on May 30, 1997. At the close of business in that year the company created 31.6% of the group's market value. At the same time, *Amazon* knocked *Yahoo's* share of value down to 68.4%. *Amazon's* share of value (**SOV**) deceased to 19.0% by 2002 and then jumped to 23.4% in 2003.

eBay first reported a monthly closing price on September 30, 1998. By the end of that year, *eBay* had created 19.3% of the strategic group value. *PriceLine* entered the game on March 31, 1999 with 4.7% of the year-end market value. Meanwhile, *Yahoo's* share of value slid to 25.2% by the close of business in 2002, rebounding to 29.6% in 2003.

Value-Sales Differentials

Table 7-3 shows each company's **VSD** beginning with the year in which both share of value and share of revenues were first reported. Also included in this table are preliminary enterprise marketing risk estimates.

It's typical of companies in newly formed, volatile strategic groups to experience extraordinarily big swings in value-sales differentials. It is also common to see associated high levels of enterprise marketing risk. So it was with these four online retailers.

Table 7-3 Online Retailer Value-Sales Differentials 1995–2003

VSD	*Amazon*	*eBay*	*PriceLine*	*Yahoo*
1995	−27.3	0.0	0.0	−72.7
1996	−44.7	−1.1	0.0	45.8
1997	−35.3	−2.6	0.0	37.9
1998	−34.2	14.0	−3.9	24.1
1999	−40.0	2.2	−11.7	49.6
2000	−32.3	20.4	−21.6	33.5
2001	−42.4	41.4	−16.5	17.5
2002	−36.3	37.7	−13.2	11.8
2003	−29.7	24.5	−8.0	13.2
Enterprise Marketing Risk (Available Data Years)	5.8	16.9	7.9	36.6

AMZN's value-sales differentials ranged from a high of −27.3 in 1995 to a low of −44.7 in 1996. Its enterprise marketing risk was lowest for this group at 5.8. *eBay's* VSDs ranged from −2.6 in 1997 to +41.4 in 2001. At 16.9 points, its marketing risk was double the *MSI* sample average. *Yahoo's* VSDs ranged from −72.7 in 1995 to +49.6 in 1999. At 36.6, *Yahoo's* enterprise marketing risk was about five times the MSI average. *PriceLine* fell in the middle of these ranges.

Risk-Adjusted Differentials

How did investors value these companies? The answers are shown in Chart 7-3.

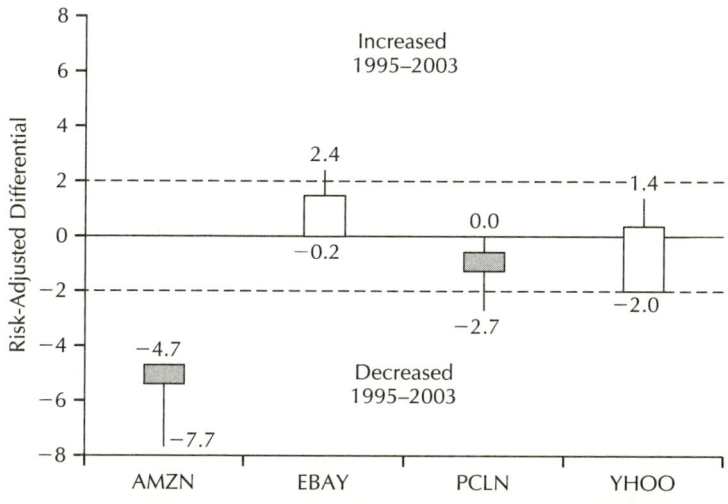

Chart 7-3 RAD Candlestick Chart of Online Retailers 1995–2003

It was not a pretty picture for *Amazon*. Shareholder value of the market leader was heavily discounted throughout the eight-year period. In 1995, the company opened with a risk-adjusted differential of -4.7. This negative differential further deteriorated to a low of -7.7, closing under -5.0.

eBay was the strongest performer in the group. Its **RAD** opened at -0.2 and closed at $+1.4$, reaching a high $+2.4$ value premium in 2001. *PriceLine* opened at -0.5 and closed at -1.0. The company saw the value of its assets discounted over the entire period. The discount reached a low of -2.7 points in 2000.

Investors discounted the market value of *Yahoo's* assets by -2.0 in the company's first year of trading and then awarded the company a premium of $+0.4$ in 2003. The premium reached a high of $+1.4$ in 1999.

After the Bubble Burst

Now let's take a close-up look at how these four companies performed after the Internet shakeout ended and recovery was underway. This period (circled in Chart 7-2) began in the fourth quarter of 2000 and extended through the first quarter of 2003.

Surprisingly, *Amazon* continued to be a bottom-feeder with significant discounts in the market value of its assets. *Amazon* generated 53.0% of the revenues, but created only 19.6% of the value in this strategic group. The company's value-sales differential was -33.4 points. *AMZN's* enterprise marketing risk was slightly below average (6.2). *Amazon's* **RADs** averaged -6.2 over the period ending March 31, 2003, with a high value of -4.7. *PriceLine's* **RADs** averaged -1.5 with a high of 0.0.

Lost Profit Opportunities

A different view of enterprise marketing performance is reported in Table 7-4, which shows the cumulative actual and maximum theoretical earnings of each online retailer in this strategic group over the ten quarters. Think of the "actual" and "maximum" values as *real*—compared with **potential**—earnings, summed over the ten quarters.

The difference between the maximum versus actual earnings measures the theoretical profit opportunities lost as a result of failing to maximize the residual after enterprise marketing expenses. By taking the ratio of maximum-minus-the-actual to actual earnings, lost profit opportunities in Table 7-4 were standardized to adjust for different scales of operation.

The results are revealing. *Amazon* and *PriceLine* suffered large theoretical lost profit opportunities. These losses are reflected in their respective ratios

Chapter 7 • In Search of Maximum Earnings 173

Table 7-4 Ten-Quarter Maximum and Actual Earnings of Online Retailers

4th Q-2000 to 1st Q-2003	Actual Earnings★	Maximum Earnings★	Maximum − Actual★	Lost Opportunity Ratio
Amazon	$ 252.3	$ 622.4	$370.1	1.47
eBay	$ 875.7	$1,128.2	$252.5	0.29
PriceLine	−$ 7.5	$ 61.5	$ 69.0	9.21
Yahoo	$ 423.5	$ 509.3	$ 85.8	0.20
Strategic Group	$1,544.0	$2,321.5	$777.4	0.50

★Ten-quarter cumulative values in millions of USD.

of 1.47 and 9.21. Though not shown in this table their corresponding relative earnings productivity ratios are −59% and −112%, respectively. *eBay* and *Yahoo's* lost earnings ratios were comparatively very small, at 0.29 and 0.20, respectively. Their corresponding relative earnings productivity ratios are −22% and −17%.

Amazon Overspending

It's not news that *Amazon* overspent on enterprise marketing. And it's not news that the company continued to pay a high price in forgone shareholder value. But it is news to find out how much the company overspent in the ten quarters ending March 31, 2003. The numbers appear in Table 7-5.

Table 7-5 *Amazon's* Overspending and Marketing Efficiency

Quarter Ending	Actual Enterprise Marketing Expenses	Maximum Earnings Marketing Expenses	Overspending on Enterprise Marketing	Share Maintenance Marketing Expenses	Enterprise Marketing Efficiency Ratio
	(1)	(2)	(3)	(4)	(5)
Dec-00	$ 283	$ 94	−$ 189	$ 478	0.59
Mar-01	$ 234	$ 80	−$ 155	$ 358	0.65
Jun-01	$ 210	$ 84	−$ 126	$ 286	0.73
Sep-01	$ 187	$ 78	−$ 109	$ 289	0.65
Dec-01	$ 217	$ 120	−$ 98	$ 541	0.40
Mar-02	$ 209	$ 108	−$ 101	$ 389	0.54
Jun-02	$ 215	$ 109	−$ 106	$ 354	0.60
Sep-02	$ 188	$ 111	−$ 77	$ 392	0.47
Dec-02	$ 269	$ 148	−$ 121	$ 664	0.40
Mar-03	$ 230	$ 135	−$ 96	$ 498	0.46
Totals	$2,243	$1,066	−$1,177	$4,249	0.55

Columns (1) and (2) show *AMZN's* actual and maximum enterprise marketing expenses from December, 2000 through March, 2003. For example, in December, 2000 the company actually spent $283 million on enterprise marketing, though it would have maximized earnings if it had spent just $94 million. Column (3) shows the extent of *Amazon's* overspending on enterprise marketing. That's the difference between its actual and maximum spending, or −$189 million in December, 2000. Column (4) reports the company's theoretical share maintenance enterprise marketing expenses. For example, if Amazon was as efficient as it was in December, 2000, it would have had to spend $478 million on enterprise marketing to maintain its 59.095-point share of group revenues.

As shown in the last row of column 3 (Table 7-5), *Amazon* overspent by a cumulative total of $1.177 billion! Okay, you say, surely Mr. Bezos has gotten religion. Sort of. By the first quarter of 2003, he overspent on enterprise marketing only $96 million compared with the $189 million in the last quarter of 2000.

AMZN's Marketing Efficiencies

Though Mr. Bezos overspent on enterprise marketing assets, he did it with even greater efficiency than you might have guessed. Look back at Column (5) (labeled "Enterprise Marketing Efficiency") in Table 7-5. In December, 2000 *Amazon's* enterprise marketing efficiency ratio was a surprising 0.59. This is the ratio of what the company actually spent ($283 million) to its theoretical share maintenance spending level ($478 million). The company spent only 59¢ on enterprise marketing forces that cost an average competitor in this strategic group $1.00. And *Amazon* became even more efficient over the next ten quarters. By the first quarter of 2003, its marketing efficiency ratio was 0.46, yielding even more bang per enterprise marketing buck than any other company in the group.

Closing the Earnings Gap

It's well known that market leadership was the driving force behind the strategy of *Amazon's* CEO. Jeffrey Bezos made this abundantly clear in his 1997 letter to shareholders (reproduced in the company's 2004 annual report):

> *We believe that a fundamental measure of our success will be the shareholder value we create over the long run. This value will be a result of our ability to extend and solidify our current market leadership position. The stronger our market leadership, the more*

powerful our economic mode. Market leadership can translate into higher revenue, higher profitability, greater capital velocity, and correspondingly stronger returns on invested capital. (Bezos 2004)

So what's happened to the company's market leadership recently? The CEO's strategy of extending and solidifying its leadership doesn't square with the more recent facts in Chart 7-4. The company's actual market share (in the white circles) was 63.41% in December, 2001. Four quarters later, in December, 2002, *AMZN's* actual share had dropped 198 basis points to 61.43%. In December, 2003, it fell an additional 484 basis points to 56.59%.

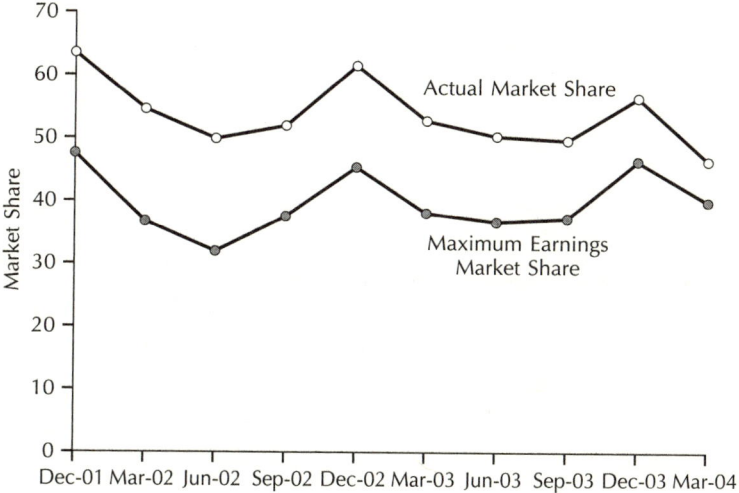

Chart 7-4 *Amazon's Actual and Maximum Earnings Share*

Compare this to maximum earnings market share (the gray circles) in Chart 7-4. In this period there was a large, but shrinking, difference between maximum earnings share and the company's actual market share. In March, 2002 the difference was 1,707 basis points. In March, 2000 the difference had shrunk to 1,409 basis points. By March, 2004 it had dropped to 626 basis points. Over the twenty-four months, this was a 63% decline in share of group revenues. Willfully or not, Mr. Bezos was trading market share for earnings in this strategic group.

Also notice in Chart 7-4 the significant seasonal swings in market share of revenues. The highest is in the fourth (holiday) quarter and the lowest in the second (mid-summer) quarter of each year. December is the fiscal year-end month for all four companies in this space.

The force behind *Amazon's* move toward its maximum earnings revenue share is revealed in Chart 7-5. The vertical axis measures *AMZN's* incremental profit and cost per basis point in thousands of current dollars.

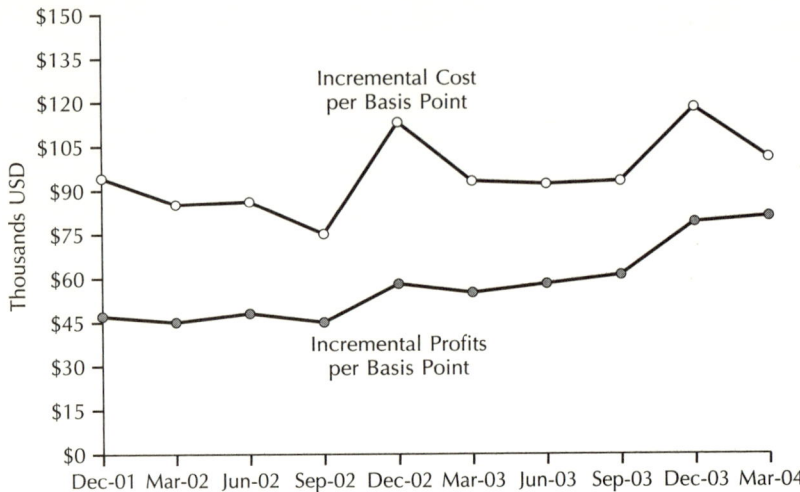

Chart 7-5   *Amazon's* Incremental Profits and Cost per Basis Point

In the fourth quarter of 2002, *Amazon* paid $113 thousand for the 6,143rd basis point. That point had an incremental profit value of just $58 thousand. Then the gap began to close, not because the cost per basis point fell. The real force behind *Amazon* closing the gap between incremental cost and profit was a systematic increase in its gross profits per point from $45 in the first quarter of 2002 to $81 thousand in the first quarter of 2004. Controlling for seasonality, the difference between its cost and profits per basis point fell from $40 thousand to $20 thousand between March, 2003 and March, 2004. Here's an important footnote to this analysis: even though *AMZN* was overspending on enterprise marketing, its efficiency ratio averaged 0.47 over the ten quarters. In other words, even though the company overspent, it continued to overspend very efficiently!

In the future you would expect that *AMZN* might maximize its earnings after enterprise marketing expenses. The trend is highlighted in Chart 7-6. Actual EBITDA was $86 million compared with a potential $122 million in December, 2002—a $36 million opportunity loss. In December, 2003, maximum earnings of $173 million were only $17 million less than potential.

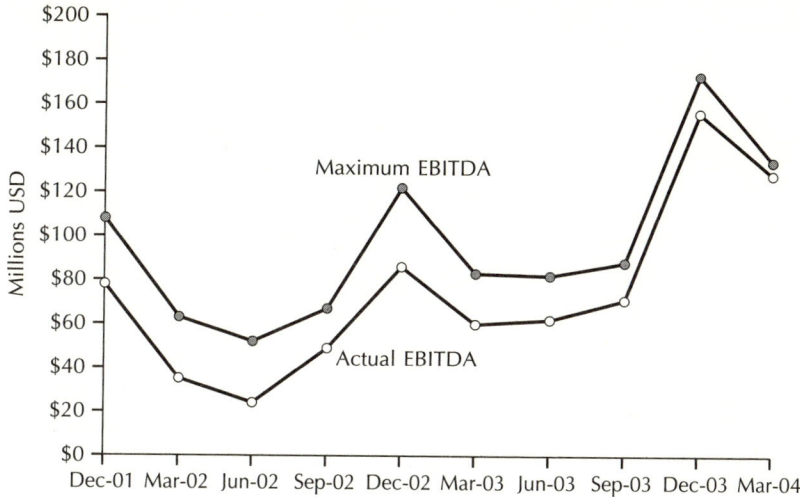

Chart 7-6 *Amazon's* Maximum and Actual Earnings

What Happened to *eBay?*

The surprising thing is that *eBay* actually underspent on enterprise marketing. The shortfall is documented in Chart 7-7. The difference between *eBay's* actual and maximum earnings market share averaged 1,244 basis points over the ten quarters from December, 2002 through March, 2004.

Chart 7-7 *eBay's* Actual and Maximum Earnings Market Share

Notice that the seasonality of *eBay's* market share is opposite that of *Amazon*. *eBay's* seasonal lows were in December of each year, probably because second-hand gifts are not as popular as new ones during the holidays. That difference between actual and maximum earnings share actually increased 120 basis points from December, 2002 to December, 2003.

Here's an important question: if *eBay* were underspending, how could management have spent more on enterprise marketing? To answer that question you would have needed to talk with heavy *eBay* sellers in March, 2003. You would have found this answer: it's the interface, stupid!

In 2003, the process of multiple and future auction listing was so primitive that frequent sellers either had to learn *HTML* programming or buy third-party software via monthly subscriptions. These ran from ten to fifty dollars a month; but with a third-party interface, *eBay* sellers could overcome the roadblocks to effective listing. The company should have invested heavily in an interface that made sales listings containing graphics and photos as easy to use for sellers (wanting to create auctions) as searching was for buyers (making purchases). Instead, in 2005 the company began the ***it*** ad campaign on television, which was designed to attract more buyers and let the sellers continue to fend for themselves!

What if a lot of those heavy users decreased their sales listings in favor of the fun (and easy) process of buying? Or shifted their advertising to *Google's AdWords?* Since *eBay* only makes money on sellers, this would have adversely affected the company's earnings—and eventually its stock price.

If you believed this analysis you would have bought a short option six months out on *eBay* in late 2004. In December, 2004, *eBay's* price hit a high of $60.59. By the end of May, 2005, its price had dropped to $30.78.

*Lesson # 7-1: Sometimes **less** is more, other times **more** is more.*

The Sundown Rule

The *Wal*Mart* Web site described the story of a pharmacist who received a call on Sunday morning saying that one of his customers had dropped her insulin down the garbage disposal. He rushed to the store, opened the pharmacy, and filled the customer's prescription. The story says that this is just one of many ways a local *Wal*Mart* store might honor what is known as the *Sundown Rule*.

The Web site also said that this was Sam Walton's translation of the proverb "never put off 'till tomorrow what you can do today." It is symbolic of the company's dedication to customer service. Coupled with its policy of "low prices, always," and aggressive expansion from its founding in rural America to global operations, *Wal*Mart* became the darling of Wall Street and one of the most valuable companies in the world. Today the company owns some 3,000 outlets in the U.S. and 1,000 internationally.

Amazing Value

On March 31, 2003, the closing price of *Wal*Mart's* common stock was $56.32. With 4,380 million shares outstanding, the company's market value was $247.0 billion. This made it the second most valuable company traded on North American stock exchanges. It was sandwiched between *GE*, the leader with a market cap of $255 billion, and *Pfizer* with $246 billion. *Microsoft* wasn't far behind with a market value of $234 billion.

Wal*Mart (ticker *WMT*) was competing in a strategic group that included *Costco, K-Mart, Sears,* and *Target.* The company was the dominant player in this group with 81.99% of the market value. In the first quarter ending March 31, 2003, *Wal*Mart's* sales were $56.7 billion, or 62.12% of total strategic group revenues. The company's value-sales differential was +19.87 points.

Over those ten quarters *Wal*Mart's* enterprise marketing risk was just 2.7. This was low compared with a large sample average of 6.6 published in *Marketing Science Institute Reports.* The result was that *Wal*Mart* sustained high-flyer status over the two and one-half years. Its risk-adjusted differential averaged +6.3 over the period from the fourth quarter of 2000 through the first quarter of 2003. Given its relatively low strategic risk, it appears more than likely that investors will sustain *Wal*Mart's* large positive **RAD**. *Wal*Mart* was a stable winner.

Enterprise Marketing Efficiency

During this same period, *Wal*Mart* was the second most efficient competitor in its strategic group. The company spent only 18.0% of sales on enterprise marketing resources compared with *Target's* 29.2%. It spent 74.6% of gross margins on enterprise marketing compared with *K-Mart's* 89.0%. These differences show up even more dramatically in *Wal*Mart's* average marketing efficiency ratio of 0.83. By comparison, *Target's* **MER** was 1.56; *K-Mart's* was 1.17. In other words, *Wal*Mart* on average spent just $0.83 for a dollar's worth of enterprise marketing resources that cost *Target* $1.56 and *K-Mart* $1.17. *Costco* was the champ of the group. They paid only $0.49 on average for a buck's worth of enterprise marketing resources.

Maximum Earnings Market Share

You would think that one of the biggest, most valuable, and most efficient companies on the planet would come very close to maximizing earnings. You might think so, but you'd be wrong. The story is told in Chart 7-8.

Chart 7-8 Wal*Mart's Actual and Maximum Earnings Share

Wal*Mart's actual share of revenues exceeded its maximum earnings share by more than 1,000 basis points in every quarter from December, 2000 through March, 2003. And it didn't get any better over the last 2½ years. Looking at same-quarter data, the gap between WMT's actual and maximum earnings share increased 22% from 1,066 points in the fourth quarter of 2000 to 1,296 revenue basis points in the fourth quarter of 2002. At the same time, the company's spending on enterprise marketing increased by 18%.

Wal*Mart theoretically could have increased earnings by $11 billion over the ten quarters if management had just taken its foot off the enterprise marketing expense pedal. And, theoretically, that $11 billion could have been used to increase shareholder wealth significantly.

Profit and Cost per Basis Point

You can see the problem clearly in Chart 7-9. In December, 2000, WMT paid $3.51 million for its last (5,465th) basis point even though it had a profit value of only $2.30 million. Let's look more closely at this result by breaking it down step by step.

Recall from Chapter 5 that the incremental cost of a basis point (1/100th of a share point) is the following rather scary formula:

$$\ddot{c} = \frac{f \times x}{(100 - m)^2}$$

In this formula the two dots over the c signify 1/100th of a share point. The sum of WMT's competitors' enterprise marketing forces is the value

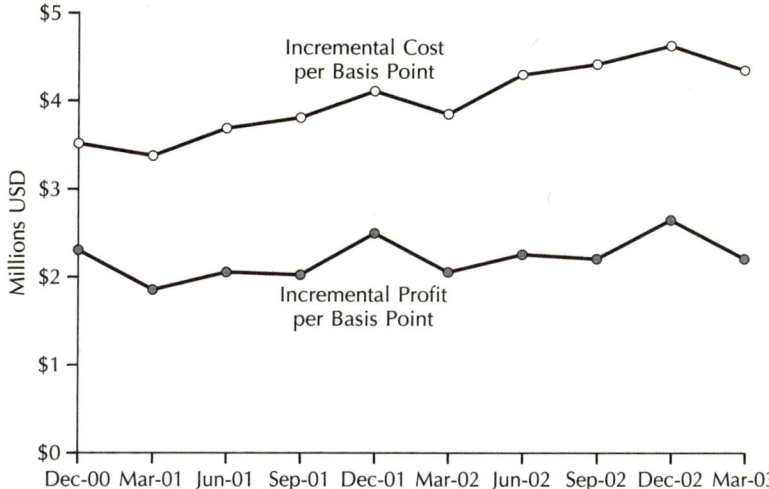

Chart 7-9 *Wal*Mart's* Incremental Cost and Profit per Basis Point

of *f*. As before, *x* is *WMT's* enterprise marketing efficiency ratio. To maintain the last basis point, *WMT* was facing $8,129 million in competitors' spending on enterprise marketing resources in the fourth quarter of 2000. Since *Wal*Mart's* enterprise marketing efficiency was 0.887, we can discount competitors' expenses by 11.3% (1.0 − 0.887).

The discounted cost of competitor's marketing resources ($f \times x$) in that quarter was $7,210 million. Competitive spending increased to $8,898 million in December, 2002, driving *Wal*Mart's* incremental cost per point up to $4.62 million, even with an improved marketing efficiency ratio of 0.835. Its incremental profit per basis point was only $2.64 million.

Now, here's the rub. *Wal*Mart* can't escape the theoretical cost of maintaining that last basis point unless management decides to give it up. Take a look at the denominator of incremental cost formula:

$$(100 - m)^2$$

Notice it's like the incremental force multiplier in Chapter 5, but it's squared and the numerator *m* is gone. That numerator got factored out when we converted share points to basis points. But it still has the intuitive meaning of the competitive multiplier. *WMT's* fourth-quarter 2000 actual share *m* was 54.65%. So the denominator in the incremental cost formula is 2056.6 = $(100 - 54.65)^2$. The number 2,056.6 is a mathematical scaling factor that has no physical form, kind of like the accountants' intangible asset. Dividing competitive spending of $7,210 million by the scaling factor yields the theoretical cost of *WMT's* last basis point [$3.51 = $7,210/2,056.6].

Remember this rule: the cost of the last basis point is a nonlinear function of two things: **competitors' spending on enterprise marketing resources** and the **company's enterprise marketing efficiency.**

Competitors' Enterprise Marketing Resources

Managers prefer to think that competitors' SG&A spending doesn't really matter. But it does. Remember the correlation between share of revenues and SG&A expenses in Chapter 1? That correlation was 0.96. We don't know which causes which, but we do know that sales and enterprise marketing expenses move in lock step.

The more important question is: what are *Wal*Mart's* strategic options? There are two and they can be tested simultaneously. First, management can ease off on SG&A spending for a few quarters and see earnings increase as share of revenue falls. Or management can boost *Wal*Mart's* gross margins by adding higher-priced merchandise lines to the mix. If *WMT* had done either, or both, of these things, theoretically its earnings would have increased significantly.

What Was Left on the Table?

*Wal*Mart's* actual earnings and maximum earnings appear in Chart 7-10. Over the ten quarters from December, 2000 to March, 2003, *Wal*Mart* management left $10,695 million in theoretical earnings on the table by overspending in enterprise marketing and underpricing merchandise lines. In that period the company actually spent $95,876 million on enterprise

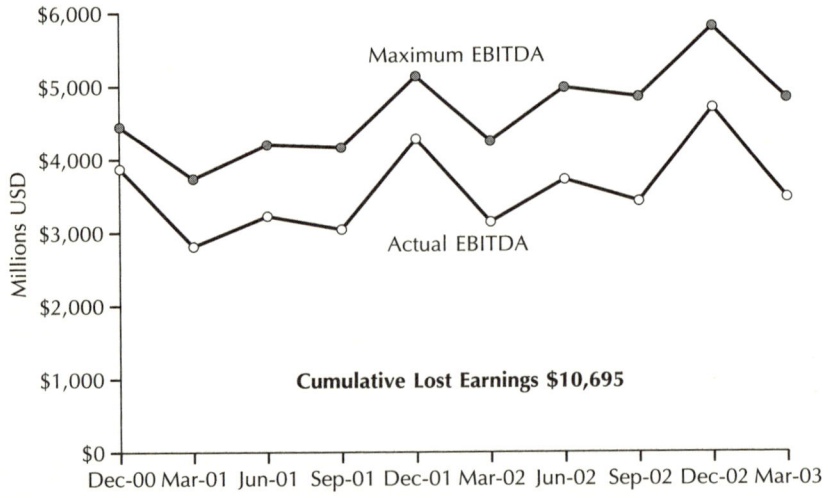

Chart 7-10 *Wal*Mart* Actual and Maximum Earnings

marketing. Theoretically, the company would have maximized EBITDA and pocketed nearly 11 billion bucks—if instead management had not spent $54,714 million. Of course, the company would have had to give up those 1,066 basis points (10.66 share points) in the bargain.

> *Joseph J. Fitzsimmons goes by the name of Jay on Wall Street. There, the* Wal★Mart Stores *veteran serves as the voice of the earth's dominant retailer. Boy, is his voice humble right now. 'My CEO has lost faith in me,' he told investors recently. 'He's done his job. Sales are up 83% since he took over five years ago, and net income is up almost 100%.' So the only reason he can think of that the stock isn't moving is because the person in charge of investor relations isn't doing a particularly good job.* (Barker 2005, 108)

It's not just that *Wal★Mart's* stock isn't moving—it's been moving down for two years from a high of $61 in January, 2004 to $45 on January 13, 2006. Did *Costco* and *Target* have a hand in this loss of shareholder value? You bet they did.

Scale Efficiencies in Enterprise Marketing?

Wal★Mart is famous for its buying efficiencies. The company has clout with vendors because of its size. It's also famous for its ability to streamline the supply chain by sharing information with its vendors. And demanding just-in-time delivery from vendors keeps inventory carrying costs at a minimum.

So how could a company with so much savvy in buying operations be overspending on enterprise marketing to such a huge degree? The answer involves a complex interaction between gross margins and SG&A expenses. Despite its size, *Wal★Mart* is less efficient in deploying its marketing forces than two of its most important competitors. Chart 7-11 tells the story.

The bars in Chart 7-11 show SG&A expenses as a percent of gross profits (2000–2003). This comparison levels the playing field among these five

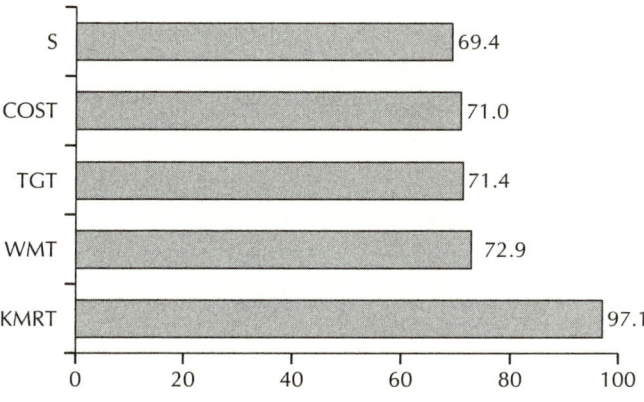

Chart 7-11 SG&A % Gross Profits

retailers. *Sears's* SG&A expenses as a percent of gross profits are 349 basis points below *Wal★Mart's*. Even *Target Stores* have a 148 basis-point advantage over *Wal★Mart Stores*. Remember the three parts of a dollar? Earnings are left over from gross profits **after** enterprise marketing expenses. No matter how big the pool of gross profits is, if you spend too much on enterprise marketing, your earnings will suffer. So much for scale efficiencies in marketing.

Why did *Wal★Mart* overspend so aggressively? It may be that management thinks higher market share means greater profits. Or maybe customer service means more to the Walton family than maximizing earnings. Or it may be that management is determined to stick to its mantra of "Always Low Price, Always." Sam Walton claimed in his book *Made in America* that his family owned 38% of *Wal★Mart* stock. If so, Sam and company could have placed a higher priority on customer service and low prices than they did on earnings—and made it stick. In any event, you should not be surprised that shareholder value suffered from January, 2004 onward and likely will continue to do so until spending and pricing are brought are brought into line.

Lesson # 7-2: Scale is no guarantee of enterprise marketing efficiency.

All the News That Fits

This analysis begins with the combined sales revenues of competitors, because all ships rise and fall with the tide. The competitors in this dual-segment communications market are *Fox Entertainment Group* (Ticker *FOX*), *Gannett Co Inc. (GCI)*, *New York Times Co. (NYT)*, and *Tribune Co. (TRB)*.

Low Tide in Communications

Theoretically, the tide has been low for these dual-segment communications companies for the past ten quarters. The nominal value of group sales grew by 21% over the period. But if all four companies had maximized earnings after enterprise marketing expenses, group revenues would have been significantly greater than they actually were. Chart 7-12 documents the degree to

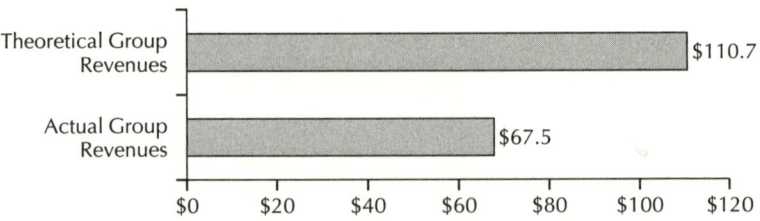

Chart 7-12 Cumulative Actual Versus Potential Group Revenues

which all four companies underperformed from the fourth quarter of 2001 (after the bubble burst) through the end of the first quarter of 2004. Cumulative group revenues should have been $107.8 billion. They actually were $65.6 billion, or 38% less than potential.

Gannett's Maximum Earnings Market Share

Based on the gap between actual and maximum earnings market share, *Gannett* delivered the worst performance in this strategic group. A comparison between *GCI's* actual and maximum earnings share is shown in Chart 7-13. The upper line is *GCI's* maximum earnings market share from the fourth quarter of 2001 through the first quarter of 2004. The lower line is its actual market share. The company consistently underperformed over the ten quarters.

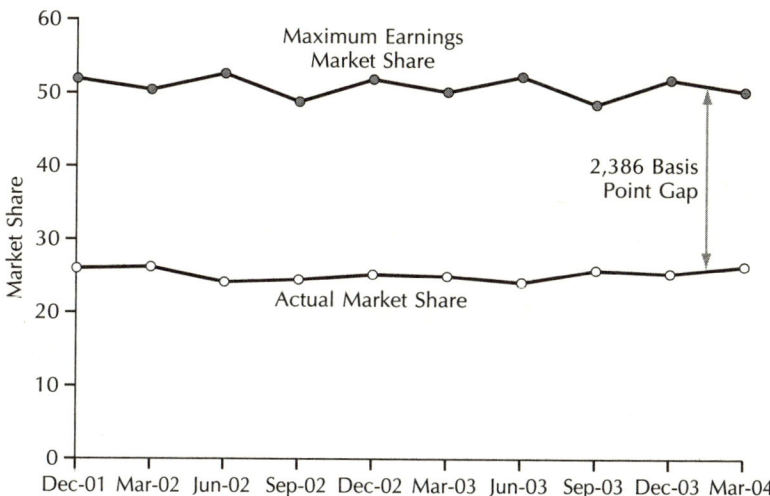

Chart 7-13 *Gannett's* Actual and Maximum Earnings Share

In the first quarter of 2004, *Gannett's* actual market share was 26.35% of the $67,493 million actual group revenues. This was 2,386 basis points less than its maximum earnings share of 50.20%. Over the ten quarters, *GCI's* actual share averaged only 52% of its maximum earnings share.

Chart 7-14 shows *GCI's* market share at the end of the first quarter of 2004. It also shows what its share would have been if management had maximized earnings after enterprise marketing expenses. At its maximum earnings market share of 50.20%, the company would have generated $826 million in EBITDA. This would have been a 44% increase over actual earnings of $573 million.

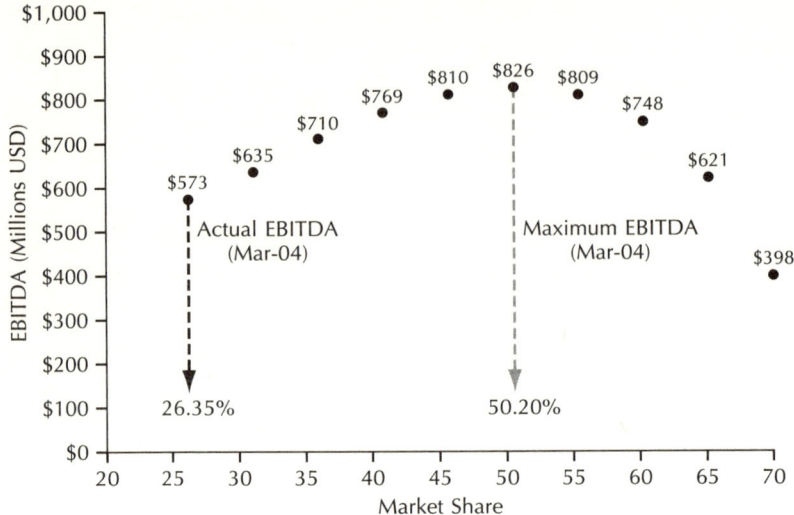

Chart 7-14 *Gannett's* Potential Earnings and Market Share

How could *GCI* increase its market share in this space from 26% to 50%? In the short term the only way to nearly double market share would be to buy a best-fit competitor. *TRB* appears to be the candidate of choice.

Would it be worth it? To place this in perspective, *Gannett's* theoretical lost earnings in the quarter ending March, 2004 were $253 million. Its cumulative lost earnings over the ten quarters amounted to $2.917 billion. This was a staggering loss in earning opportunities. It was the poorest performance among the four competitors in this space. The ten-quarter opportunity loss amounted nearly to 25% of *TRB's* shareholder value. Approaching maximum earnings via acquisition of *TRB* theoretically would have increased *GCI's* stock price to $131. On January 13, 2006, the stock closed at $64.28.

Cumulative Earnings Shortfall

A comparison of lost earnings among the four companies appears in Chart 7-15. *FOX* nearly hit the nail on the head. Its actual earnings were only 6.9% less than its maximum earnings after enterprise marketing expenses.

To a much greater degree than its competitors, *Gannett* underspent on enterprise marketing. In the first quarter of 2004, the company actually spent $283 million on selling, general, and administrative expenses. Theoretically, if the company had maximized earnings it would have spent $765 million. Even though it underspent, *GCI* spent its money efficiently. The

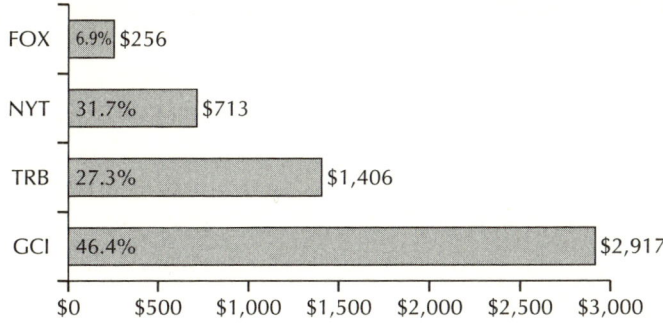

Chart 7-15   Cumulative Theoretical Shortfall in EBITDA

company's enterprise marketing efficiency ratio was 0.77. This means that *GCI* spent just 77¢ on enterprise marketing forces that cost an average competitor in this strategic group $1.00.

Put another way, *GCI* generated $6.11 in sales revenues for every dollar it spent on SG&A. The *NYT* and *TRB* didn't even come close to this level of marketing efficiency. They generated just $2.47 and $3.72, respectively, in revenues for each SG&A dollar spent. *FOX* was the leader at $8.82 per dollar of SG&A and an enterprise marketing efficiency ratio of 0.50.

Differences in Key Operating Ratios

By comparing Charts 7-16 and 7-17, you will see that *Gannett's* cost of goods sold (54.3%) was significantly greater than *Tribune's* (48.2%). Partly as a result, *Gannett* had a narrower gross margin and thus less money to spend on enterprise marketing (16.4%) than did *Tribune* (26.9%). *Gannett's* residual earnings, however, at 29.3% of revenues, were significantly better than *Tribune's* 24.9%.

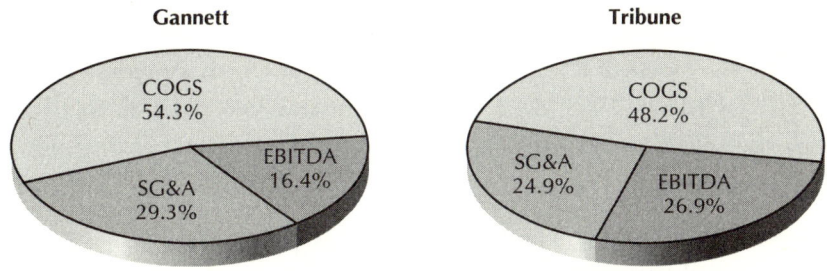

Chart 7-16   Costs and Earnings per Dollar of Sales Revenue

Combined Company Performance

All *Gannett's* numbers would have been improved if it purchased the *Tribune*. A combined *GCI/TRB* would give *Gannett*:

- a significantly lower cost of goods sold (49.5%).
- higher gross margins (50.5%).
- a big boost in enterprise marketing forces (19.6%).
- nearly maximum earnings market share (45.28%).
- increased EBITDA (30.9%).

Chart 7-17 shows the companies' stand-alone and combined sales revenues and market share based on 2003 calendar-year data.

Lesson # 7-3: Maximum earnings market share can point to merger opportunities.

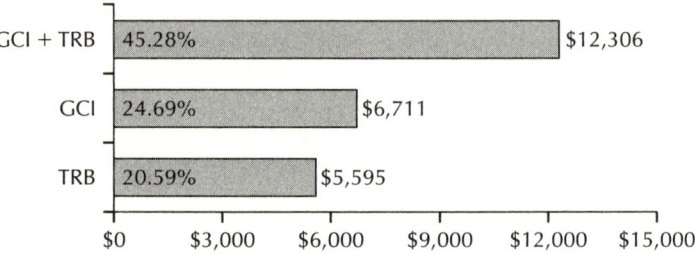

Chart 7-17   Merged *GCI* and *TRB*

Buy on the Rumor, Sell on the News

AT&T Bell Labs invented cellular service in 1947. Because the company had not capitalized on the invention, in 1994 it purchased *McCaw Cellular* for $11.5 billion. In April, 2000, *AT&T* offered a tracking stock for its wireless division that was the largest **i**nitial **p**ublic **o**ffering (IPO) in history. The 137 million shares traded that day closed at $32.19. The IPO ultimately raised $10.6 billion. Wall Street's day of *AWE* (the ticker symbol for the *Wireless* division) didn't last long. The price of these shares peaked at $35 on May 1, 2000, and closed at $16.57 the day *Wireless* became independent on July 9, 2001. By March, 2003, *AWE* was trading at around $8.00. The Wall Street hype overvalued the *Wireless* market cap at the crest of the bubble. And the press had a field day.

- *Business Week* said, "The chairman of *AT&T* has lots of experience with so-called tracking stocks—most of it bad."
- *Newsweek* said, "The valuations of *AT&T Wireless* and *AT&T Classic* seem out of whack."

The hype didn't fool the enterprise marketing metrics any more than it did the press. In the fourth quarter of 2000, *Wireless* created only 12.5% of the value in this cellular strategic group with 40.0% of the revenues. The company's **RAD** was a −2.6. Its enterprise marketing risk was a chart-busting 15.7, more than double the average risk among the 337 companies in the *MSI* sample.

The Players

On June 30, 2003, *Wireless* had 21.49 million subscribers in its base. Even more important, *AT&T's* leading-edge wireless technology (called *Edge*) was compatible with worldwide networks. Its rivals with CDMA technology were not compatible. This gave *AWE* access to the worldwide wireless users that were predicted to reach 1.2 billion by 2005.

AWE's biggest competitor was *Sprint PCS*.[4] This was the tracking stock of *Sprint's* wireless division. It had first-quarter 2003 revenues of $2.95 billon. *Nextel* was a free-standing competitor with sales in that quarter of $2.37 billion. The smallest player in this group was *U.S. Celluar (USM)* with revenues of $590 million.

Strategic group revenues grew 41% from $7 billion in the fourth quarter of 2000 to $10 billion in the first quarter of 2003. At the same time, the combined market cap of these four players declined 29% from $50 to $36 billion. You could safely say this was a turbulent time in cellular competition for customers and capital.

Enterprise Marketing Efficiency

In the first quarter of 2003, *Wireless* management spent just 42¢ of each revenue dollar on enterprise marketing resources compared to 48¢ by *Nextel* and 61¢ by *USM*. Or, in terms of marketing efficiency ratios, it cost *AWE* just $0.98 for a dollar's worth of enterprise marketing resources that cost *Nextel* $1.15, and *USM* $1.23. Despite *AWE's* relative advantage in marketing efficiency and scale economies, the company staggered in its search for maximum earnings.

AWE's Maximum Earnings Market Share

AWE's share of strategic group revenues fell 247 basis points from 42.50% in the fourth quarter of 2000 to 40.03% in the first quarter of 2003. It wasn't able to capitalize on the installed base and loyalty of its parent company *AT&T*. As you see in Chart 7-18, *AWE's* maximum earnings market share went on a roller-coaster ride during the ten quarters.

Wireless overspent on enterprise marketing in the quarter ending in December, 2000, and realized a gap between actual and maximum profit share

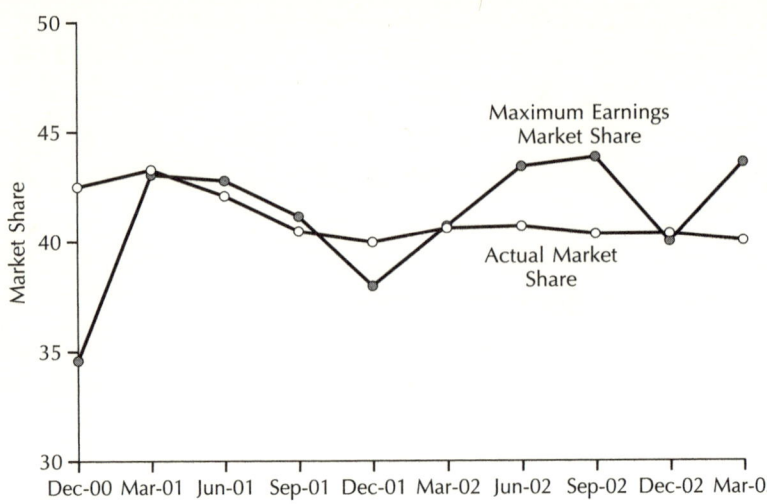

Chart 7-18 *Wireless* Roller Coaster

of +792 basis points. In March of 2002, the division was only ten basis points off the mark. By March, 2003, the company underspent on enterprise marketing, creating a gap of −356 basis points. Overall, the average difference between the *AWE's* actual and maximum earnings market share was 470 basis points.

Despite its roller-coaster search for maximum earnings in this rapidly growing strategic group, *Wireless* turned in a very respectable performance. Over the ten quarters, the company's actual EBITDA was $8.409 billion; only 0.2% less than its maximum EBITDA of $8.483 billion.

Lesson # 7-4 *Companies can maximize earnings even in a turbulent market.*

The Medicine Men

In 1996, prescription drugs weren't advertised on television at all.[5] Total prescription drug direct-to-consumer (DTC) advertising amounted to only $55.1 million. Then in 1997, the FDA eased restrictions that had banned the practice. By the end of 2002, advertising of prescription drugs on television in the U.S. totaled $1.4 billion, or 60% of the $2.5 billion spent on DTC advertising of these products. This put several drug makers into the top twenty TV-ad spenders. The addition of TV to their media portfolios raised the table stakes for players in this strategic group. And it also jump-started consumer demand.

Four firms in this group were selected from the seven pharmaceuticals in Chapter 3 (Table 3-13) for analysis here. Three of these (*GSK, JNJ,* and *NVS*) were chosen because they reported all the data in Table 4-2. A fourth (*BMY*) was added to round out the strategic group.

Market Share Attraction in Pharmaceuticals

Underlying maximum earnings market share is the assumption that sales are a strong linear function of enterprise marketing forces (selling, general, and administrative expenses). General support for this assumption appeared in Chapter 1. Chart 7-19 shows a graphic overview of recent data for pharmaceuticals from 1985 through 2004. A statistical test of these data would confirm that the linear assumption does not hold. The statistical test, however, would overlook important information. Lurking behind the clearly nonlinear spike in the data is an exception that proves the rule.

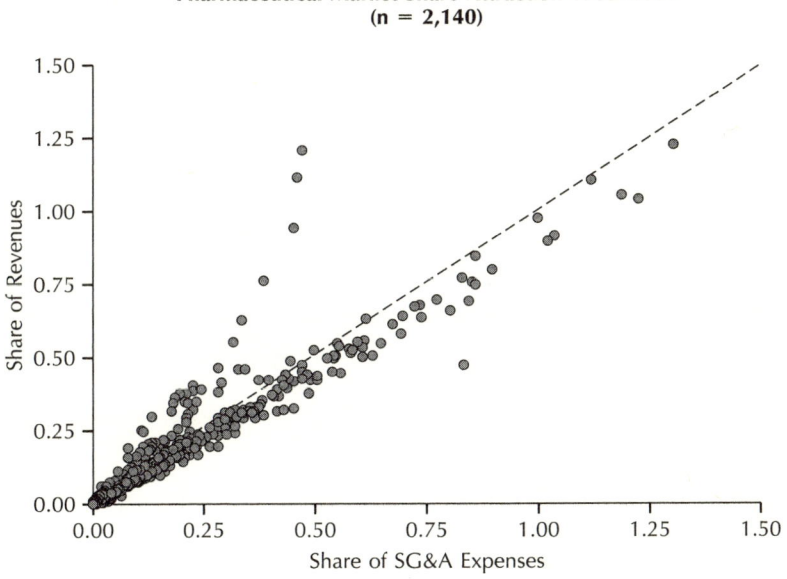

Chart 7-19 Linear Market Share Attraction?

The interesting exception is isolated from the industry data in Chart 7-20. And it's not measurement error. The ten outlying points were caused by *Merck's* 1993 acquisition of *Medco Health Solutions*. Before that acquisition, from 1985 through 1992, *Merck's* share of industry revenue and share of SG&A expenses were glued to the 90° line in the lower left-hand corner of Chart 7-20. Immediately following the company's 2003 spin-off of *Medco*, its share of revenue and SG&A expense dropped back to the 90° line. This interesting exception was the result of *Medco's* extraordinary enterprise marketing efficiency.

We can apply Gerstner's sales per dollar (**SPD**) of selling, general, and administrative expenses (from Chapter 6) to *Merck* before and after its

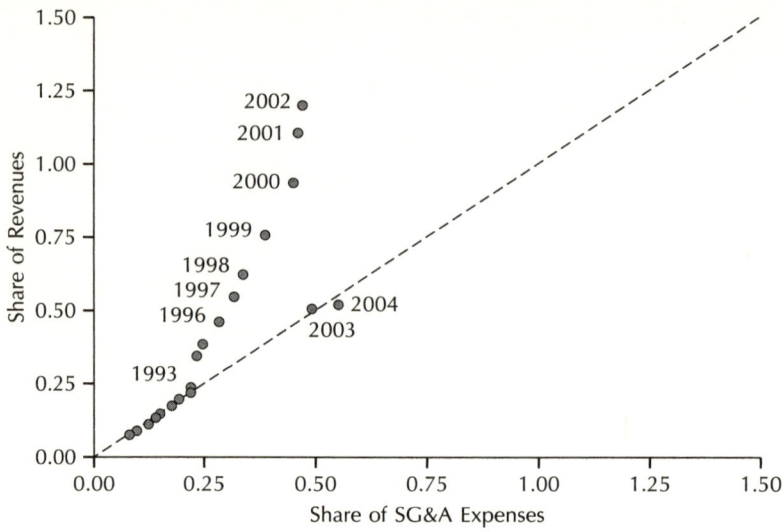

Chart 7-20 *Merck's* Non-Linear MarketShare Attraction

acquisition of *Medco* in order to show the dramatic impact it had on the company's marketing efficiency. In 1991, before the acquisition, *Merck* spent $3.6 billion on SG&A expenses and generated $8.6 billion in sales revenues. Its enterprise marketing efficiency measured in **SPD** was $2.42. After the acquisition had settled in, *Merck's* 1995 **SPD** jumped to $4.25. In 2004, after the spin-off, *Merck's* marketing efficiency dropped back to $2.26 in sales per dollar of SG&A expenses.

It's clear in Chart 7-20 that the assumption of linear market response did not hold for *Merck* in the period from 1993 through 2002.

Novartis, on the other hand, was relatively inefficient with an **MER** of 1.12. The impact of this relative inefficiency is illustrated with the classic market share attraction model in Chart 7-21. The theoretical market response function has an intercept of zero and a slope of one illustrated by the solid line in the graph. The dashed line for *Novartis* is linear but has an intercept of 1.1 and a slope of 0.9.

The high correlations between these shares of revenues and shares of enterprise marketing expsenses ensures that when *Novartis'* enterprise marketing efficiency ratio departs significantly from 1.0 in either direction, the company is more (or less) efficient than an average competitor.[6]

Having established that the linear model applies to all the pharmaceuticals except *Merck,* we can be comfortable in calibrating the interactions between marketing and finance by linking the profit and cost per market share point to maximum earnings after enterprise marketing expenses.

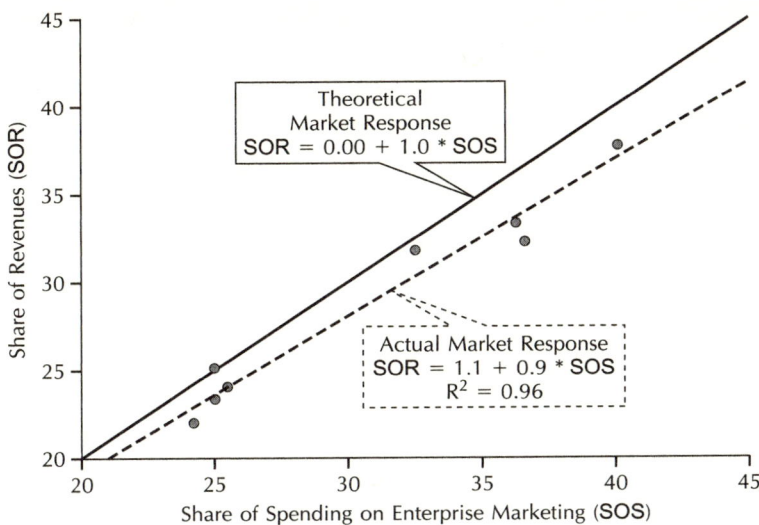

Chart 7-21 *Novartis'* Linear Market Share Attraction

Relative Earnings Productivity

As a group, these four pharmaceutical companies were adroit at maximizing their earnings after enterprise marketing expenses. The data in Chart 7-22 compare each firm's cumulative actual with its cumulative maximum EBITDA over the years from 1994 through 2003.[7] The relative earnings productivity (REP) for each company is reported at the bottom of this chart.[8]

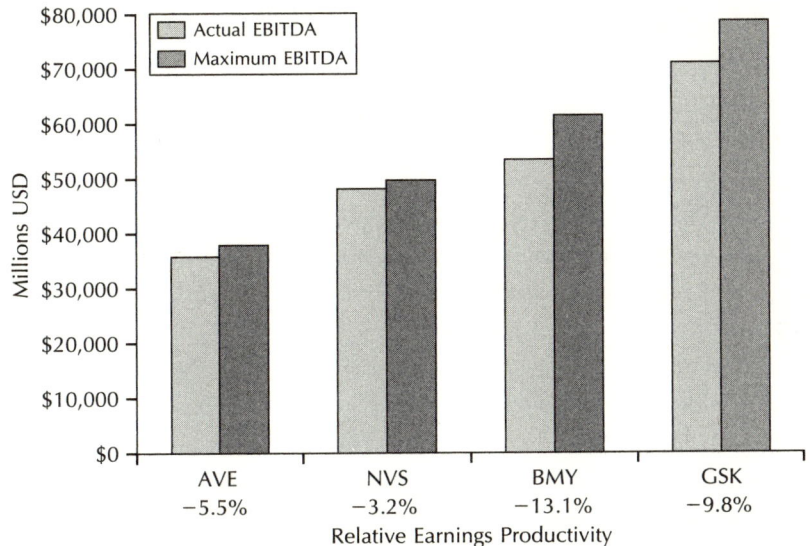

Chart 7-22 Actual Versus Maximum Earnings

The largest shortfall between actual and theoretical maximum earnings was −13.1%. *Bristol-Meyers Squibb (BMY)* actually earned $53.4 billion over the decade, compared with theoretical maximum earnings of $61.5 billion. *Novartis (NVS)* management posted the smallest cumulative shortfall (−3.2%) with actual earnings of $48.1 billion compared with maximum theoretical earnings of $49.7 billion.

It's interesting to observe that *Novartis'* actual market share was significantly less than its maximum earnings share in six of the eight years (1998–2003). These results appear in Chart 7-23.

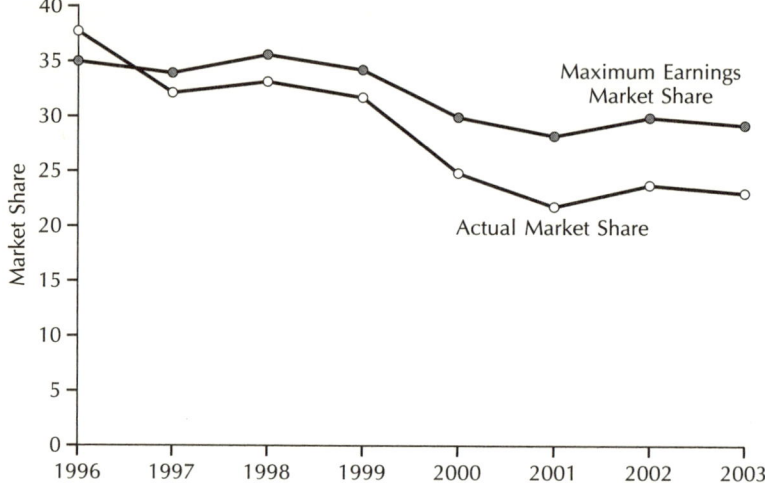

Chart 7-23 *Novartis* Actual and Maximum Earnings Share

The vertical axis is percent of actual and maximum earnings share of strategic group revenues. *Novartis* management almost hit the nail on the head in 1997 with an actual share of 32.13% compared with a theoretical maximum earnings share of 33.94%. That's a difference of only 180 basis points. In 1996, the company overspent, achieving a 37.72% share of group revenues compared with its maximum earnings share of 34.99%. The biggest gap between actual and maximum earnings share occurred in 2001. In that year the gap widened to 645 basis points or 6.45 share points.

Of course, what matters most to management and investors is the year-to-year difference between actual and maximum earnings. These results are shown in Chart 7-24. The vertical axis is EBITDA in millions of U.S. dollars. In 1996, *Novartis's* relative earnings productivity was −1.0%. Management came within 1% of achieving maximum earnings. The gap widened to −5.9% by 2003.

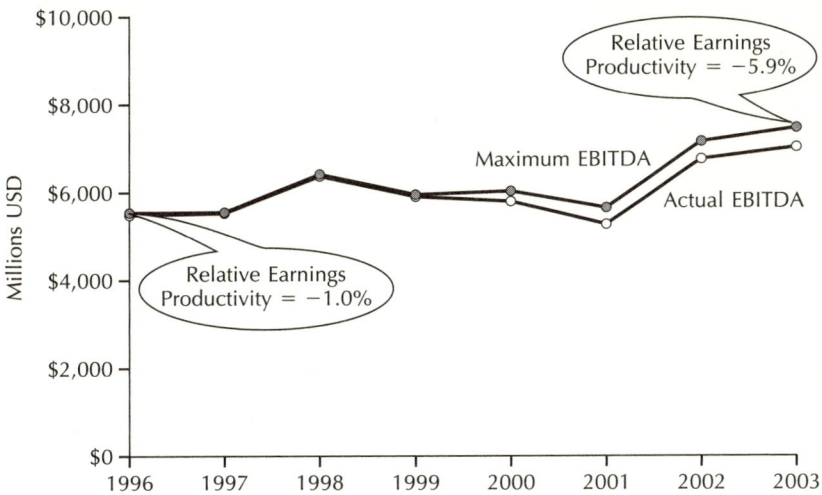

Chart 7-24 *Novartis* Actual and Maximum EBITDA

The eight-year weighted average **REP** was just −3.2%. Nevertheless it amounted to a shortfall of $1.6 billion. Can managers "fine-tune" spending on enterprise marketing forces to precisely maximize earnings over the long term? *Novartis* management came remarkably close. Out of some 200 applications of maximum earnings market share in over 30 industries, only a handful of companies delivered such consistently high relative earnings productivity.

Lesson # 7-5: Senior managers can maximize earnings over the long haul.

Higher-Order Effects

Three higher-level effects are ignored in this analysis. First, the "sum constraint" is one way of limiting the impact of changes in a company's enterprise marketing strategy on competitors' market share and their likely response. Second, the "revenue multiplier" captures the aggregate effects of changes in the total enterprise marketing expenses of all companies on total revenues and earnings in the strategic group. Third, the lagged (or carry-over) effects of enterprise marketing expenses on future market share and earnings of each company.

The Sum Constraint

Here's what the "sum constraint" in market share theory says: theoretical predictions of maximum earnings market share should lead to revenue shares that **sum to 100%**. The sum constraint was not enforced in this book. It is quite complicated to add the requirement that firms should simultaneously maximize earnings and respond to competitors' reaction to their plans in such a way that market shares in every period sum to 100%. You need to incorporate features from advanced game theory to do this.

These higher-level effects can be added to the analysis only at the cost of intuitive understanding and computational ease. You can't add the simultaneous effects of competitor response if you want to work on the back of an envelope. And financial accounting data rarely are available for a large enough number of periods to conduct econometric analyses at the level of strategic groups.

Lesson # 7-6: Simplify or forget maximum earnings market share analysis.

The Revenue-Multiplier Effect

Relaxing the sum constraint, however, produces an unexpected and useful side benefit. If the sum of maximum earnings revenue shares of the companies in a strategic group is less than 100%, this indicates that the players underspent on enterprise marketing forces and that group revenues are depressed.

For example, recall that in the recovery period from the fourth quarter of 2000 through the first quarter of 2003, *Amazon* overspent on enterprise marketing. The other players in the group underspent. This was especially true for *eBay*, which actually spent a total of $1,374 million on enterprise marketing while its theoretical maximum spending was $2,875 million. The degree to which *Amazon's* competitors underspent on enterprise marketing forces during this period of recovery from the burst bubble was sufficient to drive actual group revenues down to $14,982 million, or 9.5% below theoretical group revenues of $16,553 million. In every period except the third and fourth quarters of 2002, the sum of MEMS of the four companies was less than 100%. These results are shown in Table 7-6. We saw the same effect in the dual-segment communications group.

Table 7-6 The Impact of Underspending in Online Retailing

	AMZN	*YHOO*	*eBAY*	*PCLN*	Group SOR
Dec-00	31.5	29.0	20.6	0.0	81
Mar-01	27.4	6.4	22.9	2.7	59
Jun-01	26.1	7.9	25.3	21.4	81
Sep-01	27.7	8.5	24.3	18.2	79
Dec-01	48.1	13.5	24.7	5.1	92
Mar-02	37.7	11.6	28.3	18.2	96
Jun-02	33.1	15.6	29.8	18.5	97
Sep-02	38.4	20.6	30.5	12.0	102
Dec-02	46.0	22.6	30.3	5.8	105
Mar-03	38.9	23.4	34.8	0.0	97

Alternatively, if the sum of maximum earnings market shares of the companies in a strategic group is greater than 100%, this indicates that the players overspent on enterprise marketing forces.

Lesson # 7-7: Over (under) spending stimulates (depresses) group revenues.

Carry-Over Effects

The argument about carry-over effects between marketing and accounting has continued without resolution for decades.[9] The carry-over effect of advertising with regard to future market share has been documented in many studies. It's also clear that R&D expenses incurred today cannot possibly have an impact on sales revenues until tomorrow. But it's also true that there may be no carry-over effects. Advertising and R&D expenses will never have an impact on sales revenues if they produce only marginal (or no) improvement in preferences and product performance. And financial markets incorporate the effects, or lack of them, into stock prices. On balance, most agree you cannot depreciate enterprise marketing expenses as if they were plant and equipment. In any event the argument cannot be resolved here. You've got to farm with the tools you have or not at all.

Lesson # 7-8: Lagged effects of enterprise marketing expenses are unknown.

Any Added Information?

Does maximum earnings market share add any significant information about variations in the risk-adjusted VS differential? Even after you control for key financial ratios like capital structure and total return to shareholders? If so, can that information be used in predicting stock price? You'll find out in the final two chapters.

References

Barker, R. 2005. "Why Wal-Mart Is Still a Smart Buy." *Business Week,* May 9:108.

Bezos, J. P. 2004. *Amazon.com 1997 Letter to Shareholders* attached to the 2004 letter to shareholders. http://library.corporate-ir.net/library/97/976/97664/items/144853/2004_Annual_report.pdf

Cook, V. J., Jr. 1985. "The Net Present Value of Market Share." *Journal of Marketing* 49 (Summer): 49–63.

Greenhouse, S. 2005. "How Costco Became the Anti-Wal-Mart." New York Times, July 17, 2005.

Hansell, S., and G. Rivlin. "As It Goes Public, *Google* Says It Is Worth Up to $36 Billion." *New York Times,* July 27, 2004, Section C.

Jackson, D. 2003. "Cell Wars: *AWE + NXTL + PCS + USM* December 2000–March 2003." *Bottom Line Marketing Report* 1, No. 2, December: Masters of Business Administration Program, Tulane University.

King, L. 2003. "Pharmaceuticals Prescribe Success: *BMY + JNJ + MRK + PFE* 1991–2000." *Bottom Line Marketing Report,* 1, No. 4, December: Masters of Accounting Program, Tulane University.

End Notes

[1] SEC: http://www.sec.gov/Archives/edgar/data/1288776/000119312504073639/ds1.htm

[2] *Google's* auction price closed at $85 on August 18, 2004. The next day the stock (ticker GOOG) opened on NASDAQ at $135.91. At 11:41 a.m., the stock was traded at $141.91.

[3] On its Web site, *Google* reports 2003 sales revenues of $1.466 billion. These are not included in Chart 7-1. The lion's share of sales, $1.421 billion, was from advertising revenues.

[4] This section is based in part on Jackson 2003.

[5] This section is based in part on Lauren King, "Pharmaceuticals Prescribe Success: *BMY + JNJ + MRK + PFE* 1991–2000," *Bottom Line Marketing Reports,* Vol. 1, No. 4, December 15, 2003; Masters of Accounting Program, Tulane University.

[6] The reason *Eating Places* and *Integrated Systems Design* have relatively low correlations is that the costs of people are assigned to the cost of goods rather than selling, general, and administrative expenses.

[7] *Novartis* began trading on North American exchanges as an ADR in 1996, so it reported only eight years of data.

[8] Relative earnings productivity is scaled to have a maximum value of 0.0% and a minimum value of 100%. The scaling equation is REP = -1 + (Actual earnings/ Maximum earnings).

[9] Carry-over effects were included in Cook 1985.

CHAPTER 8

HIGH-FLYERS AND BOTTOM-FEEDERS

When it comes to creating shareholder value, the lion's share of companies is populated with average Joes. Forget about these guys for the moment. What we want to know now is:

- Who are the high-flyers and the bottom-feeders?
- Do the big players tend to be high-flyers?
- Are the small fries usually the bottom-feeders?
- Do you find more of each in large strategic groups (or small ones)?

A study published by the *Marketing Science Institute,* a marketing think-tank based in Cambridge, Massachusetts, provides some answers to these questions.

The *MSI* Sample

The properties of financial data required a two-stage sampling process. Both samples were drawn from the *COMPUSTAT* database using *Standard & Poor's Research Insight* (2002).

Calibration Sample

In the first stage of the sampling process, a calibration sample was created. This sample included all companies that reported sales revenue and market value. The Global Industry Classification System (GICS) was used to define sub-industries. The sample frame used to identify the sub-industries consisted of the sixty-seven companies that were members of the *Marketing Science Institute* in August, 2002. A total of thirty-eight *MSI* members were free-standing publicly traded companies that reported stock price, number of common shares outstanding, and sales revenues in the *COMPUSTAT* database in each year from 1991 through 2000.[1] These companies are listed in Appendix 8-A with ticker symbols in brackets.

Competing Companies. The ticker symbol of each of these 38 *MSI* member companies was entered to prompt the *Research Insight* software *(Standard & Poor's* 2002b). For example, selecting the "Find Similar Companies" option for a *GICS* sub-industry with DD *(DuPont)* as a prompt identified twenty-one competitors in the diversified chemicals database. The list included both U.S.-based firms such as *Dow Chemical Company* and foreign firms such as *Akso Nobel NV*, which is listed on the NASD exchange as an American Depository Receipt (ADR). The 38 company prompts returned 29 *GICS* sub-industries out of the total of 122 in the database. The number of firms identified in this way as competitors ranged from a low of 3 in the "Personal Products" sub-industry to a high of 198 in the "Telecommunications Equipment" sub-industry.

Sampling Limits. Due to mergers, acquisitions, failures, IPOs, and new as well as discontinued ADR listings, the number of companies with ten years of continuous data was reduced significantly in many *GICS* sub-industries.[2] Each sub-industry list was sorted from highest to lowest fiscal-year 2000 market cap. Every company in this list was included in the calibration sample if its market cap was at least 50% of the next largest company, up to a maximum of 25 firms in each sub-industry. A 25-firm cutoff was adopted to focus the sample on firms that management might consider to be competitors.

Business Methods. In some cases, the list of companies in the sub-industry was trimmed further due to fundamental differences in the business model that could distort the research findings. For example, advertising agencies were defined as a separate market within the advertising sub-industry to distinguish them from companies that were primarily market research suppliers. In addition, packaged meat manufacturers were deleted from the packaged goods and meats sub-industry because the gross margins of highly processed packaged foods are much larger than the gross margins for packaged raw meats. In short, the process was tempered by judgment in an effort to define managerially meaningful markets. The calibration sample consisted of 337 firms in 29 markets.

Analysis Sample

In the second stage an analysis sample was drawn. This sample included only those companies from the calibration sample that also reported the data needed to determine if both financial and enterprise marketing factors offered significant information about variations in the VS differential. These data requirements were rather strict. In addition to sales revenue, shares outstanding, and stock price, all companies in the analysis sample were required to report *COMPUSTAT* line items for selling, general, and administrative expenses; cost of goods sold; and operating income before depreciation. The analysis sample consisted of 100 firms in five markets drawn from the companies in the calibration sample.

The Big Picture

Only a few companies were able to sustain risk-adjusted value premiums greater than +2.0 over the long haul—adding support to the proposition that goodwill is fickle and intangible market values are fleeting. At the same time, few companies were able to endure risk-adjusted value discounts less than −2.0 over the long haul—adding support to the idea that tangible assets can be cement shoes. As Table 8-1 shows, only 31 of the 337 firms in the sample maintained risk-adjusted differentials greater or less than two.

The twenty-nine strategic groups in the study published by *MSI* (Cook 2003) are listed alphabetically in the first column of Table 8-1. The next two columns list the *GICS*[3] number from which each strategic group was formed and the number of firms in the sample. The last three columns list the number of firms in the sample that were, respectively, high-flyers, average Joes, and bottom-feeders.

Life in the Ad Lane

The first row of Table 8-1 lists five companies in a strategic group of advertising agencies. These five firms are identified by their ticker symbols in Chart 8-1.

Over the decade from 1991 through 2000, the *Omnicom (OMC) Group* created an average of 34% of the capitalized value in this strategic group with an average of only 26% of the sales revenues. Its lowest risk-adjusted VS differential (+1.75) occurred in 1996. This almost made the *OMC Group* a high-flyer.[4] *OMC's* largest **RAD** was +4.48. Its ten-year average was +3.0. In addition, its enterprise marketing risk of 2.4 was well below the *MSI* sample average of 6.6.

Omnicom's share of market value increased over the decade from 25.3% to 44.5%. The company's market cap increased from $906 million in 1991 to $14.7 billion in 2000. At the same time, *OMC's* share of sales revenues in this strategic group increased from 17.9% to 33.6%. As Chart 8-1 shows, this represented extraordinary performance in both capital and customer markets.

There were no pure "average Joes" in this ad agency group. The *Interpublic Group of Companies (IPG)* straddled the line midway between high-flyer and average Joe. The *WWP Group (WWP)* and *Cordiant Communications Group (CDA)* bounced back and forth between bottom-feeder and average Joe status. The last two firms were traded on U.S. exchanges as ADRs.

Interpublic's share of revenues increased from 23.6% in 1991 to 30.7% in 2000. Over the same period, its share of capitalized value fell from 60.3%

Table 8-1 A Distribution of High-Flyers, Average Joes, and Bottom-Feeders

Strategic Group	GICS Number	Firms in Sample	High-Flyers RAD > +2	Average Joes RAD ±2	Bottom-Feeders RAD < −2
Advertising Agencies	25401010	5	1	3	1
Automobile Manufacturers	25102010	7	1	5	1
Banks	40101010	25	1	24	0
Broadcasting & Cable TV	25401012	7	0	8	0
Computer Hardware	45202010	8	0	7	0
Consumer Electronics	25201010	5	0	5	0
Distillers & Vintners	30201020	3	0	3	0
Diversified Chemicals	15101020	9	0	8	1
Diversified Financial Services	40201020	17	1	16	0
Household Appliances	25201040	16	0	15	1
Household Products	30301010	5	0	5	0
Industrial Gases	15101040	4	0	4	0
Industrial Machinery	20106020	23	0	22	2
Integrated Oil & Gas	10102010	7	0	7	0
Integrated Telecommunications Services	50101020	11	0	11	0
IT Consulting & Services	45102010	9	0	9	0
Life & Health Insurance	40301020	6	0	6	0
Packaged Foods	30202030	8	1	7	0
Personal Products	30302010	3	1	0	2
Pharmaceuticals	35202010	9	0	9	0
Photographic Products	25202020	3	0	3	0
Property & Casualty Insurance	40301040	18	2	13	3
Publishing	25401040	18	0	17	1
Restaurants	25301040	25	1	23	1
Semiconductors	45205020	25	1	23	1
Soft Drinks	30201030	8	1	4	3
Specialty Chemicals	15101050	25	1	22	2
Telecommunications Equipment	45201020	25	0	25	0
Tires & Rubber Products	25101020	3	0	3	0
Totals:	29	337	12	306	19
Percent:		100%	3%	91%	6%

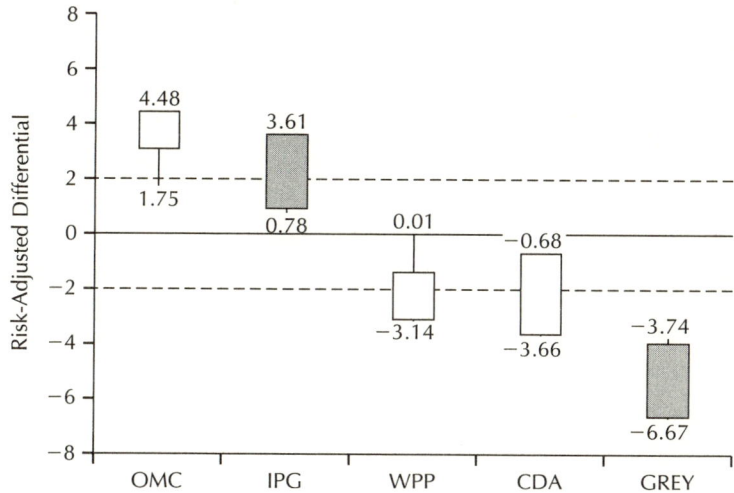

Chart 8-1 RAD Candlestick Chart in Ad Agencies 1991–2000*

*Company tickers ordered left-to-right $14,674M to $657M fiscal year-end 2000 market cap.

to 39.7%. The company's value-sales differentials fell from 36.6 to 9.0, yielding a higher-than-average enterprise marketing risk coefficient of 10.2. This combination of increasing market share and falling market value made *IPG* a very risky bet. *IPG's* risk-adjusted differentials fell from +3.61 to +0.78, signaling a sharp fall in its value premium over the decade.

Cordiant Communications suffered a drop in its market value from 9.0% to 0.5%—and a similar decline in its share of revenues from 20.0% to 4.2%. This combination produced a large negative **VSD** in each year with a lower-than-average marketing market risk of 3.0. *CDA* straddled the border between average Joe and bottom-feeder categories with a highest **RAD** of −0.68 and a low of −3.66 points. The *WPP Group* fared a bit better. Its share of value increased dramatically from 1.5% in 1991 to 11.7% in 2000. At the same time, its share of revenues fell from 30.9% to 24.7%. In every year except 1996, *WPP* posted negative **RAD** values with a relatively high enterprise marketing risk coefficient of 9.4 points.

The only clear-cut bottom-feeder in this ad agency group was the *Grey Global Group (GREY)*, even though its revenues grew from $528 million to $1.2 billion. The company's highest **RAD** was a −3.74; the lowest was a −6.67, with an extremely low enterprise marketing risk of 0.9 points. Chances are that *Grey* will remain stuck on the bottom of this strategic group without a fundamental change in its financial and/or enterprise marketing strategies. Such a change took place on May 3, 2005 when *Grey* shareholders agreed to merge with the *WPP* group.

The companies in Chart 8-1 are rank-ordered from left to right by their market cap in 2000. *OMC's* market cap was $14.7 billion. *GREY's* was $657 million. The seeming relationship between a high-flying big cap company and a bottom-feeding small cap company is purely accidental. Or, at best, is it unique to this group of ad agencies. This is the only one of the twenty-nine strategic groups where direct relationship between **RAD** and market cap was found in the *MSI* sample.

Toyota's on Top

A group of automobile manufacturers appears in the second row of Table 8-1. There were seven firms in the strategic group over the period 1991-2000. *Toyota Motors,* as we already have seen, was the high-flyer in this market. *General Motors* was the bottom-feeder. The other five firms were average Joes. They all experienced risk-adjusted VS differentials between +2.0 and −2.0 in each of the ten years.

It's Easier to Fall Than Fly

If you count the entries in the last three columns of Table 8-1, you will find that only twelve companies posted **RADs** greater than +2.0 in every year of the decade. These companies were consistently awarded value premiums over the long run. A greater number of companies (nineteen) experienced significant and consistent value discounts (**RAD** < −2.0). While the *MSI* sample is relatively small, this result does suggest it's easier for management to fall down than to fly.

Viewed another way, 306 companies (91% of the sample) were consistently bounded by ±2 **RAD** over the ten years. This finding is consistent with the Fama and French (2000) conclusion that earnings are "mean reverting." Risk-adjusted differentials also are mean reverting.

The Best a Man Can Get

The highest flyer of them all was *Gillette*. Its strategic group was occupied by two other competitors—*Avon Products* and *Alberto-Culver*. Over the decade, *Gillette* created an average of 78.4% of the year-end capitalized values in this group. The company did this on an average of 55.0% of group revenues. Its VS differentials averaged 23.4 points. The year-to-year standard deviation in the company's unadjusted VS differentials was only 2.0. The low standard deviation indicates that investors regard *Gillette* as a low enterprise marketing risk company. They believe it is likely to sustain its value premiums into the future.

Chapter 8 • High-Flyers and Bottom-Feeders   205

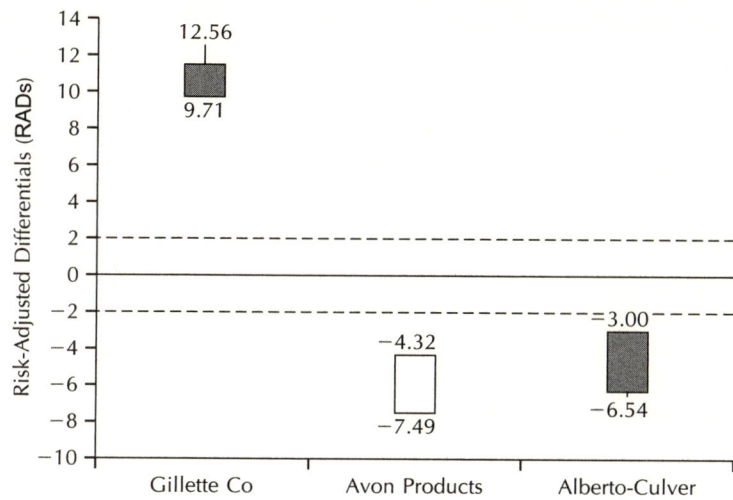

Chart 8-2   RAD Candlestick Chart in Personal Products

Gillette's risk-adjusted differential was 11.5 in 1991. It dropped a bit to 9.7 by 2000. These values define the top and bottom of the gray (down) candle in the upper left-hand corner of Chart 8-2. *Gillette's* average risk-adjusted differential was 11.5. It's highest **RAD** (+12.6) occurred in 1995.

An update on these three companies showing the tends in risk-adjusted differentials appears in Chart 8-3. At the end of the second quarter in 2003,

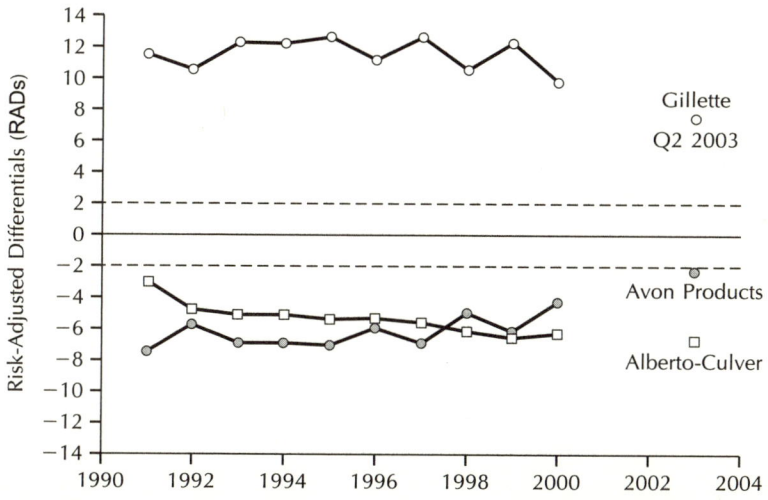

Chart 8-3   Risk-Adjusted VS Differentials in Personal Products

Gillette's risk-adjusted VS differential was still up in the stratosphere. It was 7.6 standard deviations above the expected value of zero. *Gillette* was acquired by *Procter & Gamble Co.* in October, 2005 for $57 billion.

Avon Products and *Alberto-Culver* were, of course, blown out of the water by Gillette's performance in this strategic group.

Between fourth quarter of 2000 and the second quarter of 2003, *Avon Products* continued its recovery from bottom-feeder status that began in 1997. Meanwhile, *Alberto-Culver* continued to receive ever-greater discounts on its market value.

The Scorecard of High-Flyers

The mean value share, revenue share, VS differential, strategic risk, market value, and sales revenues of the twelve high-flying companies are listed in Table 8-2. The companies are rank-ordered by their average share of revenues over the period 1991 through 2000. All of these high-flyers experienced enterprise marketing risks below the *MSI* sample average except *Berkshire Hathaway,* which experienced risk.

McDonald's created 72.5% of the market value on 41.8% of group revenue. The standard deviation (enterprise marketing risk) in *McDonald's* unadjusted differentials was less than the sample average ($\sigma = 4.8$), indicating it is likely to sustain its mean risk-adjusted value premium of 6.4. *McDonald's* lowest RAD was 5.2 and its highest was 8.4 points.

Coca-Cola created 65.9% of the market value in the soft drink group with 31.5% of sales revenues. The standard deviation in *Coca-Cola's* unadjusted VS differentials was 3.2. Its mean RAD over the period 1991–2000 was 10.7 points. *Toyota Motors* and *Campbell Soup* also were high performers posting both large values of RAD and low enterprise marketing risks. *Toyota* created 33.9% of the value in autos with just 15.5% of sales. *Omnicom Group* appears next in Table 8-2, followed by *Campbell Soup Company,* which created 13.1% of the value in packaged foods on 7.1% of sales revenues.

Exceptional performance also was observed in the property and casualty market. *Berkshire Hathaway* created 43.1% of the market value in this strategic group with 16.3% of the sales revenues. A small player in the property and casualty space, *MBIA* created 4.3% of the value on 1.0% of group revenues.

Overall, it appears that share of sales revenues has little to do with earning sustained risk-adjusted value premiums. Big players don't always win. And small ones don't always lose.

Table 8-2 A Scorecard of High-Flyers in the *MSI* Sample

Company:	Value Share Mean '91–'00	Revenue Share Mean '91–'00	Value-Sales Differential Mean '91–'00	Value-Sales Differential Risk '91–'00	Risk-Adjusted Value-Sales Differential $Mill Mean '91–'00	Risk-Adjusted Value-Sales Differential $Mill Low	Risk-Adjusted Value-Sales Differential $Mill High	2000 $Mill Market Cap	2000 Revenue
Gillette Co	78.4	55.0	23.4	2.0	11.5	9.7	12.6	$ 38,050	$ 9,295
Mcdonald's Corp	72.5	41.8	30.7	4.8	6.4	5.2	8.4	$ 44,584	$ 14,243
Coca-Cola Co	65.9	31.5	34.4	3.2	10.7	9.3	12.7	$151,112	$ 20,458
Berkshire Hathaway	43.1	16.3	26.8	6.5	4.1	2.6	5.3	$108,253	$ 33,871
Toyota Motor Corp	33.9	15.5	18.4	4.2	4.4	3.1	6.2	$118,366	$119,656
Omnicom Group	33.8	26.4	7.5	2.4	3.0	3.0	1.8	$ 14,674	$ 6,154
Campbell Soup Co	13.1	7.1	6.0	1.5	5.8	4.6	7.6	$ 14,551	$ 6,267
Sigma-Aldrich	5.4	1.9	3.5	0.8	4.1	2.0	5.6	$ 3,036	$ 1,096
Fifth Third Bancorp	5.8	1.6	2.2	0.6	3.6	2.6	5.4	$ 27,815	$ 4,276
MBIA Inc	4.3	1.0	3.3	0.6	5.1	3.8	6.9	$ 7,612	$ 1,057
Linear Technolog	2.8	0.7	2.1	0.5	4.0	2.4	4.9	$ 14,648	$ 706
Eaton-Vance	0.3	0.2	0.2	0.04	3.1	2.0	5.0	$ 2,268	$ 430

The Bottom-Feeders

Investors discounted the market value of nineteen companies in the *MSI* sample. These firms are listed in Table 8-3 from highest to lowest share of revenues. Many of these companies are household names.

Electrolux, in a strategic group with sixteen other household appliance manufacturers, created only 21.3% of the market value on 45.8% of the revenues. The company's market cap at the end of its 2000 fiscal year was $4.5 billion compared with its sales revenues of $13.2 billion.

Avon averaged 18.3% of value and 34.2% of sales revenues in the personal products group. Notice in the last two columns of Table 8-3 that *Avon's* market cap in 2000 was almost twice its sales revenues ($11.4 vs. $5.7 billion). Yet its market value was small relative to *Gillette's* $38.0 billion and its sales were relatively large. In the same group, *Alberto-Culver* had 3.5% of value and 10.2% of sales.

CNA Financial in the property and casualty group created only 7.8% of the value with 26.5% of the sales in the period from 1991 through 2000. Its market cap was less than half its sales revenues in 2000. Investors heavily discounted *CNA's* shareholder value relative to its market power.

General Motors averaged 15.1% of the value on 25.3% of revenues in the automobile market. The company created only $28.8 billion in market value compared with $180.6 billion in sales revenues. GM's v/r ratio was just 0.16: by far the lowest observed among the bottom feeders in this study. Investors continue to tell *GM* to sell off assets and cut costs in the face burning cash at $2 billion per quarter (Bloomberg 2006).

Among the nineteen firms with sustained discounts, their share of sales revenues ranged from a high of 45.8% to a low 0.4%. It appears that both market share and market value has little do with sustained discounting of shareholder value.

Did the Big Players Always Win?

There is considerable speculation about whether being a market leader is particularly desirable. As Jack Welch often said during his long tenure as CEO of *General Electric*, if a business couldn't be number one or number two in a category, they should "fix it, sell it, or close it down." While testing that hypothesis was not the purpose of the study published by *MSI,* the data from this sample do provide some insight on the question.

The mean share of sales revenues of companies in the top 10% of the sample is 29.0%. Those in the bottom 10% had a mean share of

Table 8-3 Scorecard of Bottom-Feeders in the *MSI* Sample

Company:	Value Share Mean '91–'00	Revenue Share Mean '91–'00	Value-Sales Differential Mean '91–'00	Value-Sales Differential Sigma '91–'00	Risk-Adjusted Value-Sales Differential Mean '91–'00	Risk-Adjusted Value-Sales Differential High	Risk-Adjusted Value-Sales Differential Low	2000 $Mill Market Cap	2000 $Mill Revenue
Electrolux Ab-Adr	21.3	45.8	−24.5	5.7	−6.1	−5.6	−8.5	$ 4,474	$ 13,182
Avon	18.3	34.2	−16.0	2.6	−6.2	−4.3	−7.5	$11,376	$ 5,714
CNA Financial Corp	7.8	26.5	−18.7	3.4	−5.4	−3.5	−6.7	$ 7,107	$ 15,614
General Motors Corp	15.1	25.3	−10.2	2.2	−4.8	−2.5	−6.0	$28,777	$180,557
St. Paul Cos	6.0	11.0	−5.0	1.3	−3.8	−2.0	−5.7	$11,750	$ 8,608
Alberto-Culver	3.5	10.2	−7.4	1.4	−5.3	−3.0	−6.5	$ 2,261	$ 2,247
Skf Ab-Adr	3.6	8.7	−5.1	1.0	−5.1	−4.1	−7.0	$ 908	$ 4,297
Grey Global Group	2.7	7.6	−4.9	0.9	−5.3	−3.7	−6.7	$ 657	$ 1,247
FMC	2.5	5.2	−2.8	0.8	−3.4	−2.3	−5.1	$ 2,184	$ 3,926
Pepsiamericas Inc	1.4	4.5	−3.1	0.9	−3.6	−2.1	−5.3	$ 2,557	$ 2,528
Timken Co	2.2	4.1	−1.9	0.4	−4.6	−3.1	−6.5	$ 896	$ 2,643
First American Corp/CA	1.1	3.1	−2.5	0.4	−6.0	−4.5	−7.3	$ 2,088	$ 2,934
Ferro Corp	1.5	2.6	−1.1	0.3	−3.8	−2.1	−5.3	$ 797	$ 1,447
Coca-Cola Btlng Cons	0.2	1.4	−1.2	0.2	−5.6	−4.5	−7.1	$ 242	$ 995
Stepan Co	0.4	1.1	−0.7	0.1	−6.1	−4.2	−7.9	$ 219	$ 699
Chart House Enterprise	0.2	0.7	−0.5	0.1	−5.0	−3.8	−6.5	$ 47	$ 142
National Beverage Corp	0.1	0.7	−0.6	0.1	−8.1	−6.1	−9.6	$ 163	$ 426
Playboy Enterprises	0.5	0.6	−0.4	0.1	−4.5	−2.9	−5.6	$ 233	$ 308
Microsemi Corp	0.1	0.4	−0.3	0.1	−4.2	−3.1	−5.7	$ 384	$ 248

revenues of 0.1%. This difference is statistically significant ($p < 0.00$) using the larger standard error of the two sub-samples. The mean risk-adjusted differential of the market leader sub-sample was -0.73, while the mean risk-adjusted differential of the market follower sub-sample was -0.25. These differences were not statistically significant ($p > 0.41$). However, the total returns to the shareholders of the market share leaders was 77.53%, while the total returns to the shareholders of the market laggards was 28.45%. Statistically this difference is only marginally significant due to the large variation within the two small sup-samples. The difference is very significant managerially. In this sample the big players win on shareholder returns.

Group Size Has No Big Effect

The mean and standard deviation of the risk-adjusted differentials by market cap—rank-ordered from the most (twenty-five) to the least (three) number of companies in each market—are shown in Table 8-4. Variations from the total sample mean (-0.3) and standard deviation (2.5) of **RAD** suggests both are robust in relation to market cap and number of firms in the twenty-nine markets. Only two markets (soft drinks and personal products) contain standard deviations that are significantly different from the total sample results.

The correlation coefficients among number of firms, market cap, and mean **RAD** in Table 8-4 are all between ± 0.21. These results suggest that industry group size does not have a big effect either on the mean or standard deviation in risk-adjusted differentials across groups.

Market Cap Has No Effect

Evidence that the risk-adjusted VS differential is robust across firms with large and small market caps is provided by comparison of the minimum and maximum values of **RAD** by firm within a strategic group over time.

The pattern shown in Chart 8-4 for diversified chemical manufacturers is typical of all twenty-nine strategic groups in the study. The vertical axis in this Candlestick chart is centered on zero and ranges from positive $+6$ to negative -6 values of **RAD**. The companies are identified by ticker symbols and are rank-ordered from left to right by their 2000 market value. These range from a high of $50.37 billion for *DuPont (DD)* to a low of $106 million for *Penford Corporation (PENX)*.

The white candles are companies that experienced an increase in **RAD** over the decade. Those with gray candles experienced a decline in **RAD**. The wicks represent the highest and lowest values of **RAD** for each company.

Table 8-4 Big and Small Strategic Groups Are Not Much Different

Strategic Group	Sample Market Capitalization (in billions of dollars) 2000		Number of Firms	Risk-Adjusted VS Differentials	
	Biggest Cap	Smallest Cap	Sample	Mean	Sigma
Banks	$ 95.18	$ 5.21	25	.1	1.5
Restaurants	$ 44.60	$ .02	25	−1.4	2.4
Semiconductors	$202.32	$ .32	25	−.3	2.0
Specialty Chemicals	$ 7.98	$ .04	25	−.4	2.5
Telecommunications Equipment	$ 98.31	$ .12	25	−.1	1.5
Industrial Machinery	$ 17.98	$ .74	23	−.3	2.5
Property and Casualty Insurance	$108.25	$ 1.20	18	−.6	3.1
Publishing	$ 16.62	$ .23	18	−.5	2.1
Diversified Financial Services	$229.37	$ 1.63	17	.5	1.8
Household Appliances	$ 4.54	$ .006	16	−.1	2.4
Integrated Telecommunications	$161.63	$ 4.92	11	.4	1.9
Diversified Chemicals	$ 50.37	$ .11	9	−1.0	1.9
IT Consulting and Services	$ 26.94	$ .67	9	−.1	1.5
Pharmaceuticals	$290.22	74.87	9	−.2	1.8
Computer Hardware	$149.12	$ .76	8	−.2	1.6
Packaged Foods	$ 45.94	$ 2.48	8	1.2	2.3
Soft Drinks	$151.11	$ .04	8	−1.9	5.3
Automobile Manufacturers	$118.37	$10.94	7	−.7	3.0
Broadcasting and Cable TV	$ 37.41	$ 2.10	7	.0	1.3
Integrated Oil and Gas	$302.21	$ 6.44	7	−.7	2.2
Life and Health Insurance	$ 55.75	$ 2.12	6	−.1	1.5
Advertising	$ 14.67	$ .66	5	−.8	3.1
Consumer Electronics	$ 62.61	$ 1.37	5	.3	1.3
Household Products	102.26	$ .85	5	−.2	1.2
Industrial Gases	$ 9.40	$ .64	4	−.2	1.4
Distillers and Vintners	$ 4.56	$ .08	3	.3	1.7
Personal Products	$ 38.05	$ 2.26	3	.0	8.4
Photographic Products	$ 21.23	$ .26	3	−.6	1.7
Tires and Rubber Products	$ 3.60	$ .69	3	.4	1.6
Total Sample	$302.21	$ .006	337	−.3	2.5

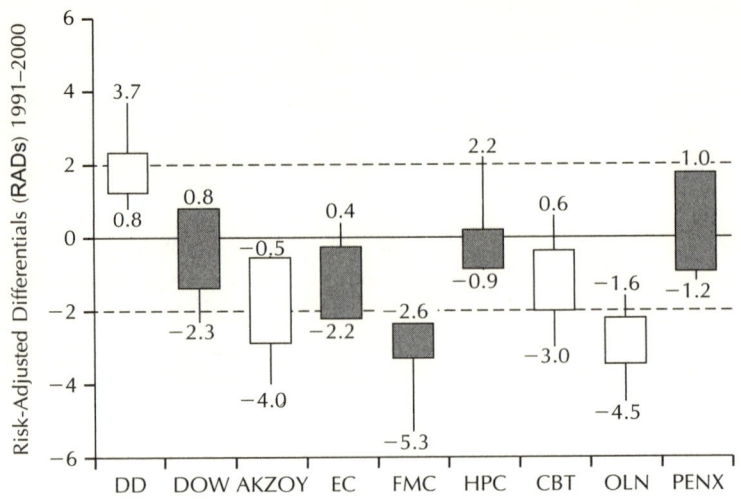

Chart 8-4 RAD Candlestick Chart in Diversified Chemicals*

*Company tickers ordered left-to-right $50,370M to $106M fiscal year-end 2000 market cap.

For example, *DuPont's* RAD increased from +1.2 in 1991 to +2.4 in 2000; however, *DD's* highest RAD was +3.7 in 1998 and its lowest RAD was 0.8 in 1995. Throughout the decade, investors rewarded *DuPont* with risk-adjusted premiums.

The range between the highest and lowest values of RAD is roughly similar across firms. The difference between the highest and lowest RAD in this group ranged from −5.3 to +3.7. This demonstrates that enterprise marketing risk adjustments are effective in standardizing measured differentials. In addition, with respect to market capitalization, among the sample firms the candles appear to be randomly distributed around zero.

Notice that investors systematically discounted the value of the *FMC Corporation* (ticker *FMC*) over the entire decade. This company was one of the nineteen bottom-feeders in the study.

A similar pattern of minimum and maximum values of RAD was also observed in the much larger semiconductor market, occupied by twenty-five firms. The results appear in Chart 8-5. Again, the companies are identified by their ticker symbol. The firms are rank-ordered left to right by fiscal year-end market capitalization.

The companies range in size from *Intel Corporation (INTC)*, with a 2000 market cap of $202 billion, to *Standard Microsystems Corporation (SMSC)*, with a market cap of $323 million.

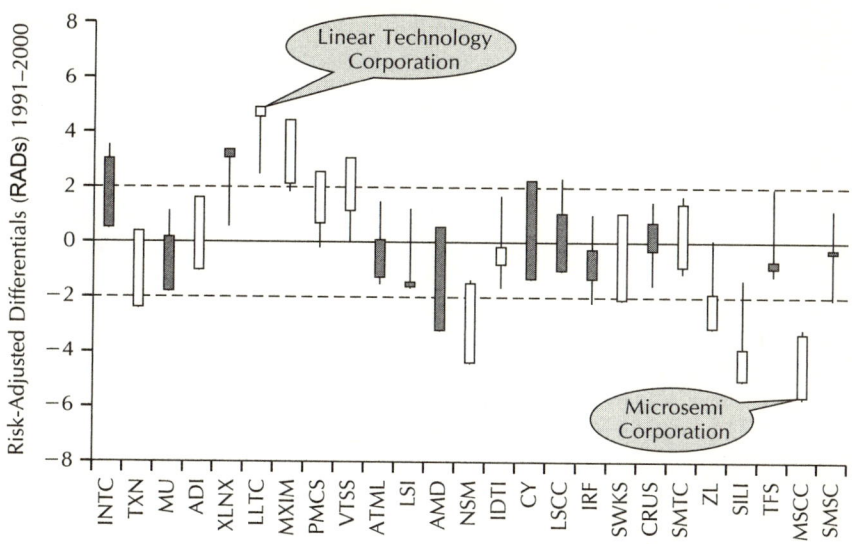

Chart 8-5 RAD Candlestick Chart in Semiconductors*

*Firms are rank-ordered left-to-right from highest ($202.3 Bill) to lowest ($0.323 Bill) market cap.

The semiconductor group contains almost three times as many firms as the diversified chemicals group. It happens that the largest market cap is also four times greater.

Even so, the highest and lowest values of **RAD** in semiconductors display effectively the same range as seen in all other industry groups. The bars also appear to be randomly distributed around zero with respect to market capitalization.

Chart 8-5 highlights some interesting differences among the companies in this group. As you might expect to find, investors rewarded *INTEL Corporation* (INTC) with significant value-sales premiums over the ten years. But the size of those premiums declined from +3.0 in 1991 and +0.5 in 2000. Differentials of all the companies with shaded candlesticks fell from 1991 to 2000.

Linear Technology Corporation (LLTC) earned value premiums greater than +2.0 throughout the ten-year period from 1991 to 2000. And the range between its beginning value in 1991 (+4.5) and ending value in 2000 (4.9) was unusually small, though the company fell to +2.45 in 1996.

At the other extreme, the *Microsemi Corporation* (MSCC) was the only pure bottom-feeder in this strategic group. The market systematically discounted its value over the entire period. But the company did show significant gains. It began the decade with a **RAD** of −5.7 and ended up at −3.3. All of the companies with white candles experienced increases over the decade.

What It Adds Up To

High-flyers earn exceptional and sustained value premiums over and above their market power. Alternatively, bottom-feeders are heavily and systematically discounted by investors. The trick is to discover the mix of product and stock market value drivers that produce exceptional, sustained high and low performance.

Financial Forces Mediate

By definition, a company's share of market value is dependent on the market value of all the other firms in its strategic group. These in turn are influenced by the company's and its competitors' earnings. In other words, "the stock market tries to infer a firm's costs and demand (and hence future profitability) based on the firm's realized profits and those of its rivals." (Rotemberg and Scharfstein 1990, 369) There are, however, financial forces that come into play.

Constant Growth Model

The classic constant growth model of firm valuation (Brigham and Gordon 1968, 91, equation 16) sets the current market price per share as a function of the retention rate; earnings per share before interest and taxes; the leverage-free cost of capital; interest rate; the firm's debt-equity ratio; and the rate of return on common equity investment.

The *ex post* price per share plus dividends paid per share equals total return to shareholders (b). Total return captures "price appreciation plus reinvestment of dividends and the compounding effect of dividends paid on reinvested dividends." (*Standard and Poor's* 1998) Total return to shareholders is one of the powerful forces influencing a company's market value.

Another powerful financial force is the ratio of debt to total invested capital (e). This is comparable to the debt-equity ratio in the Gordon growth model. Debt to equity is widely used as a measure of leverage in finance literature (Brander and Lewis 1986). When more debt than equity is used to finance competitive strategies, the market return to shareholders is expected to decrease since debt service becomes relatively more important.

These financial forces will mediate any relationship between VS differentials and maximum earnings market share.

Is the Glass Half Empty or Half Full?

How do enterprise marketing metrics stand up against total return to shareholders and capital structure? Do they add any information about variations in the value-sales differential that's not captured in the constant growth model?

The *MSI* study of the 100 companies in the analysis sample was a first step in sorting out the influence of enterprise marketing and corporate financial metrics on risk-adjusted VS differentials. That study did not incorporate the maximum earnings metric as presented here. Instead, a proxy was used to represent this variable. The proxy was the difference between a company's average profit per basis point and the average cost per basis point—roughly the denominator and numerator in the maximum earnings market share formula.

Descriptive Statistics in the *MSI* Study

Descriptive statistics from this study for five peer groups are shown in Table 8-5 on the following page. The mean of risk-adjusted VS differentials is not significantly different from zero in any of these markets. In row two the mean change in risk-adjusted differentials is zero with a standard deviation of 1.0 in each of the five markets. This result was expected.

The profit and cost per basis point ranged from a high of $8.08 and $3.21 million, respectively, in commercial banks—to a low of $1.11 and $.69 million in household appliances. Note that the profit per basis point is not a function of the size of the market alone. For example, the profit per basis point in semiconductors, a market of twenty-five firms, was $2.43 million, compared with $2.62 million in diversified chemicals, a market of eighteen firms. The profit—minus the cost per basis point—was greatest in commercial banks ($4.87 million) and smallest in household appliances ($.43 million).

The year-to-year changes in the profit minus cost per basis point ranged from a high of $750,000 in commercial banking to a low of $20,000 in diversified chemicals.

Banks were the most highly leveraged firms in the *MSI* sample, with an average long-term-debt-to-total-invested-capital ratio[5] of 150.9. The average debt-to-capital ratio of firms in the four other markets is 30.2.

The highest total shareholder returns over the period 1992–2000 averaged 64.8% in the telecommunications equipment group. Household appliance firms yielded the lowest total returns (+13.6%) over the period.

Table 8-5 Descriptive Statistics in the *MSI* Study

Variable (Std Dev)	Commercial Banks	Diversified Chemicals	Household Appliances	Semiconductors	Telecom Equipment
		Means 1992–2000 (Millions USD)			
Risk-Adjusted VS Differential	0.14 (1.51)	1.04 (1.88)	−0.03 (2.03)	−0.26 (2.01)	−0.15 (1.56)
Δ Risk-Adjusted VS Differential	0.01 (1.02)	−0.03 (0.95)	−0.10 (1.01)	0.03 (0.95)	0.00 (1.01)
Profit per Basis Point	$8.08 ($4.13)	$2.62 ($.69)	$1.11 ($.29)	$2.43 ($1.21)	$3.32 ($1.76)
Cost per Basis Point	$3.21 ($1.62)	$1.22 ($.19)	$.69 ($.09)	$1.07 ($.47)	$1.93 ($.76)
Profit Minus Cost per Basis Point	$4.87 ($2.68)	$1.40 ($.79)	$.43 ($.29)	$1.36 ($.90)	$1.39 ($1.34)
Δ Profit Minus Cost per Basis Point	$.75 ($.93)	$.02 ($.26)	$.03 ($.12)	$.23 ($.40)	$.20 ($.72)
Debt to Total Capital	150.9 (73.7)	53.0 (19.8)	48.8 (43.2)	19.9 (21.5)	22.2 (21.7)
Δ Debt to Total Capital	3.21 (49.3)	1.04 (15.4)	−.74 (33.7)	−.97 (14.5)	−2.17 (17.6)
Total Return to Shareholders	30.6 (36.1)	16.3 (29.5)	13.6 (45.4)	55.4 (106.7)	64.8 (214.9)
Δ Total Return to Shareholders	−6.05 (46.5)	−3.24 (44.1)	−5.62 (62.5)	−4.32 (162.4)	−8.36 (326.6)
No. Obs.	225	81	144	225	225

Changes in debt-to-capital ratios (Δe) and total return (Δb) exhibit very large coefficients of variation. For example, the mean change in debt-to-capital in household appliances is only −.74 points per year, while the standard deviation is 33.7 points. The mean year-to-year change in total return are very small in each of the five strategic groups. The standard deviations in each market are large. For example, the standard deviation in total returns in the telecommunication equipment market is 326.6. The smallest standard deviation in total returns is in the diversified chemical strategic group (44.1). These results were traced to large year-to-year changes in company dividend payout ratios not reported in Table 8-5.

Regression Results in the *MSI* Study

Table 8-6 shows the *OLS* regression intercepts, standardized slopes, and *t*-statistics for the measured independent variables.[6] The intercept is not significant in any of the markets. All three variables offer information about changes in risk-adjusted VS differentials.

First, the change in profit minus cost per basis point has a positive and significant slope in all five markets. Moreover, the slopes are quite similar, ranging from a low of 0.14 in telecommunications equipment to a high of 0.24 in commercial banks. The results are more robust in banks ($t = 3.70$) and semiconductors ($t = 3.86$) than in diversified chemicals ($t = 2.27$), household appliances ($t = 2.42$), and telecommunications equipment ($t = 2.41$).

There was little evidence of multicollinearity between changes in the profit minus cost per basis point and the other independent variables in the regression (condition indexes were less than 2.0 for all the variables in each industry).

Second, the change in one-year total return to shareholders also has a positive and significant slope in all five markets. Again, the slopes are quite

Table 8-6 Regression Results in *MSI* Study

	Commercial Banks	Diversified Chemicals	Household Appliances	Semiconductors	Telecom Equipment
Intercept	−.14	−.00	−.07	−.09	.05
(*t* Statistic)	(−1.69)	(−.00)	(−1.25)	(1.31)	(.80)
Change in Profit Minus Cost per Basis Point	.24*** (3.70)	.20* (2.27)	.18* (2.42)	.24** (3.86)	.14** (2.41)
Change in One-Year Total Return	.43*** (6.65)	.36** (4.22)	.48*** (6.70)	.46*** (7.60)	.43*** (7.26)
Change in Debt-to-Capital Ratio	.07 (1.10)	−.39*** (−4.29)	−.08 (−1.13)	.04 (.70)	−.17** (−2.89)
R^2	.16	.47	.28	.21	.22
No. Obs.	225	81	144	225	225
F	15.4***	24.6***	20.0***	21.2***	21.9***

Each equation also included (1) an annual dummy variable to control for time trend, (2) a monthly dummy to control for fiscal year end, and (3) a code dummy to control for *SIC* differences within the *GICS* sub-industry. None of these dummy variables were significant in any of the equations.

*$p < .05$; **$p < .01$; ***$p < .001$; *t*-statistics in parentheses

similar, ranging from a low of .36 in diversified chemicals to a high of .48 in household appliances. The results are robust ($t > 4.0$) in all five markets. There also was little evidence of multicollinearity between changes in total return and the other independent variables.

Third, the slopes for changes in the debt-to-capital ratio are negative as expected but significant in only two of the five markets: -0.39 in diversified chemicals and -0.17 in telecommunications equipment. The leverage variable contains little significant information about the $\Delta\rho$ in the other three markets.

Overall, the estimation results are highly significant. Adjusted R^2s are substantial[7] and significant in all five markets: In commercial banks $R^2 = .16$ ($F = 15.4$); in diversified chemicals $R^2 = .47$ ($F = 24.6$); in household appliances $R^2 = .28$ ($F = 20.0$); in semiconductors $R^2 = .21$ ($F = 21.2$); and in telecommunication equipment $R^2 = .22$ ($F = 21.9$).

Perhaps the most striking feature of the results shown in Table 8-6 is the relative magnitude of the slopes for the significant enterprise marketing and financial variables. The mean of the slopes for changes in profit minus cost per basis point β_{1j} is 0.20 in the five markets. The mean of the slopes for the changes in total returns to shareholders β_{2j} is 0.43. On average, the profit minus cost per basis point offers almost half as much information about variations in risk-adjusted VS differentials as does total return to shareholders.

Is the glass half empty or half full? That depends on your point of view. Even after controlling for total returns and capital structure, the impact of enterprise marketing on shareholder value is large and statistically significant.

What's Up Next?

Now it's time for the final act. In the next chapter we combine risk-adjusted differentials and relative earnings productivity to show how management can create, or destroy, shareholder value.

Appendix 8-A: *MSI* Sample Frame

AT&T [T]
Bank of America [BAC]
Bank One Corporation [ONE]
Bristol-Meyers Squibb [BMY]
Chevron Corporation [CVX]
Citigroup [C]

The Clorox Company [CLX]
The Coca-Cola Company [KO]
Colgate-Palmolive Company [CL]
The Dow Chemical
   Company [DOW]
DuPont Company [DD]

Eastman Kodak Company [EK]
Electrolux [ELUX]
Ford Motor Company [F]
General Mills Inc [GIS]
General Motors
 Corporation [GM]
The Gillette Company [G]
Goodyear Tire & Rubber [GT]
Hewlett-Packard Company [HPQ]
IBM Corporation [IBM]
Intel Corporation [INTC]
J.P. Morgan Chase & Co [JPM]
Johnson & Johnson [JNJ]
Merck & Company, Inc [MRK]

Motorola, Inc [MOT]
NFO World Group [IPG]
PNC [PNC]
PepsiCo [PEP]
Pharmacia/Monsanto [PHA]
Praxair, Inc [PX]
Procter & Gamble Company [PG]
Royal Philips Electronics [PHG]
The Timken Company [TKR]
Unilever [UN]
Wells Fargo & Company [WFC]
Verizon Communications [VZ]
WPP Group PLC [WPPGY]
W.R. Grace & Company [GRA]

References

Bloomberg. 2006. "General Motors Has Fifth Straight Quarterly Loss Amid Cuts." Article retrieved January 29, 2006 (http://quote.bloomberg.com/apps/news? pid=10000006sid=aLcf TN4pJIRU&refer=home).

Brander, J. A., and T. R. Lewis. 1986. "Oligopoly and Financial Structure: The Limited Liability Effect." *The American Economic Review* 76 (December): 956–970.

Brigham, E. F., and M. J. Gordon. 1968. "Leverage, Dividend Policy, and the Cost of Capital." *The Journal of Finance* 23 (March): 85–103.

Cook, V. J., Jr. 2003. "Marketing's Impact on Firm Value: The Value-Sales Differential." *Marketing Science Institute Reports* 03 (2): 55–78.

Fama, E. F., and K. R. French. 1992. "The Cross-Section of Expected Stock Returns." *The Journal of Finance*, 47 (2):   .

———. 2000. "Forecasting Profitability and Earnings." *Journal of Business* 73 (April): 161–175.

Rotemberg, J. J., and D. S. Scharfstein. 1990. "Shareholder-Value Maximization and Product-Market Competition." *The Review of Financial Studies* 3 (3): 367–391.

Standard & Poor's. 1998. *COMPUSTAT North America Data Guide*. Englewood, Colo.: The McGraw-Hill Companies, Chapter 16, 24.

———. 2002. *Research Insight: A Primer for Getting Started*. The McGraw-Hill Book Companies.

End Notes

[1] This sampling requirement leads to a survivor bias in the results presented here.

[2] To minimize the loss of firms in each sample market, a single missing value between two observations is replaced with the mean of these observations. A single missing value at the beginning or the end of the ten-year series was replaced with the prediction of a best-fitting equation if the R^2 was greater than 0.9.

[3] **G**lobal **I**ndustry **C**lassification **S**ystem.

[4] Strictly speaking, the cut-point for the lowest Rho was pinned at +2.0. This means that the probability the observed value is greater than zero is 0.975.

[5] LTDCAP in *COMPUSTAT* is Total Long-Term Debt divided by Total Invested Capital multiplied by 100. Invested capital is the sum of long-term debt, preferred stock, minority interests, and common equity.

[6] The regression model was $\Delta\rho_j = \alpha_j + \beta_{1j}(\Delta\ddot{p}_{ijt} - \Delta\ddot{c}_{ijt}) + \beta_{2j}(\Delta b_{ijt}) - \beta_{3j}(\Delta e_{ijt}) + \varepsilon_j$.

[7] For comparison, note that the widely accepted capital-asset pricing model predicts that "expected returns on securities are a positive linear function of their market βs"; yet, "when the tests allow for variation in β that is unrelated to size, the relation between β and average return for 1941–1990 is weak, perhaps nonexistent, even when β is the only explanatory variable." (Fama and French 1992, 427 and 464)

CHAPTER 9

COMPETITIVE STOCK VALUATION

Probably the most widely used management guide to creating shareholder value is Alfred Rappaport's (1998) book. The key drivers in his shareholder valuation model are company sales, sales growth rate, operating profit margin, incremental fixed capital investment, incremental working capital investment, income tax rate, and the cost of capital.

There are important similarities between Rappaport's approach and the competitive stock valuation approach introduced in this chapter. First, and most important, is the prominent role played by sales revenues, sales growth rate, and operating profit margin. These three drivers also are prominent in competitive stock valuation. The reliance Rappaport places on incremental analysis is the second similarity between his approach and competitive stock valuation.

In addition to the similarities, there are several important differences between Rappaport's approach and the one introduced here. First, investment requirements are excluded. The reason is that—whereas Rappaport assumes there will be changes in capital requirements—I assume a company does not significantly change its scale of operations or underlying capital requirements. You will recall that the phrase "within the feasible range" was used several times in the past eight chapters of this book. Second, in contrast to Rappaport's approach, the time value of money is used only to estimate the present value of a predicted stock price.[1] Otherwise the time value of money is ignored. This is because the focus of competitive stock valuation is different from Rappaport's focus. My analysis links enterprise marketing expenses to shareholder value. These expenses do not appear on the balance sheet and, therefore, are not treated as a capital investment. Further, my analysis is based on **market shares** rather than **dollar values.** If the enterprise marketing expenses of all competitors were discounted at the same weighted average cost of capital, market shares would remain unchanged. As a result I do not need to rely on discounted cash flows.[2] To the degree that these factors become important in an analysis of competitive valuation strategies, I leave them to financial management.

My approach is not a substitute for Rappaport's financial valuation model. It is instead a supplement designed to provide a new perspective on how competitive advantages influence shareholder value. Here is the common ground we share:

> *It is . . . productivity that the stock market reacts to when pricing a company's shares. Embedded in all shares is an implied long-term forecast about a company's productivity*—that is, its ability to create value in excess of the cost of producing it. When the stock market prices a company's shares according to a belief that the company will be able to create value over the long term, it is attributing [this belief] to the company's long-term productivity or, equivalently, a sustainable competitive advantage. In this way, productivity is the hinge on which both competitive advantage and shareholder value hang. (Rappaport 1998, 69)

So it is that my competitive valuation model integrates the marketing theory of competitive advantage with the creation of shareholder value.

Competitive Stock Valuation Model

The five steps in this model are shown in Chart 9-1. The first step is to identify a group of competitors and forecast the growth rate of their combined sales revenues. This step is critical. Top-line growth is a key to success. "Large companies need to pay at least as much attention to top-line growth as to increasing the bottom line." (Smit, Thompson, and Viguerie 2005, 36) And the tail-wind factor—growth in strategic group revenues—creates a favorable environment for sales growth for every company.

Chart 9-1 Competitive Stock Valuation

The second step is to calculate each company's **maximum earnings market share** (**MEMS**) using the incremental analysis introduced in previous chapters. MEMS is a sophisticated form of strategic benchmarking analysis. It equates the incremental cost of a market share point with incremental earnings after selling, general, and administrative and other enterprise marketing expenses. This is the point where earnings are maximized.

The third step is to calculate each company's earnings at that share of revenues where earnings are maximized. Company sales revenues are the arithmetic product of strategic group revenue and maximum earnings market share. Earnings at this level of sales depend upon expected changes in operating gross margins as well as upon competitors' enterprise marketing expenses.

The fourth step is to estimate each company's historical value-sales differential and relative earnings productivity. The difference between a company's share of the strategic group's capitalized value and share of sales revenue is adjusted for enterprise marketing risk. The "enterprise marketing risk" required to make this adjustment is the standard deviation in a company's observed value-sales differentials. Relative earnings productivity is the difference between a company's actual earnings and its maximum potential earnings in the strategic group.

The final step is to forecast the strategic group's combined shareholder value and each company's share of that value. I assume that enterprise marketing risk is independent of **MEMS**. A company's share of group capitalized value is the arithmetic product of its risk-adjusted differential and enterprise marketing risk added to its maximum earnings market share. Given the number of common shares outstanding at the end of the forecast period, worst, best, and expected stock prices are predicted.

The Missing Link

Suppose investors actually could detect when a company is close to maximizing earnings, as well as when it's not. If investors could read these tea leaves, they should be able to anticipate future risk-adjusted VS differentials and relative earnings productivity.

The closer a company gets to maximizing earnings, the greater will be its differentials, other things being equal. If investors pick up on the proximity of a company's earnings relative to its maximum potential, then its risk-adjusted differential will be higher. Alternatively, if a company is far off the maximum earnings mark, it will experience lower risk-adjusted differentials.

Anecdotal Evidence

If relative earnings productivity and risk-adjusted differentials are to be useful, we should be able to find at least anecdotal evidence to support our expectation that these enterprise marketing metrics are related.

Let's revisit that epic battle for your desktop. Table 9-1 shows what happened to *IBM* over the decade beginning in 1991 and ending in 2000. The second column of the table reports *IBM's* risk-adjusted differentials in the strategic group that includes *Compaq, Dell,* and *Hewlett-Packard.* The third column contains *IBM's* actual earnings minus its theoretical maximum earnings from Chapter 7, *The Battle for Your Desktop.*

Table 9-1 *IBM's* Performance

	Risk-Adjusted Differential	Actual-Maximum Earnings
1991	0.04	−$7,488
1992	−2.28	−$5,327
1993	−1.09	−$4,701
1994	−0.54	−$2,197
1995	−0.86	−$1,019
1996	0.33	−$ 938
1997	0.01	−$ 533
1998	0.22	−$ 255
1999	−0.93	−$ 67
2000	1.40	−$ 1

IBM's risk-adjusted differentials opened at +0.04, then fell dramatically to −2.28, then bounced around zero and ended the decade at +1.40. The difference between the company's actual earnings and its theoretical maximum earnings in 1991 was −$7,488 million. In short, *IBM* left $7.5 billion in theoretical earnings on the table in 1991. The lost earning opportunities declined steadily over the decade, ending at just over −$1 million in 2000.

The numbers in Table 9-1 are shown in Chart 9-2. It appears as if there is a fairly strong positive correlation between the downward trend in lost profit opportunities (the white circles approaching $0 on the right-hand axis) and the upward trend in *IBM's* risk-adjusted differential (the white circles). There is. But with this small sample ($n = 10$) the correlation (0.45) is not statistically significant.

But don't be misled. The world isn't this predictable. We saw in Chapter 6 that *IBM's* strategy produced remarkable results. The company began the decade with that huge $7.5 billion theoretical lost-profit opportunity. Through some combination of luck, competitive pressure, and management

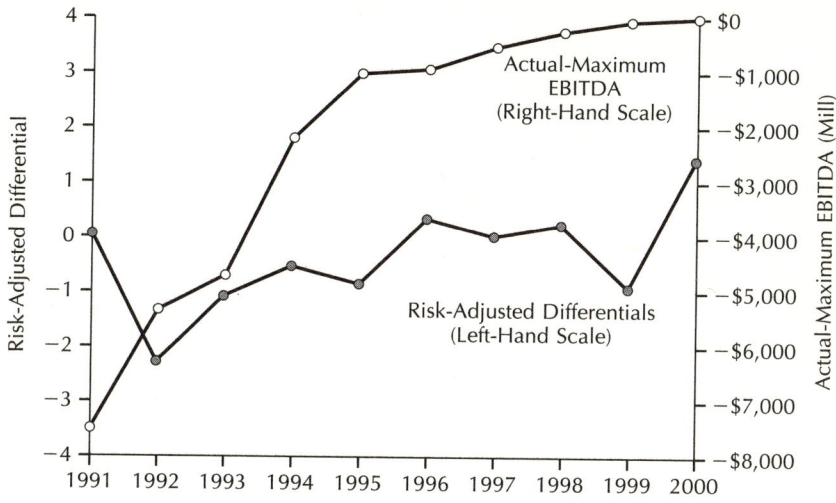

Chart 9-2 Trends in *IBM's* Enterprise Marketing Metrics

audacity the company brought its profit and cost per basis point into line. It was the only company in the desktop group that did so. In addition, the result in Chart 9-2 isn't that strong.

If investors had read these tea leaves correctly, *IBM's* risk-adjusted differential would have taken off. By the year 2000, the company should have earned high-flyer status. It didn't quite make it. A single force, however solid it appears to be, rarely moves investors to bid up a company's stock price.

I Gotta Check My Auction—Revisited

We'll use *Amazon* to dig more deeply into the details of the competitive valuation process. Let's take it step by step, according the outline in Chart 9-1:

 Strategic Group Revenues

The dashed line in Chart 9-3 tracks actual group sales revenues from the fourth quarter of 2000 (period 1) through the first quarter of 2003 (period 10). The solid line tracks the forecast of group sales revenue four quarters ahead to the first quarter of 2004 (period 14). Two things are apparent: group revenues are on the upswing and sales are seasonal. It's often true that quarterly sales data are seasonal. If so, we need some method for capturing seasonality.

Unfortunately, with only ten observations we don't have enough degrees of freedom to use quarterly dummy variables to separate seasonal effects from the trend.[3] But we can forecast quarterly sales as a rolling four-quarter percentage change pegged to the average annual growth in sales. This captures both the upward trend and seasonal properties. It also produces a

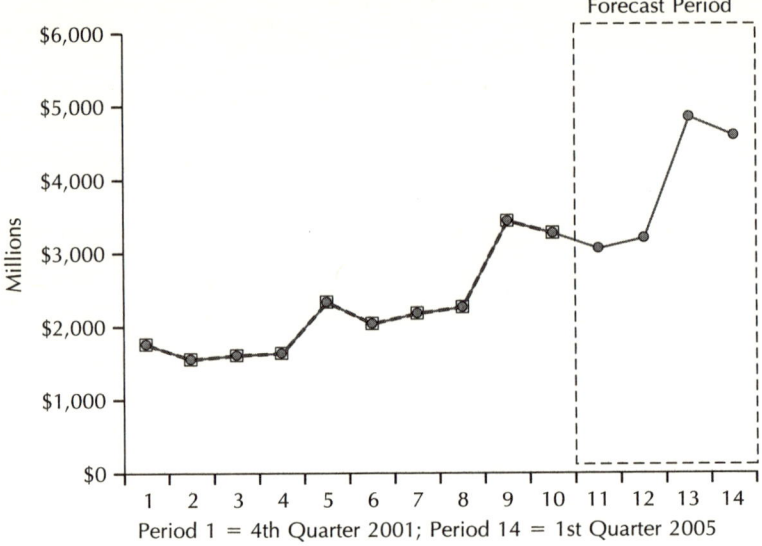

Chart 9-3 Actual and Forecast Online Retailer Group Revenues

reasonable result. Using this method to forecast first quarter of 2005 (period 14) group sales revenues returns an estimate of approximately $4.6 billion. This is based on the average of six annual quarter-to-quarter revenue growth rates of 41% beginning with December, 2002.

2 Company Maximum Earnings Market Share

I make a fundamental assumption here: *Amazon* management will set its enterprise marketing expenses to maximize earnings over the four quarters. This is a pretty strong assumption, particularly in view of the CEO's commitment to market leadership. Nevertheless, I'll make the assumption in order to check the theoretical implications of this enterprise marketing strategy.

Further, I assume that Mr. Bezo's commitment to minimizing costs by reducing *Amazon's* cost of goods sold will increase the company's operational efficiency—and therefore increase its gross margins by 0.5% per quarter.

The forecast growth of group revenues will likely motivate competitors to increase their enterprise marketing expenses. Remember that the correlation between SG&A expenses and sales revenues is 0.96. The historical growth rate of competitors' SG&A expenses over the same period was 44%. In a rapidly growing market, competitors anticipate the need for even higher spending levels. As competitors observe that *AMZN* is reducing its enterprise marketing expenses as a percent of its sales revenue, will they increase their own investments at a more prudent rate? Or will they assume this represents an opportunity to gain share? They will notice the trend, but we don't know how they'll react. So let's assume that competitors will increase enterprise marketing expenses over the four quarters at the historical average with a multiple of 1.44.

The interaction among these assumptions produces a surprising result: *Amazon's* forecast maximum earnings market share in the first quarter of 2005 falls 626 basis points from 46.96% to 40.67%.

 Earnings After Enterprise Marketing Expenses

The left-hand column of Table 9-2 shows *Amazon's* income statement based on actual market share in the first quarter of 2004. The right-hand column displays its maximum earnings market share in the first quarter of 2005 derived from the assumptions described previously.

The first thing to note in Table 9-2 is the forecast increase in group sales revenues from $3.259 billion to $4.596 billion. Next, you will see a decline in *AMZN's* actual market share from 46.96% in the first quarter of 2004 to a maximum earnings market share of 40.67% in the first quarter of 2005.

Since strategic group sales are forecast to grow faster than market share declines, the net result is an increase in *AMZN* sales revenues from $1.530 to $1.868 billion. A subtle but critical transition has just taken place in the stock valuation process. **I did not forecast Amazon's sales revenues.** Instead, I calculated the company's maximum earnings market share of forecast group sales revenues. Then I multiplied forecast group revenues by that market share to forecast Amazon's sales revenues. This is something you probably have not done before because market share typically is considered

Table 9-2 *Amazon's* Actual and Maximum Earnings

US Dollars in Millions	Actual 3/31/2004	Expected 3/31/2005
Group Revenues	3,259	4,594
AMZN Market Share	46.96%	40.67%
AMZN Sales Revenues	1,530	1,868
AMZN COGS	1,152	1,397
Gross Profits	379	471
Enterprise Marketing Expenses	251	280
Maximum Earnings	128	192
Earnings to Revenues	3.9%	4.2%
Enterprise Marketing Expenses to Revenues	7.7%	6.1%

just an interesting historical fact in financial analysis. It is not a variable in any financial valuation models.

Gross profits also are predicted to increase from $379 million to $471 million. Even enterprise marketing expenses are predicted to increase—but not as a percentage of sales. More important is the fact that forecast earnings are up to 4.2% from 3.9% of sales. And enterprise marketing expenses are down to 6.1% from 7.7% of sales. These results would be reflected in a higher stock price if Amazon actually were to adopt a maximum earnings enterprise marketing strategy.

Will the change in company sales revenues cause an incremental change in either fixed or working capital requirements? Probably not, because I assume the company will operate within its feasible range. If this assumption does not hold true, the impact of both changes in capital requirements and the time value of money must be added to this analysis. Since Amazon would shed 629 basis points in revenue share it might even experience a decrease in capital requirements, further enhancing the returns to this strategy.

At this point in the competitive stock valuation, we could calculate maximum earnings in the same manner for each future period, incorporate the effects of changes in capital requirements, and discount the cash flows—in order to estimate *AMZN's* shareholder value. Instead, I'm now going to chart a radically new path to equity pricing.

 Risk-Adjusted Differential and Earnings Productivity

I extend the competitive stock valuation model by simply rearranging the relationship between risk-adjusted differentials and maximum earnings market share. Recall from Chapter 2 that the **r**isk-**a**djusted **d**ifferential is the difference between **s**hare **o**f **v**alue and **s**hare **o**f **r**evenue divided by enterprise marketing risk:[5]

$$RAD = (SOV - SOR)/RISK$$

Since I assume management is maximizing earnings, I can add a "hat" to the **SOR** term and solve for **SOV**. The result is:

$$SOV = RAD \times RISK + S\hat{O}R$$

Think for a moment about the three terms on the right-hand side of this formula. We have a historical estimate of the firm's enterprise marketing risk. We also have an estimate of the firm's maximum earnings share of revenues ($S\hat{O}R$) which we assume is independent of risk. Theoretically, the firm's share of value is simply its risk-adjusted differential multiplied by enterprise marketing risk and added to maximum earnings market share. Not only is this simple; it also makes sense. For example, when a company's marketing

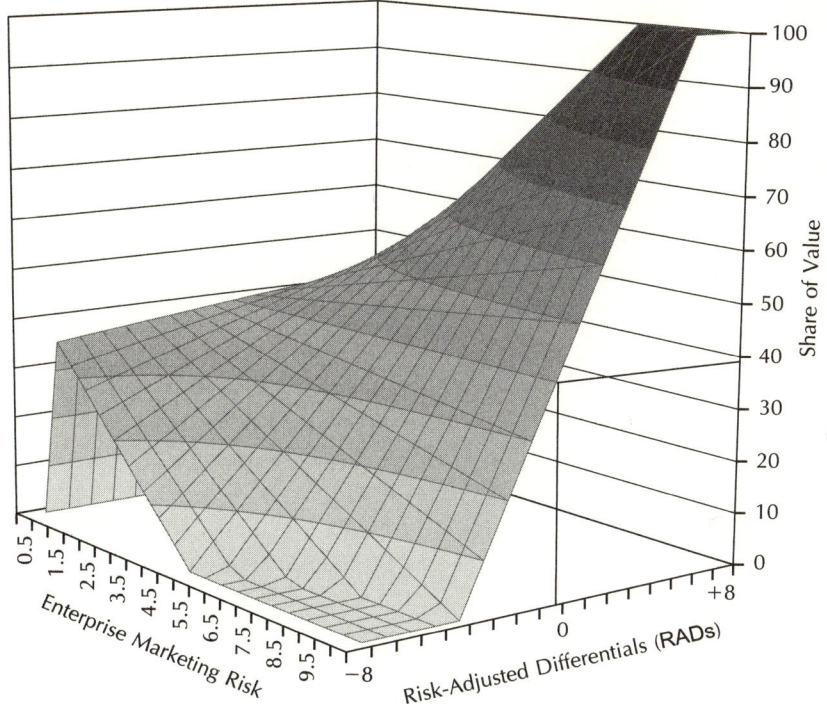

Chart 9-4 Variations in Share of Value at SOR = 40%

risk is zero, share of market value equals its share of group revenue. In this event, the risk-adjusted differential is zero.

Now let's take a close look at the relationship between enterprise marketing risk, share of market value, and risk-adjusted differentials. Chart 9-4 plots these relationships over a wide range of values.

As you might expect, when marketing risk gets large, for any given share of revenues, share of value deviates more from share of revenues. And, as risk-adjusted differentials become more (or less) than zero, share of value again varies more (or less) from share of revenues. Chart 9-4 plots all possible shares of value at different levels of marketing risk and risk-adjusted differentials for a maximum earnings market share equal to 40%. This is very close to maximum earnings market share predicted above for *Amazon*.

As this surface map in Chart 9-4 shows, when RAD equals zero, share of value equals share of revenue over all levels of enterprise marketing risk. At the lowest level of risk (0.5), share of value ranges from 36% to 44%. At the highest level of enterprise marketing risk (9.5), share of value ranges from 0% to 100%. For unit changes in risk-adjusted differentials, share of value increases (decreases) by the level of risk. For example, when risk is 5.0, share of value ranges—by increments of 5—from 0% to 80% for unit changes in risk-adjusted differentials.

What we don't know (and this is critical) is the company's **future** risk-adjusted differential. In other words, how will **RAD** change as investors become aware that a company is maximizing earnings?

In this example, what will *Amazon's* risk-adjusted differential be if it maximized earnings? We don't have an equation for that. And there are too few observations to estimate a regression.[5] Faced with limited information, we can do two things. First, we can estimate likely outcomes from the historical data. Second, we can hypothesize the implications of these likely outcomes.

I've developed two ways to estimate future risk-adjusted differentials: confidence intervals and free-hand directional vectors.

Confidence-Interval Estimates

Recall that the standard deviation in a company's risk-adjusted differentials is exactly 1.0. This is true of all firms in any industry over any time period. This property makes it easy to set confidence intervals around any risk-adjusted differential, given its expected value. The most recent **RAD** is probably the best predictor of the future. Using this assumption, Chart 9-5 shows a 98% confidence-interval (±2 sigma) estimate of *Amazon's* first-quarter 2004 **RAD** of −3.5. In the worst case (minus two sigma), *AMZN's* risk-adjusted differential is −5.5. In the best case (plus two sigma), the company's **RAD** is −1.5.

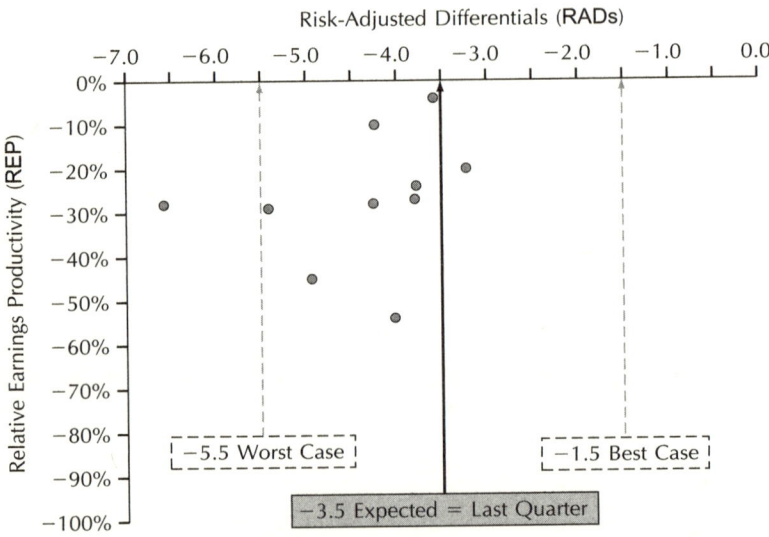

Chart 9-5 *AMZN* Confidence-Interval Estimates

The vertical axis in Chart 9-5 is *AMZN's* relative earnings productivity (REP). The horizontal axis is its risk-adjusted differentials (RAD). *AMZN's* REP ranged from −54% (its worst performance) to −4% (its best performance). Its RAD ranged from a high of −3.2 to a low of −6.6. Notice that all of the lines in Chart 9-5 terminate at zero. That's because the best management can do is to maximize earnings after enterprise marketing expenses. As a result, if management had maximized earnings, the difference between *Amazon's* actual and maximum earnings would have been zero on March 31, 2005.

There is a problem with confidence-interval estimates of RAD. This method ignores information about **trends** in risk-adjusted differentials and relative earnings productivity. The historical points in Chart 9-5 appear to be shifting in a bottom-to-top and left-to-right direction. To use a geographic metaphor, the RAD-REP coordinates are shifting in a **northeast** direction.

Freehand Directional Vectors

The vectors in Chart 9-6 are **freehand** lines fitted to the *Amazon* data. But they are not subjective. The direction is clear from the dated points in this chart. The upper-left-hand boundary of the envelope is created with lines that fall exactly along this outside edge. Points projected on the upper side of the envelope are defined entirely by three RAD-REP coordinates: −28%, −10%, and −4%, corresponding with December, 2001, December 2003, and March 2004 respectively. This line cannot be moved without violating

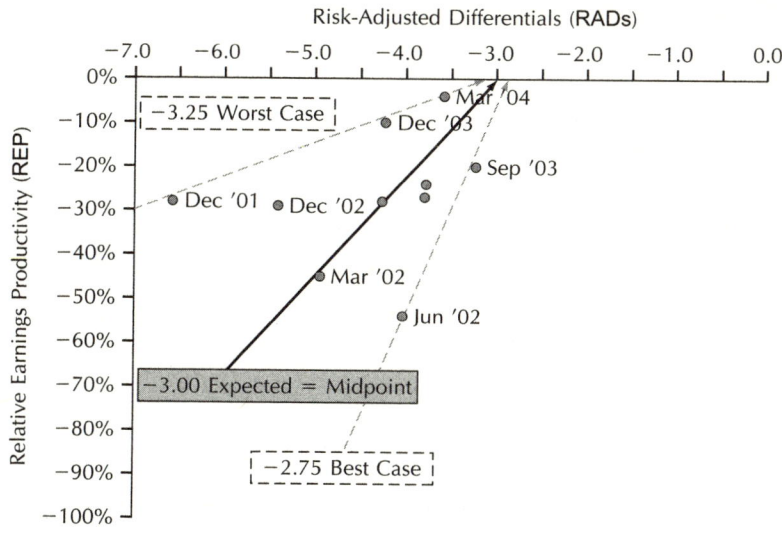

Chart 9-6   *Amazon* Freehand Directional Vectors

one of these three conditions: the **upper boundary** of this envelope demonstrates a **northeast drift.** This vector points to a worst-case RAD of −3.25.

Similarly, the points projected on the lower right-hand side of the envelope are defined by the coordinates −54% and −20%, corresponding with June, 2002 and September, 2003. This vector points to the best-case RAD of −2.75. The expected value (−3.00) is the midpoint between these best- and worst-case projections. Even if *Amazon* management actually were to maximize earnings, past performance has cast a long shadow over the near-term earnings expectations of investors.

 Strategic Group Market Value

Group market value can be forecast with a number of different functions. Again, we were limited to ten observations in forecasting future market value. So the best way to proceed is to make three different forecasts: a best-case, expected, and worst-case forecast using appropriate functions. Selection of the "appropriate functions" is a judgment call. In the example illustrated by Chart 9-7, an exponential, linear, and log function were selected.

The exponential function has a high R^2 (0.84). But this function forecasts an increase in market value from $93 billion to $166 billion in four quarters. This forecast is neither reasonable nor likely in normal times.

The linear function has the highest R^2 (0.86). This function forecasts an increase in strategic group market value from $93 billion to about $122 billion. This is reasonable, and it falls between the exponential and log function forecasts.

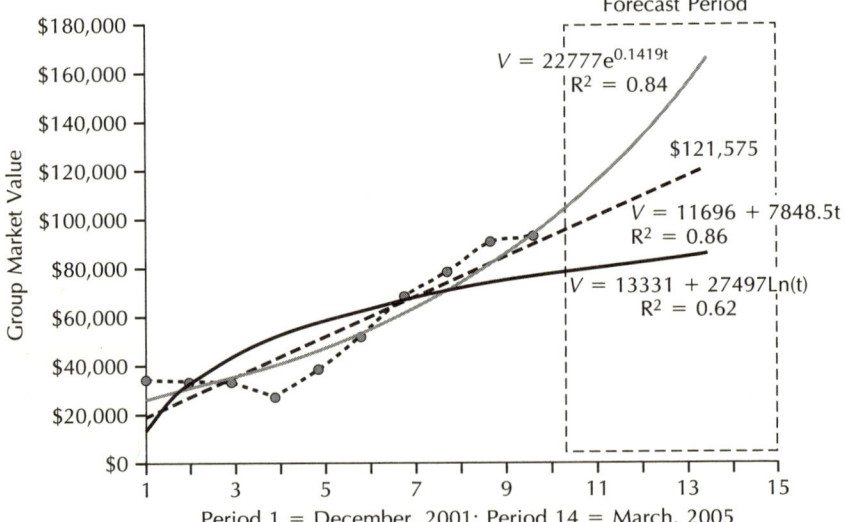

Chart 9-7 Online Retailer Group Market Value

The R^2 of the log function is the lowest of the three (0.62). This equation yields an estimated group market value of $86 billion, which represents a significant decrease. All things considered, we would have to go with the linear forecast of $121,575 million.

Amazon's Competitive Valuation

Using the relationship $SOV = RAD \times RISK + S\hat{O}R$, we can value *Amazon* at different levels of **RAD**. The results appear in Table 9-3.

Amazon's enterprise marketing risk is held constant at its ten-quarter historical estimate (7.84). The company's risk-adjusted differentials are varied in steps from a low of −4.0 through a high of +0.0 on the assumption that these values will bracket actual performance.

Which share of value between these end points is most likely to occur? The theory combined with the projections in Chart 9-6 gives us some clues. First, investors will bid up the company's stock price if they believe management is maximizing earnings. Second, as the difference between actual and maximum earnings approaches zero, share of value will reach higher levels.

Table 9-3 displays, for the risk-adjusted differentials projected with freehand vectors in Chart 9-6, *Amazon's* price per share if (1) group market value increased to $121,575 million, (2) group sales revenues were $4,594 million, (3) management achieved maximum earnings market share at 40.67%, and (4) enterprise marketing risk was unchanged at 7.84.

If investors believed *Amazon* would achieve maximum earnings market share at 40.67%, in the best case they would have bid up its share price 32% from $43.28 in the first quarter of 2004 to $57.33, corresponding with an increase in share of market value to 19.09%. This represents an increase of twenty-five basis points over its share of value in the first quarter of 2004. At this point, *AMZN's* shareholder value would have been $23,214 million.[6]

Table 9-3 *Amazon's* Theoretical Valuations First Quarter 2005

Share of Market Value	Risk-Adjusted Differential	Enterprise Marketing Risk	Maximum Earnings Share	Forecast Shareholder Value	Forecast Share Price	
9.29	−4.0	7.84	40.67	$11,293	$ 27.89	
15.17	−3.25	7.84	40.67	$18,446	$ 45.56	Worst
17.13	−3.00	7.84	40.67	$20,830	$ 51.45	Expected
19.09	−2.75	7.84	40.67	$23,214	$ 57.33	Best
24.98	−2.0	7.84	40.67	$30,367	$ 75.00	
32.82	−1.0	7.84	40.67	$39,904	$ 98.55	
40.67	0.0	7.84	40.67	$49,441	$122.11	

Alternatively, if investors had believed the worst case, they would have bid *Amazon's* price down to $45.56 a share, and its market value would have been $18,446 million.

If investors believed *Amazon* actually would maximize earnings into the indefinite future, they would have bid its price up accordingly. But they didn't. And even if they believed management was committed to maximizing earnings, the theory says *AMZN's* expected shareholder value would be $20,830 million.

The Price of Market Leadership

On August 5, 2005, *AMZN's* share price closed at $45.27. With 411.9 million shares of common stock outstanding on that day, its market cap was $18,647 million. Strategic group market value was $124,409 million. *Amazon's* risk-adjusted differential was −3.3 points. And its share of revenues had slipped to 40.53 without maximizing earnings. The worst case was realized.

How much longer will shareholders allow the company to pay the price of market leadership with their money? The prognosis is not favorable. *Amazon's* share of market value slipped to 14.7% on that day, down from 24.75% in August, 2004. On January 27, 2006 as I finalized the proofs for this chapter *AMZN* closed at $45.22. With 414.47 million shares outstanding its market cap was $18.74 billion. The value of the online retail group had increased $138.39 billion. On that day Amazon created only 13.5% of the group's value.

Taking Stock

At this point, it's a good idea to take stock of where we are. First, our purpose is to document the way that prudent management of enterprise marketing expense can create shareholder value. A predicted stock price is the result of this exercise, rather than its purpose.

Second, competitive stock valuation boils down to the relationship between risk-adjusted differentials and relative earnings productivity. Given the limited number of observations, two methods are available for identifying the underlying relationship between these enterprise marketing metrics.

As you've seen, the first is to set confidence-interval estimates around the last observed **RAD**. This method is both objective and easy to apply, because the standard deviation in value-sales differentials for any company is exactly one. A 98% confidence interval around the last observed **RAD** is ±2 standard deviations.

The other method is to capture any additional information apparent in the data by creating freehand directional vectors in order to define an envelope of company performance. While the word "freehand" suggests that this is a subjective method, it is only a little less precise than the confidence-interval (CI) method. More important, it allows one to capture and use the additional information available in the data.

One of these methods will always be appropriate for defining the relationship between risk-adjusted differentials and relative earnings productivity for a company. The question is which method to use?

Risk-Adjusted Differentials and Relative Earnings Productivity

Chart 9-8 illustrates the underlying patterns that might be observed empirically—and the appropriate estimation method for each pattern.

Theoretically, there are six possible underlying patterns. These are labeled in bold initials in Chart 9-8. These labels represent each of the following patterns and estimation methods:

1. Topped-Out (**TO**): increasing RADs and maximum REP > Confidence Interval (CI) estimates.
2. Northwest (**NW**): declining RADs and increasing REP > Freehand Vectors (FV) estimates.
3. Northeast (**NE**): increasing RADs and increasing REP > FV estimates.
4. Southwest (**SW**): decreasing RADs and decreasing REP > FV estimates.

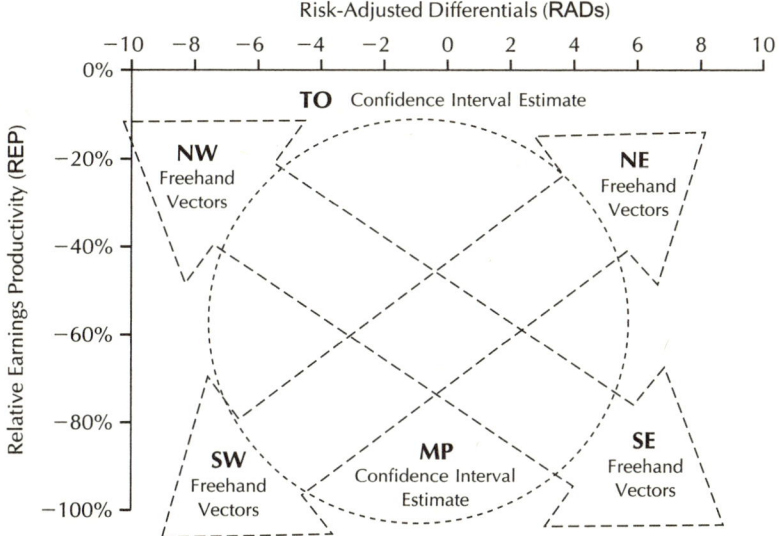

Chart 9-8 Observed Patterns and Estimation Methods

5. Southeast (**SE**): increasing **RADs** and decreasing **REP** > FV estimates.
6. Martingale Process (**MP**): short trends and abrupt shifts > CI estimates.

Let's review each one of these patterns with an empirical example drawn from the previous chapters and a short discussion of the management implications of each one.

Novartis's Topped-Out Performance

Over time, a company that continuously maximizes earnings should experience steadily increasing stock price. This is exactly what's happened to *Novartis* in recent years. Chart 9-9 illustrates the situation.

Chart 9-9 shows a scatter diagram of the company's risk-adjusted differentials and its relative earnings productivity. We take the most recent risk-adjusted differential as the expected future value of **RAD**. Recall the standard deviation in **RAD** is one. We then define a 98% confidence interval by two standard deviations below (as the worst-case) and two above (as the best-case) future value of **RAD**.

Applying the competitive valuation model in order to forecast the company's stock price in 2007 yields Table 9-4, the table of theoretical valuations.

On October 26, 2005 *Novartis* ADR shares closed at $53.28. The future value of the most likely share price in 2007 is $111.49. Discounted at an assumed WACC of 5%, the present value of this share price is $91.72. The worst-case future price is $89.11. The best-case future price is $133.87.

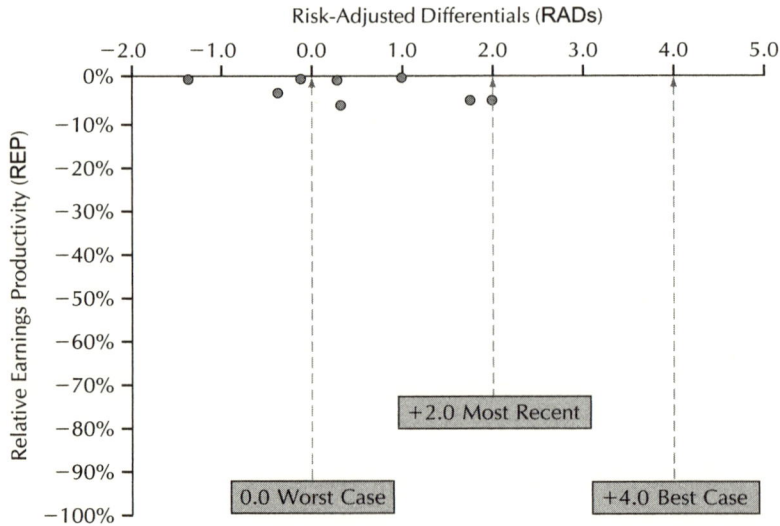

Chart 9-9 *Novartis's* RADs and REP

Table 9-4 *Novartis'* Theoretical Valuation 2007

Share of Market Value	Risk-Adjusted Differential	Enterprise Marketing Risk	Maximum Earnings Share	Shareholder Value	Forecast Share Price*	PV of Share Price*	CASE
33.55	0.0	4.21	33.55	$219,909	$ 89.11	$ 73.31	Worst
37.77	1.0	4.21	33.55	$247,523	$100.30	$ 82.52	
41.98	2.0	4.21	33.55	$275,136	$111.49	$ 91.72	Most Likely
46.19	3.0	4.21	33.55	$302,750	$122.68	$100.93	
50.41	4.0	4.21	33.55	$330,364	$133.87	$110.14	Best

*Assuming *Novartis's* shares outstanding remain at 4,268 thousand and the WACC = 0.05.

What will *Novartis* look like if management continues to maximize earnings over the ensuing four years? Table 9-5 provides a snapshot of the company's actual 2003 and expected 2007 performance in this strategic group.

Notice the "top line" in this table is not company sales. It is strategic group revenues. Company sales are a function of maximum earnings market share. Strategic group revenues were forecast to grow by 22% to $132.2 billion. The company's maximum earnings market share of group revenues will be 33.55%. That's an increase of 46% over its actual share of revenues in 2003.[8] This will generate revenues of $42.6 billion, an increase of 71%. The resulting production efficiencies will drive cost of goods sold down 23% and increase gross margins from the current 81% to 92% of revenues.

The combined impact of growth in group revenues, market share, sales, and the decline in cost of goods sold is a 94% increase in gross profits. Driving the increase in market share to maximum earnings is a doubling of enterprise marketing resources. As a result, earnings are forecast to increase

Table 9-5 *Novartis's* Actual and Maximum Earnings

Novartis ADR (Millions of USD)	Actual 2003	Expected 2007	Change '03 to '07
Strategic Group Revenues	$107,974	$132,246	22%
NVS Market Share	23.03%	33.55%	46%
NVS Sales Revenues	$ 24,864	$ 42,599	71%
NVS COGS	$ 4,758	$ 3,673	−23%
Gross Profits	$ 20,106	$ 38,926	94%
Enterprise Marketing Expenses	$ 13,081	$ 27,044	107%
Maximum Earnings	$ 7,025	$ 13,657	94%
Earnings to Revenues	28.25%	32.06%	13%
Enterprise Marketing Expenses to Revenue	52.61%	63.48%	21%
Stock Price	$ 45.89	$ 111.49	143%

94%. The ratio of earnings to revenues increases 13%, while the ratio of enterprise marketing expenses to revenues increase 21%. The result is an enterprise marketing return of 143%—measured by a predicted increase in stock price from $45.89 to $111.49.

Can managers "fine-tune" spending on enterprise marketing resources to maximize earnings precisely over the long term? *Novartis* management came remarkably close. Out of some 200 different company applications in over 30 industries, only a handful of companies delivered such consistently high relative earnings productivity.

Since this appears to be a rare case, what is management to do if the company falls far short of maximizing earnings?

Hewlett-Packard's Northwest Drift

A northwest drift in the data identifies improving levels of earnings productivity accompanied by deterioration in stock price. This is probably a **public- and investor-relations problem.** Either the company has been the subject of bad press for some time, or investors are not aware of the improvement in relative earnings productivity, or they don't believe the improvement can be sustained. Or all three of these forces may be simultaneously at work. Freehand directional vectors can be applied to this pattern.

Recall from Chapter 6 the high levels of relative earnings productivity under Carly Fiorina's management of *Hewlett-Packard*. Removing the disastrous second quarter of 2002 immediately following the merger with *Compaq*, the resulting **RAD-REP** chart appears in Chart 9-10.

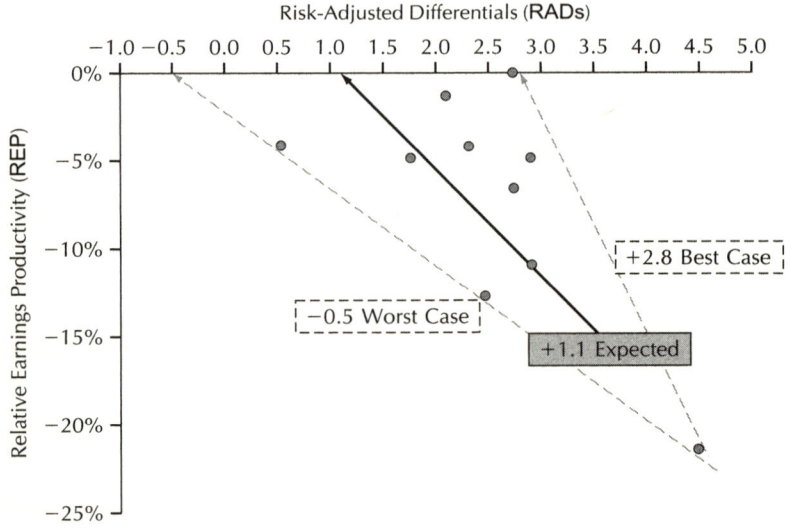

Chart 9-10 *HPQ's* Northwest Drift

This is a classic northwest drift. Despite high and improving levels in earnings productivity, investors continued to punish HPQ's stock relative to its market power. After the −21.5% REP in the second quarter following the merger, the company's earnings continued to improve.

Considering the bad press Ms. Fiorina continued to receive, and investors' failure to reward the company's performance under her leadership, this appears to be case of bad PR—coupled with poor investor relations.

Yahoo's Northeast Drift

A northeast drift in the data identifies improvements in both relative earnings productivity and stock price. This suggests investors are both aware of improvements in REP and believe these improvements can be sustained. Freehand directional vectors can be applied successively to this pattern.

The drift in *Yahoo's* risk-adjusted differentials and relative earnings productivity shown in Chart 9-11 is similar to *Amazon's*.

Like *Amazon*, the best case points to increasing risk-adjusted differentials. But unlike *Amazon*, *Yahoo's* differentials are positive. The expected case (the last observed RAD) was +3.75. In addition, relative earnings continued to improve significantly from −27% to −1% in the best case. Even the worst case points to a risk-adjusted differential of +2.75.

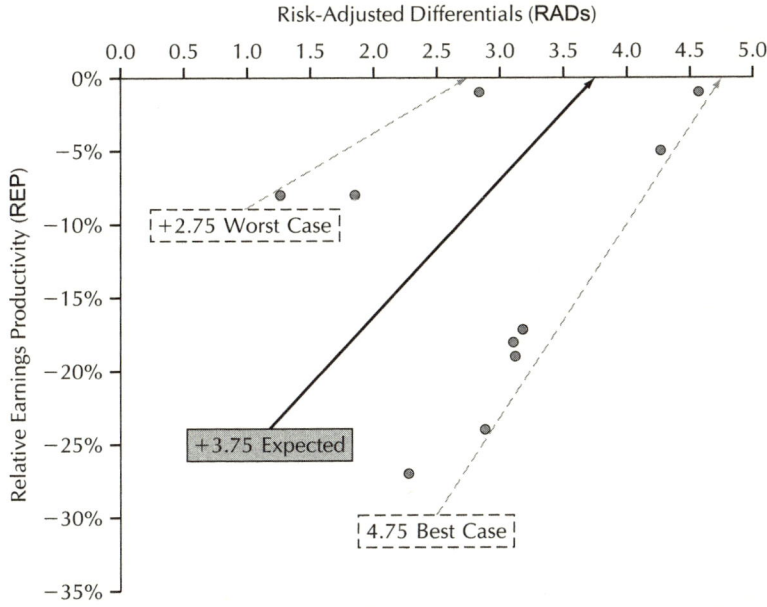

Chart 9-11 *Yahoo's* Northeast Drift

Investors historically have awarded *Yahoo* with a significant value premium over and above its market power. Indications are they will continue to do so, unless *Yahoo* falls victim to the ongoing assault seen in *Google*'s elevated and increasingly aggressive spending on enterprise marketing resources.

Wal*Mart's Southwest Drift

A southwest drift in the data identifies deteriorating **REP** and a falling stock price. Investors are aware of the fall in earnings productivity and are bidding down the company's stock price. Investors appear to believe the fundamentals are so out of balance that management cannot maximize earnings—at least in the short term. Directional vectors also are appropriate when this pattern is observed.

Chart 9-12 shows the data for *Wal*Mart* covering the period from the fourth of quarter 2001 through the first quarter of 2004. As relative earnings productivity deteriorated from December, 2001 through March, 2004, investors bid down the company's stock price. Its risk-adjusted differentials reflect the reality of these actions.

Should management be concerned about this pattern? Yes. Will *Wal*Mart's* risk-adjusted differentials continue to shift to the west while its relative earnings productivity drifts south? That depends on what corrective actions management takes.

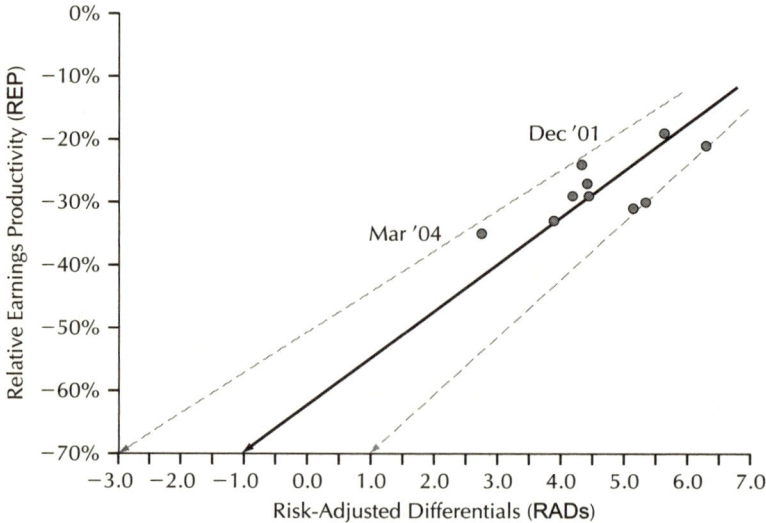

Chart 9-12 *Wal*Mart's* Southwest Drift

Honda's Southeast Drift

A southeast drift in the data is a wake-up call to management. Relative earnings productivity is deteriorating; yet investors are not aware of the trend. Management has time to fix the fundamentals. Freehand vectors are appropriate when this pattern is observed.

Chart 9-13 shows the southeast drift in *Honda Motor Company's* numbers from 1993 through 2002. Why are investors unaware of this trend? Probably for reasons that are the mirror image of their lack of awareness when a northwest drift occurred in the case of *HPQ*. In that case, investors either were unaware that *Hewlett-Packard* was close to maximizing earnings or they didn't believe the company could sustain that performance because it was getting bad press. In the case of *Honda*, either they are unaware that the company is drifting farther and farther away from maximum earnings or they think it's a temporary departure from its previous performance. Either investors aren't reading the tea leaves correctly, or the company is getting great press—or both.

So investors are happy. Should *Honda* management be concerned? Yes. Managers had better take action to correct the slide in relative earnings productivity that began in 1993 and continued through 2002. They may already have done so.

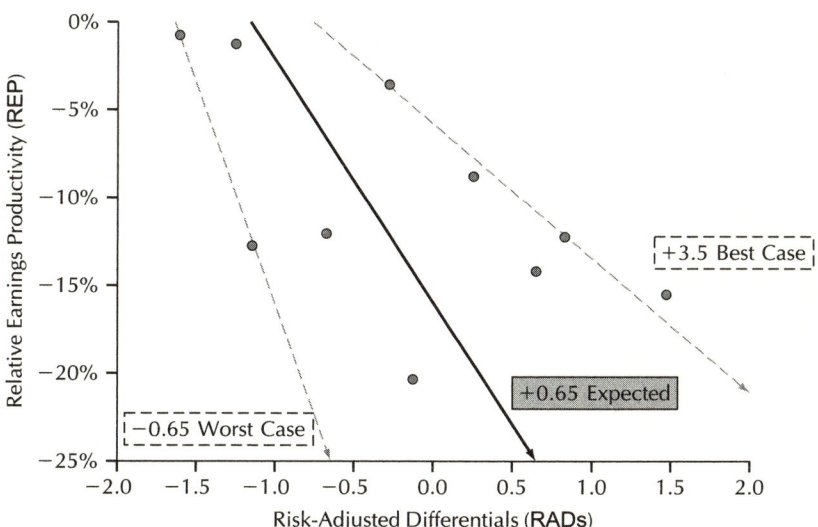

Chart 9-13 *Honda's* Southeast Drift

PriceLine's Martingale

A *Martingale pattern* exists when there are short-lived trends where risk-adjusted differentials and relative earnings productivity move together, but these trends are interrupted by dramatic and unexpected changes. Confidence-interval estimation is appropriate when this pattern is observed.

Chart 9-14 illustrates the case of *PriceLine*. The company's performance can be approximated by a Martingale process. In seven of the ten quarters, the company came very close to maximizing earnings. For example, in March, 2002 the company's **REP** was just −1%. This means that actual earnings were 99% of maximum potential earnings in that quarter. In June, 2002, actual earnings were $9.47 million compared with maximum earnings, which were $9.48 million. Its **REP** was virtually zero. The problems investors had with this pattern are in the fourth quarter of 2001 (when actual earnings were off by 295% of potential) and the first quarter of 2003 (when they were off by more than 900%). Unanticipated negative results like these undermine investor confidence in a company's performance.

A Martingale is similar to a random walk—with one important difference. In a Martingale there are back-to-back periods where the expected relationship is observed. In the case illustrated by Chart 9-14, after

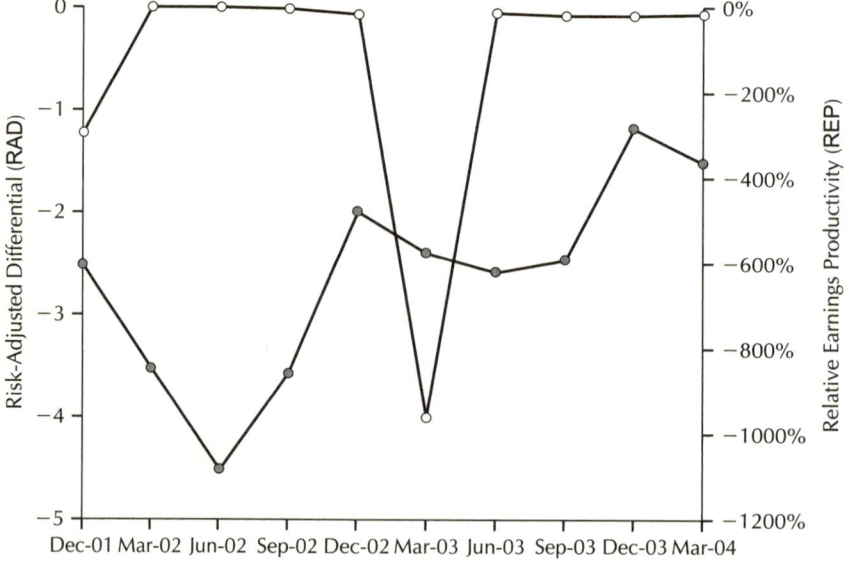

Chart 9-14 *PriceLine's* Martingale

each "crash" in relative earnings productivity, investors regained some confidence and began to bid up *PriceLine's* stock price. You can see this between June and December of 2002 before the second earnings crash in March of 2003. And again from June of 2003 through March of 2004.

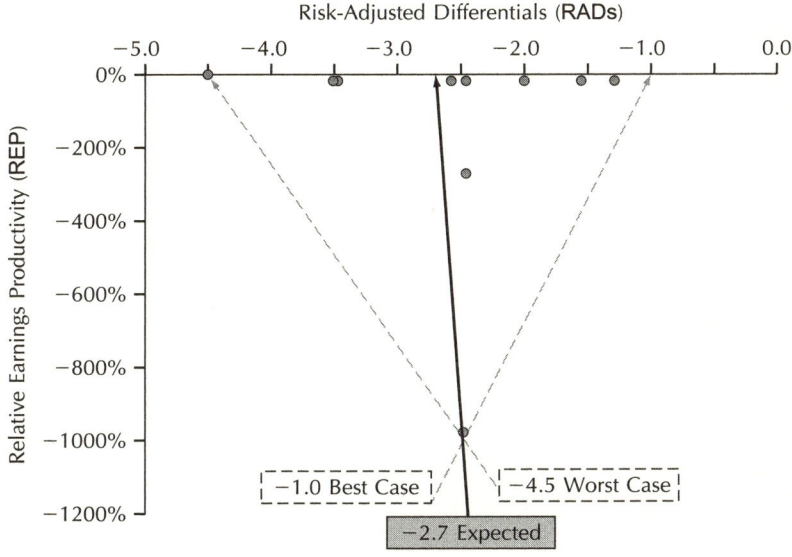

Chart 9-15 *PriceLine* Lacks a Meaningful Performance Envelope

The difficulty of creating directional vectors with a Martingale pattern shows up dramatically in Chart 9-15. The freehand directional vectors in this chart are meaningless. While it's possible to create a performance envelope with these data, it is not meaningful because there are no directional drifts. Eight observations are spread across the risk-adjusted differential axis at nearly zero relative earnings productivity while the other two are off the scale.

In cases like *PriceLine* you should use the confidence-interval estimate of **RAD**. Chart 9-16 shows this method for *PriceLine* in the first quarter of 2004. Management should be very concerned with a Martingale pattern. This pattern is more common than you might think. In fact, in a study of the profit-maximizing behavior of senior managers in simulated markets, Utsey (1987) found that the Martingale pattern was common.

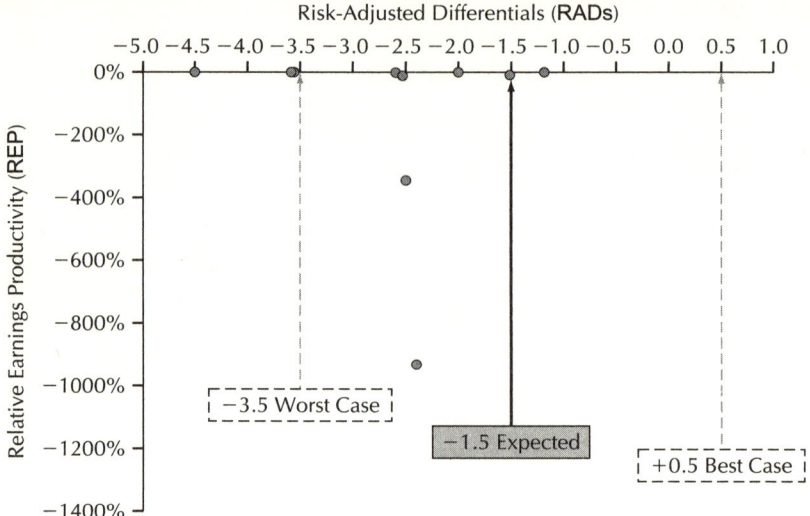

Chart 9-16 *PriceLine* 98% Confidence-Interval Estimate of RAD

A Closer Look at Directional Vectors

The cases requiring freehand directional vectors are more complex than confidence-interval estimates because fitting freehand vectors appears to be subjective. The "freehand" method is data-driven and only a little less precise than confidence-interval estimates, but it does not rely on a "statistical analysis." Freehand vectors do, however, make efficient use of the limited information. A closer look at the case of *Amazon* will make this point.

There was a clear shift to the northeast that corresponded with *AMZN's* improving relative earnings productivity from −45% in the first quarter of 2002 (March '02) to −4% in the first quarter of 2004 (March '04). Over the same time period, *Amazon's* risk-adjusted differentials also improved from −4.94 in March, 2002 to −3.59 in March, 2004.

Recall that in Chart 9-6 *AMZN's* worst-case freehand vector fit snugly against the three upper-left-hand points that defined the edge of the envelope. The same was true of the best-case freehand vector, but it fit tightly to the two points on the lower-right-hand edge of the envelope. These vectors were freehand, but each one was precisely defined by the performance envelope and could not logically be placed in any other position given the information contained in the ten observations. There were no degrees of freedom in these freehand vectors. The +0.26 correlation coefficient between **RADs** and **REPs** in this example is not significant because the sample is so small, but the directional drift was significant.

Now consider the misplaced directional vectors in Chart 9-17. The worst-case vector in this example points toward −6.5, but it is not anchored on the **RAD** dimension because it is not defined by two or more points on the envelope. The best-case vector is anchored to −4% and −20% on the envelope. But it fails to capture the directional drift that is better defined by the relative earnings productivity values of −20% in June of 2003 and −54% in September of 2002.

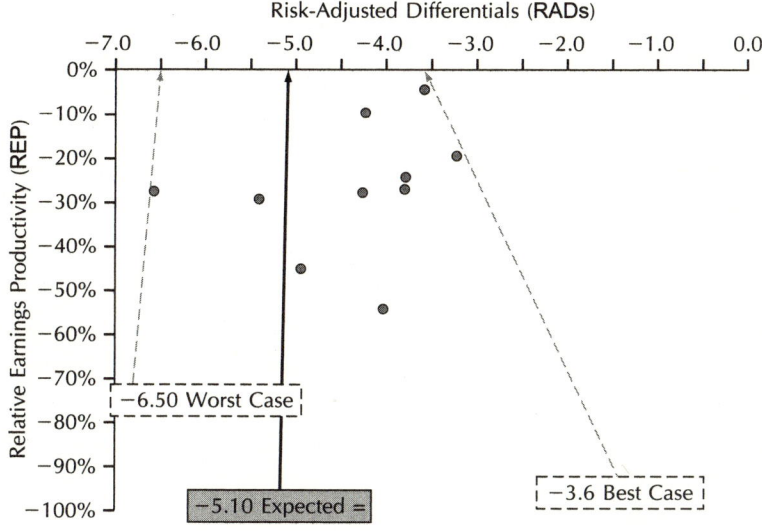

Chart 9-17 *Amazon's* Misplaced Freehand Vectors

When the freehand vectors are misplaced, the expected case scenario also will also be misplaced. If you look closely at what the data are saying, freehand directional vectors can provide useful information about the relationship between risk-adjusted differentials and relative earnings productivity.

Longer-Term Shareholder Value

You probably noticed that the Novartis and Honda examples above were based on annual data. Predicting longer-term shareholder value requires several changes in the analysis. The key changes are: use of annual data, a simplified forecasting methodology, and present value discounting of stock price.

Annual Data

The use of annual data simplifies the problem. It also expands the set of companies available for analysis. The problem is simplified because seasonal effects are eliminated. The set of companies is expanded because most foreign companies that trade as ADRs on U.S. stock exchanges only report annual financial accounting data. This is why *Novartis* and *Honda* were based on annual data. A small, but important, complication is also introduced. COMPUSTAT uses different variable numbers for annual and quarterly data.

Forecasting Methodology

Forecasting is simplified with annual data because we can use the concept of compound annual growth rate (CAGR) in place of regression analysis on the small samples typically available for the analysis of maximum earnings market share. CAGR rates are equivalent to rate of return and so they are widely used in financial reporting and analysis. CAGR is simply the nth root of a ratio of the future value and current value of a series.[8]

Present Value Discounting

A *Bottom Line Marketing* report on *Whole Foods'* performance in a strategic group including *Albertson's, Kroger,* and *Safeway* tracked the company's historical performance from 1995 through 2004 (Gehring et al. 2004). It also predicted the company's stock price in 2009 if management were to maximize earnings.

Chart 9-18 shows *Whole Foods* maximum earnings market share based on annual data. The scenario behind these estimates is a CAGR on three inputs: group revenues of 0.1%; *WFMI* gross margins of 0.08%; and competitors' enterprise marketing resources of 3.1%. Based on this scenario, *WFMI* should extend its market share from 2.84% (with sales of $3,865 million) to 8.69% (with sales of $17,184 million) at the end of 2009. This yields a compound annual growth in sales revenues of 35%. It was estimated that the company would need to build/acquire about 350 new outlets to achieve this target share of market—assuming $38 million annual sales per new store. The compound annual rate of growth in new stores would be 26%.

In the case of *Whole Foods Market, Inc.,* maximum earnings market share is a long-term target. We cannot predict, with MEMS analysis, the path toward this target or the substantial increases in fixed and working capital required to reach it. Neither can we assess the feasibility of recruiting and training the people necessary to reach the target. These issues are the domains of finance and

Maximum Earnings Market Share

[Chart showing market share rising from ~3% at December 31, 2004 to ~8.5% in 2009]

Chart 9-18 *Whole Foods* Maximum Earnings Market Share

human resource management. What this analysis can do is provide management with an enterprise marketing road map for long term organic growth.

Even so, we can assume *WFMI's* basic business model will not change, the number of common shares outstanding will remain at about 62.4 million (or adjustments will be made for stock splits), and the company's weighted average cost of capital will remain at 9%. If these assumptions hold, the present value of *Whole Foods'* stock price at the close of business in 2009 would be around $270. That is, if management maximized earnings after the cost of enterprise marketing expenses and built/acquired stores such that its economic value added is also maximized. *WFMI* was well on its way toward this goal when its stock closed at $150.87 on December 27, 2005. **The next day the company's stock was split two for one.**

Value Added

Remember the story of Linda Tan from Chapter 1? She's the MBA from the University of Hong Kong who, as a financial news reporter, was assigned the job of assessing which company created or destroyed value for investors. You will recall that the "value creators" she used were sales revenues, net income, earnings per share, return on capital, return on assets, market value of equity, share price, price-earnings ratio, financial risk (beta), and debt-to-equity ratio.

Recall too that the classic constant growth model of firm valuation forecasts current market price per share as a function of the retention rate, earnings per share before interest and taxes, the leverage-free cost of capital, the interest rate, the firm's debt-equity ratio, and the rate of return on common equity investment.

Rappaport's more recent, managerially oriented valuation model took us right up to the point of building the effects of competitive advantage into the valuation process. The value-sales principle, the rule of maximum earnings, and competitive stock valuation formally incorporate the impact of competitive advantage. At this point, enterprise marketing and corporate finance can become partners in creating shareholder value.

Chief marketer officers can make a great contribution to this partnership by embracing the financial statistics that already are provided by the company to the SEC and the financial community—and by relating such financial measures to the capability-building and brand-building activities that enterprise marketing brings to the corporate table.

This book has focused on an effort to do exactly that; in other words,

> ... to effectively utilize key numbers from the corporation's financial statements, such as the heretofore cryptic SG&A (Sales, General, and Administrative) expense item, to determine when and how valuable intangible assets are being built via enterprise marketing management. In this new view of the future, the mission of enterprise marketing is to visualize alternative paths to maximum shareholder wealth. This can be accomplished only by filling the empty spaces between finance and marketing with knowledge about company fortunes. (Cook, Moult, and Spaeth 2005, 39)

Company fortunes depend on the interactions between the disciplines of enterprise marketing and corporate finance. Earnings cannot be maximized by financial management alone. Since corporate finance operates at the enterprise level, so must marketing—if the two disciplines are to become partners. The link is that selling, general, and administrative expenses capture all the costs of the people involved in creating and managing the enterprise marketing resources that create intangible shareholder value. Forging this link probably requires the creation of a new C-level executive position: the Chief Enterprise Marketing Officer (CEMO).

References

Cook, V. J., W. Moult, and J. Spaeth. 2005. "When Marketing Science Meets Corporate Finance." The annual meeting of the *Institute for Operations Research and Management Science,* San Francisco, California, November 16, 2005; in the session on "Frontiers in Enterprise Marketing."

Gehring, W., A. Nakamura, A. Oeing, and L. Z. Rees. 2004. "Whole Foods Market" *Bottom Line Marketing Reports* 2, No. 4, December: Master of Business Administration Program, Tulane University.

Rappaport, A. 1998. *Creating Shareholder Value: A Guide for Managers and Investors.* New York: The Free Press.

Smit, S., C. M. Thompson, and S. P. Viguerie. 2005. "The Do-Or-Die Struggle for Growth." *The McKinsey Quarterly* 3.

Utsey, M. F. 1987. "Profit Potential as a Martingale Process." *Journal of Business Research* 15 (December): 531–544.

End Notes

[1] Stock prices five years into the future are discounted to their present value using the company's weighted average cost of capital.

[2] Of course, if the weighted average cost of capital differs among competitors, market shares will be modified somewhat by these differences.

[3] Severe data limitations like these are common and limit the opportunities for using more sophisticated forecasting models.

[4] Expanded, this formula is:

$$\rho_{ijt} = \frac{\left(v_{ijt} / \sum_{i=1}^{n} v_{ijt}\right) \times 100 - \left(r_{ijt} / \sum_{i=1}^{n} r_{ijt}\right) \times 100}{\sigma(\delta_{ij})}$$

[5] Having a limited number of observations is typical in the analysis of strategic groups because of the dynamic nature of membership.

[6] Given that the number of *AMZN* shares outstanding remained at 404.894 million.

[7] This forecast increase in market share and sales revenues will likely require a change in plant and equipment values—as well as other balance sheet values that are outside the scope of this competitive valuation.

[8] CAGR is the nth root of future value (FV) divided by the (PV). In Excel, this is coded as CAGR = (FV/PV)^(1/n) − 1, where n represents the number of years. For a complete explanation, see http://www.moneychimp.com/articles/finworks/fmpresval.htm.

Appendix A

Definitions and Derivations[1]

r_i Company *sales revenue* from the income statement or calculated as $r_i = \dot{m}_i \times R_j$ where R_j is strategic group revenues.

o_i Company *cost of goods* sold from the income statement.

$\dot{g}_i$ Company *Gross margin* $\dot{g}_i = t_i/r_i$ where $0 \leq \dot{g}_i \leq 1$.

s_i *Selling, general, and administrative expenses* from the company income statement are enterprise marketing resources.

R_j *Total revenue* in strategic group j for a given time period calculated from the income statements of n companies as $R_j = \sum_{i=1}^{n} r_i$.

m_i Company *share of revenue* expressed as an integer $m_i = (r_i/R_j) \times 100$ where $0 \leq m_i \leq 100$.

$\dot{m}_i$ Company *share of revenue* expressed as a proportion $\dot{m}_i = r_i/R_j$ where $0 \leq \dot{m}_i \leq 1$.

t_i Company *total gross profits* calculated from the income statement as $t_i = r_i - o_i$; or from group revenue and company revenue share as $t_i = \dot{m}_i \times R_j \times \dot{g}_i$.

$\dot{p}_i$ Company *incremental gross profit* per revenue **share** point $\dot{p}_i = (R_j \times \dot{g}_i)/100$.

$\ddot{p}_i$ Company *incremental gross profit* per revenue **basis** point $\ddot{p}_i = (R_j \times \dot{g}_i)/10000$.

f_i Company *enterprise marketing expenses* from the income statement.

f *Enterprise marketing expenses* of n competitors from their income statements calculated as $f = \sum_{l=1}^{n} f_l$ where $i \neq l$.

y_i Company *theoretical enterprise marketing expenses* required to achieve a target share m of revenues is $y_i = (m_i/(100 - m_i)) \times f$; f not discounted for enterprise marketing efficiency. This expression may be factored to simplify: $y_i = \dfrac{f_i \times m_i}{(100 - m_i)}$

x_i Company *marketing efficiency ratio* $x_i = s_i/y_i$.

---

[1] Note: the subscript i is for a company, subscript j is for a strategic group of which the company is a member, subscript l identifies competing companies, and implicit time subscripts apply to any quarterly or annual period.

Appendix A • Definitions and Derivations

$\dot{k}_i$ Company cost of 1st revenue **share** point $\dot{k}_i = (f \times x_i)/100$

$\ddot{k}_i$ Company cost of 1st revenue **basis** point; $k_i = (f \times x_i)/100$

$\dot{c}_i$ Company incremental cost per revenue **share** point $\dot{c}_i = \dfrac{100 \times f \times x_i}{(100 - m_i)^2}$.

$\ddot{c}_i$ Company incremental cost per revenue **basis** point $\ddot{c}_i = \dfrac{f \times x_i}{(100 - m_i)^2}$.

a_i Company earnings after enterprise marketing expenses calculated from the income statement as $a = t - s$.

$\hat{m}_i$ Company maximum earnings market share $\hat{m}_i = 1 - \sqrt{\dfrac{\dot{k}_i}{\dot{p}_i}}$ (see derivation below).

v_i Company shareholder value is $v_i = u_i \times q_i$; where u = price per share and q = number of common shares issued minus number of treasury shares held (i.e. common shares outstanding).

V_j Total shareholder value of a strategic group j for a given time period is calculated for n companies as $V_j = \sum_{i=1}^{n} v_i$.

δ_{ij} The competitive value-sales differential (δ_{ij}) for company i in strategic group j populated by n firms in any given period is:

$$\delta_{ij} = (v_i/V_j - r_i/R_j) \times 100.$$

ρ_{ijt} Risk-adjusted VS differential is calculated by dividing observed values of δ_{ij} by their standard deviation over time: $\rho_{ijt} = \delta_{ijt}/\sigma(\delta_{ij})$. Also referred to as **RAD**.

b_i Company debt to total capital from the balance sheet.

e_i Company total return to shareholders is stock price appreciation plus dividends.

$\hat{t}_i$ Company total gross profits at maximum earnings market share (see derivation below).

$\hat{s}_i$ Company enterprise marketing expenses at maximum earnings market share.

$\hat{a}_i$ Company's maximum earnings after enterprise marketing expenses calculated as $\hat{a} = \hat{t} - \hat{s}$.

To derive maximum earnings market share, start with a company's earnings after enterprise marketing expenses (for simplicity all subscripts are implicit):

1. $a = t - s$, where a is EBITDA, t is gross profits, and s is SG&A (enterprise marketing) expenses.

   Express earnings after enterprise marketing expenses as a function of market share:

2. $a = \dot{g} \times R \times \dot{m} - \dfrac{f \times x \times \dot{m}}{1 - \dot{m}}$, where $\dot{g}$ is percent gross margin, R is strategic group revenues, $\dot{m}$ is percent share of revenues, f is

competitors' enterprise marketing expenses and x is the enterprise marketing efficiency ratio (x). The second term on the right-hand side (enterprise marketing expenses as a function of market share) is derived by solving for s in the expression $x = s/y$ and inserting the factored definition of y.

Then the rate of change in earnings is the first derivative of the earnings function wrt $\dot{m}$:

3. $a' = \dfrac{\dot{g} \times R \times (1 - \dot{m})^2 - f \times x}{(1 - \dot{m})^2}$

Maximum EBITDA occurs when the marginal earnings after enterprise marketing expenses is zero:

4. $0 = \dot{g} \times R - \dfrac{f \times x}{(1 - \hat{m})^2}$

Solving for maximum earnings market share $\hat{m}$ gives:

5. $\hat{m} = 1 - \sqrt{\dfrac{f \times x}{\dot{g} \times R}}$

Expressing equation 5 in terms of company earnings per share point $\dot{p}$ and cost of the first share point $\dot{k}$ gives:

6. $\hat{m} = 1 - \sqrt{\dfrac{\dot{k}}{\dot{p}}}$

QED.

INDEX

A
accounting, and enterprise marketing expenses, 86–87
ADRs, *see* American depository receipts
advertising agencies, 201–204
Agarwal, M. K., 3, 28
aggregation level, 12–13
aggressive competitive response, 128–129
Agres, S., 12, 26
airline industry, 3–5, 30–40, 44–45, 49–50, 109–135
Alberto-Culver, 204–206, 208–209
Albertsons.com, 99, 106
Amazon.com, 165–178, 225–235
American depository receipts (ADRs), 90–93
Amgen, 75, 82
annual data, use of, 246
AT&T Bell Labs, 188
automobile industry, 79–82, 90–93, 204, 208–209, 241
average Joes, 48
Avon Products, 204–206, 208–209

B
balance sheet, 8–9
Banham, R., 9, 26
Bank One Corp., 95–98
banking industry, 95–98, 215–218
Barker, R., 183, 197
Barney, J. B., 15, 17, 27
Barret, A., 87, 106
Barrett, Colleen C., 117–118
Barwise, P., 111, 133
Bell, D., 143, 163
Bergen, M., 15, 27, 82
Berkshire Hathaway, 206–207
Bezos, J. P., 173–175, 197
Bhojraj, S., 61, 82
big P (profit), 12
biotechnology companies, 40–41, 72–77
Bloomberg.com, 208–209, 219
Bolten, S., 44, 50
book value, 2
bottom-feeders, 48–49, 208–209
Brander, J. A., 214, 219
Brigham, E. F., 214, 219
Bristol-Myers Squibb, 166, 190–195
Britannica.com, 99, 107
Bruton, J. G., 153, 163
Burkenroad Reports, 78
Buzzell, Robert D., 11, 27

C
Calabrese, M., 153, 163
Campbell Soup Company, 206–207

Canion, Rod, 151
capital asset pricing model (CAPM), 9–10
carry-over effects, 197
Chaikin, D., 92, 107
Chan, S. H., 2, 27
chemical industry, 56–61, 210–218
Chonglerttham, S. O., 153, 163
CNA Financial, 208–209
CNET News.com, 137, 163
Coca-Cola, 206–207
Comerica Inc., 95–98
Comerica.com, 107
communications companies, 52–56, 66, 165, 184–188, 215–218
Compaq Computer, 136–164
competition, views of, 52–56
Competitive Advantage Through People (Pfeffer), 84
competitive enterprise matrix, 14–17, 95, 100
competitive stock valuation model
 Amazon.com, 225–235
 relative earnings productivity (REP), 235–244
 risk-adjusted differential (RAD), 235–244
 steps in, 222–223
compound annual growth rate (CAGR), 246
computer companies, *see* personal computer companies
confidence-interval estimates, 230–231, 244–245
constant growth model, of firm valuation, 214
Consumer Discretionary sector, 65
consumer product intangibles, 6
Consumer Staples sector, 65
Cook, V. J., Jr., 14, 27, 46, 50, 133, 197, 201, 219, 248
Cordiant Communications Group, 201–204
core metrics, 12–13
corporate finance, 8–12, 17, 93–95
cost and profit schedules, intersection of, 122
cost of good sold (COGS)
 airline industry, 117–118
 Gannett Co. Inc., 187
 grocery chains, 102–104
 operations management, 16, 93–95
 personal computer companies, 162
 Tribune Co., 187
cost of services sold, 117–118
cost per basis point
 Amazon.com, 176
 Compaq Computer, 150
 Hewlett-Packard, 147
 IBM, 141
 MSI study, 215–218
 review of, 160–161
 Wal★Mart, 180–182
cost per point (CPP), 21–22
Costco, 165, 178–184

253

254　INDEX

CPP, see cost per point
cumulative earnings shortfall, in dual-segment communications companies, 186–187

D

Dahlhoff, D., 3, 28
Daiberl, S., 12, 26
Daimler-Chrysler, 79–82, 90–93
debt to total invested capital ratio, 214
debt-equity ratio, 214
debt-to-capital ratio, 215–218
Dell, 136–164
Dell, Michael, 137
dell.com, 137, 164
desktop market, 136–164
diversified chemical manufacturers, 56–61, 210–218
Dodson, M., 153, 163
Dorfman, R.T., 13, 27
double-entry accounting, 8
dual-segment communications companies, 165, 184–188, see also media companies
Dunn, Pattie, 157
DuPont, 210–214

E

earnings before interest, taxes, depreciation, and amortization (EBITDA)
　computer companies, 145, 147–148, 153–154
　corporate finance and, 93–95
　definition, 17
　dual-segment communications companies, 187
　enterprise marketing expenses and, 124–128
　grocery chains, 104
earnings productivity, and competitive stock valuation model, 228–230
eBay.com, 165–178
EBITDA, see earning before interest, taxes, depreciation, and amortization
efficient factor markets, and airline industry, 119–120
Electrolux, 208–209
energy sector, 64
enterprise marketing, 16–17
enterprise marketing efficiency
　Dell, 155–156
　measurement of, 20–21
　online retailers, 174
　Wal*Mart, 183–184
　wireless phone services, 189
enterprise marketing expenses
　accounting and, 86–87
　airline industry, 120–121
　automobile industry, 90–93
　banking industry, 95–98
　differences in, 97
　earnings before interest, taxes, depreciation, and amortization (EBITDA) and, 124–128
　financial management, 87
　grocery chains, 99–105
　measurement of, 105–106
　seven components of, 89
enterprise marketing performance, in airline industry, 123–124
enterprise marketing risk, adjusting for, 44–45
enterprise market shares, 18–19
executive action, domains of, 16–17, 93–95
Exitexchange.com, 90, 107
expense ratio, 71

F

Fama, E. F., 10, 27, 204, 219–220
Farley, J. U., 111, 133
Farris, P., 14, 27
Fiat S.p.A, 79–82, 90–93
finance, and knowledge gap with marketing, 8–12
financial accounting, 17
Financial Accounting Standards Board (FASB), 86
financial analysts' reports, 78–79
financial management, and enterprise marketing expenses, 87
financials sector, 66
Fiorina, Carleton S., 157
firm valuation, constand growth model of, 214
Fitzsimmons, Joseph J., 183
Fletcher, R., 27, 86, 107
flotation costs, 87
Forbes.com, 31, 50
force principle, 110–119, 121–122, 160–161
Ford Motor Company, 79–82, 90–93
forecasting methodology, 246
Foster, B. P., 27, 86, 107
four Ps, 10, 12
Fox Entertainment Group, 165, 184–188
freehand directional vectors, 231–232, 244–245
French, K. R., 10, 27, 204, 219–220

G

Gale, B.T., 27
Ganesan, S., 11, 28
Gannett Co. Inc., 165, 184–188
Gehring, W., 246, 248
General Motors, 79–82, 90–93, 204, 208–209
Genetech, 76, 82
Gerstner, L.V., Jr., 137–139, 144–145, 164
GICS, see Global Industry Classification Standard
Gillette, 204–206
Gimbel, B., 130, 133
GlaxoSmithKline, 166, 190–195
Global Industry Classification Standard (GICS), 61–62
goodwill, 40
Google.com, 165–178
Gordon, M. J., 214, 219
Greenhouse, S., 165, 197
Grey Global Group, 201–204
grocery chains, 99–105
gross margin, and enterprise marketing, 88

Gruca, T. S., 11, 27
Gupta, S., 12, 27

H
Hall, R., 107
Hansell, S., 167, 197
Hansen, R. S., 87, 107
Harvard Management Update, 107
health care sector, 65–66, 72–77
Hewlett, Bill, 145
Hewlett-Packard, 136–164, 238–239
high resource equivalence (HIRE), 70, 73–74
high-flyers, 47, 206–207
Ho, M., 2, 27
Honda Motor Company, 79–82, 90–93, 241
household appliance manufacturers, 215–218
hub-and-spoke air networks, 114–115
Hudson, R. L., 50, 51

I
IBM, 136–165, 224–225
incremental cost function, 127–128
incremental cost per basis point
 Amazon.com, 176
 computer companies, 141, 147, 150
 review of, 160–161
 Wal*Mart, 181
incremental force, 113
incremental profit function, 126–128
incremental profit per basis point, 141, 147, 150, 176, 181
indirect competitors, 75–76
industrials sector, 5–6, 64
industry groups, in Global Industry Classification Standard, 62
Information Technology sector, 63–71
initial public offering (IPO), and AT&T, 188
intangible assets, 2–12, 84–85
intangible value intuition, 40–44
INTEL Corporation, 213–214
interest expense, in banking industry, 96–97
Internet software and services sub-industry, 63–71
Interpublic Group of Companies, 201–204
IT Services sub-industry, 63–71
Ittner, C. D., 13, 27

J
Jackson, D., 197
Johnson & Johnson, 166, 190–195

K
Keaney, R. L., 143, 163
Kelly, Gary C., 128
Kentor, C., 27
Khan, A. E., 115, 133
King, L., 197
Kirkpatrick, D. D., 53, 83
Klein, T., 4, 16, 28
Klock, M., 51
K-Mart, 165, 178–184

knowledge gap, between marketing and finance, 8–12
Kroger.com, 107

L
Larcker, D. F., 13, 27
Lasica, J. D., 53, 82
Lear, R. W., 137, 164
Lee, C. M. C., 61, 82
Lehmann, D. R., 12, 27
Levine, Michael E., 39
Lewis, T. R., 214, 219
Licking, E., 87, 106
Linear Technology Corporation, 213–214
Little, J. D. C., 143, 163
Loomis, C. J., 157, 164
Lovelock, Christopher H., 30, 50
low resource equivalence (LORE), 70, 75
LUV, *see* Southwest Airlines

M
mail-order industry, 3–4
Malter, A. J., 11, 28
Mandlebrot, B., 50, 51
market cap, 210–214
market commonality, 63–77
market share attraction, and pharmaceuticals, 191–193
marketing, and knowledge gap with finance, 8–12
marketing efficiency ratio (MER), 20, 112–113, 142–143, 148–150, 179
marketing mysteries, 106
Marketing Science Institute (MSI) study, 199–220
Martingale pattern, 242–244
mass retailers, 165, 178–184, 240
Mastrapasqua, F., 44, 50
materials sector, 64
maximum earnings market share (MEMS)
 airline industry, 119–124
 competitive stock valuation model, 223
 definition, 22–24
 dual-segment communications companies, 185–188
 formula, 123
 mass retailers, 179–180
 online retailers, 175, 177
 personal computer companies, 140–141, 146, 149, 152–154
 review of, 160–161
 wireless phone services, 189–190
maximum earnings rule, 109–135, 161
Maynard, M., 31, 39–40, 50, 128–129, 133
McDonald's, 206–207
mean value-sales differential, 43–44
media companies, 52–56, *see also* dual-segment communications companies
medium resource equivalence (MERE), 70, 74–75
Megna, P., 51
MEMS, *see* maximum earnings market share
MER, *see* marketing efficiency ratio

Merck, 166, 190–195
merger opportunities, 188
Michaelson, G. A., 111, 133
Michaelson, S. W., 111, 133
Microsemi Corporation, 213–214
"Momentum Theory of Goodwill" (Nelson), 40
Moult, W., 12, 26, 248

N
Nakamura, A., 246, 248
Nelson, R. H., 40, 51
New York Times Co., 165, 184–188
Newton, K., 160, 164
Nextel, 165–166, 188–190
Nissan Motors, 79–82, 90–93
Novartis, 166, 190–195, 236–238

O
Oeing, A., 246, 248
Oler, D. K., 61, 82
Omnicom Group, 201–204, 206–207
ongoing costs, 85–90
online retailers, 165–178, 225–235, 239–240
online services, 3, 59
operations management, 16, 93–95
outdoor advertising peer group, 78–79
Overfelt, M., 100, 107

P
Pacioli Factor, 8–9
Packard, Dave, 145
Palda, K. S., 72, 82
Parsons, Richard D., 53
peer group member, 38
Penford Corporation, 210–214
people, as enterprise marketing assets, 130
periodicity, in desktop market, 163
personal computer companies, 136–164, 224–225, 238–239
personal products companies, 204–206
Peteraf, M. A., 15, 17, 27, 82
Pfeffer, J., 84, 89, 107
Pfeifer, P., 14, 27
pharmaceuticals
  competitive stock valuation model, 236–238
  market commonality in, 72–77
  maximum earnings market share analysis in, 166, 190–195
  traditional marketing and, 87–90
PIMS (Profit Impact of Marketing Strategy studies), 11
Porter, M. E., 11, 27
potential competitors, in biotechnology sub-industry, 75–76
PPP, *see* profit per point
prepackaged software group, 69–71
present value discounting, 246–247
price of entry, 122
price/earnings ratio, 38
PriceLine, 165–178, 242–244

price/revenue ratio, 38
principle of force, 110–119, 121–122, 160–161
private investment in public equity (PIPE), 87
Prnewswire.com, 51
product markets, 34
product quality, 10
profit (big P), 12
Profit Impact of Marketing Strategy (PIMS) studies, 11
profit per basis point
  Amazon.com, 176
  MSI study, 215–218
  personal computer companies, 141, 147, 150
  review of, 160–161
  Wal*Mart, 180–182
profit per point (PPP), 22
profit per share point, 118–121
profit ratio, 71
promotions, 10

R
RAD, *see* risk-adjusted differential
Rao, V. R., 3, 28
Rappaport, A., 221, 248–249
Rees, L. Z., 246, 248
Rego, L. L., 11, 27
Reibstein, D., 14, 27
relative earnings productivity (REP), 20–24, 193–195, 235–244
resource equivalence guidelines, 70–71
resource equivalence ratios, 76–77
return to shareholders, in *MSI* study, 215–218
revenue dollar, 94, 97–98, 101–102
revenue per share point, in airline industry, 116–117
revenue ratio, 71
revenue-multiplier effect, 196–197
Ricchiuti, Peter, 78
Ries, A., 110, 133
risk-adjusted differential (RAD)
  advertising agencies, 201–204
  airline industry, 44–45
  automobile industry, 79–82
  chemical industry, 60–61
  competitive stock valuation model, 228–230, 235–244
  grocery chains, 104–105
  interpretation, 44–50
  MSI study, 199–220
  online retailers, 171–172
  personal computer companies, 156–158, 224–225
  personal products companies, 204–206
  standardized measure, 19
Rivlin, G., 167, 197
robustness, and number of competitors, 79–82
Rollins, Kevin, 158
Rosen, Ben, 151
Ross, S. A., 13, 28
Rotemberg, J. J., 214, 219
rule of maximum earnings, 109–135, 161

S

sales per dollar (SPD), 20
sales revenues, and personal computer companies, 138, 162
Sanabria, Raul, 164
scale efficiencies, 183–184
Scharfstein, D. S., 214, 219
Schultz, D. E., 26, 28
Sears, 165, 178–184
sectors, in Global Industry Classification Standard, 62
segment profit-and-loss (P&L) statements, 8–9
selling, general, and administrative (SG&A) expenses, 16–17, 85–95, 144, 162, 187
semiconductor companies, 213–218
Serwer, A., 158, 160, 164
share of market, 138, 170
share of revenue (SOR), 18–19, 34, 143, 169
share of spending (SOS), 143, 151–152
share of value (SOV), 18–19, 34, 170
shareholder valuation model, of A. Rappaport, 221–222
shareholder value
    creation of, 84–85
    longer-term, 245–247
    online retailers, 168
    sources of, 2–6
    Wal★Mart, 183–184
Shering Group AG, 75, 83
Silo Problem, 9–10
Sinegal, Jim, 165
Smit, S., 222, 249
SNL.com, 96, 107
software companies, 63–71
SOR, see share of revenue
Sorkin, A. R., 53, 83
SOS, see share of spending
Southwest Airlines, 1, 4–5, 30–40, 44–45, see also airline industry
Southwest.com, 51
SOV, see share of value
Spaeth, J., 12, 26, 248
Sprint, 165–166, 188–190
stable markets, strategic groups in, 72–77
stand-alone enterprise, 38
Standard & Poor's, 60, 62, 199, 214, 219
Steiner, P. O., 13, 27
stock markets, 34
Stout, W. D., 27, 86, 107
strategic groups, 15, 63–77, 199–220, 232
Stuart, Je. A., 12, 27
sum constraint, 195–196
supermarket chains, see grocery chains
Sutton, D., 4, 16, 28

T

Tan, Linda, 2, 8, 247–248
tangible assets, value of, 2–6
tangible value intuition, 39–40

Target, 165, 178–184
telecommunications companies, 66, 215–218
Terman, Fred, 145
Thompson, C. M., 222, 249
time horizon, 12–13
Tobin, J., 44, 51
Torregrosa, P., 87, 107
Toyota Motor Company, 79–82, 90–93, 204, 206–207
traditional marketing, and pharmaceutical industry, 87–90
Tribune Co., 165, 184–188
Trout, J., 110, 133

U

U S Bancorp, 95–98
underspending, and online retailers, 196
U.S. Securities and Exchange Commission, 39, 51
USM, 165–166, 188–190
utilities sector, 66
Utsey, M. F., 243, 249

V

value added, 247–248
value ratio, 70–71
value/revenue ratios, 58–59, 97
value-sales differential (VSD)
    airline industry and, 36–39
    definition, 19
    grocery chains, 104–105
    mean, 43–44
    online retailers, 170–171
    personal computer companies, 156–158
value-sales principles, 31–32
van Nierop, E., 14, 27
variables, errors in, 25–26
Viguerie, S. P., 222, 249
Villalogna, B., 8, 28, 51
volatile markets, and strategic groups, 63–71
VSD, see value-sales differential

W

Wal★Mart, 165, 178–184, 240
Walton, Sam, 178, 184
Wang, K., 2, 27
Webster, F. E., Jr., 11, 28
Welch, Jack, 208
Wells Fargo & Company, 95–98
Wellsfargo.com, 96, 107
Whole Foods Market, Inc., 246–247
Wireless, 165–166, 188–190
wireless phone services, 165–166, 188–190
WWP Group, 201–204

Y

Yahoo.com, 165–178, 239–240
York, Jerry, 144

ABOUT TEXERE

Texere, a progressive and authoritative voice in business publishing, brings to the global business community the expertise and insights of leading thinkers. Our books educate, enlighten, and entertain, and provide an intersection where our authors and our readers share cutting edge ideas, practices, and innovative solutions. Texere seeks to cultivate, enhance, and disseminate information that illuminates the global business landscape.

www.thomson.com/learning/texere

ABOUT THE TYPEFACE

This book was set in 10.5 point Bembo. Bembo was cut by Francesco Griffo for the Venitian printer Aldus Manutius to publish in 1495 *De Aetna* by Cardinal Pietro Bembo. Stanley Morison supervised the design of Bembo for the Monotype Corporation in 1929. The Bembo is a readable and classical typeface because of its well-proportioned letterforms, functional serifs, and lack of peculiarities.

Library of Congress Cataloging-in-Publication Data

Cook, Victor J.
  Competing for customers and capital / by Victor J. Cook.
    p. cm.
  Includes index.
   ISBN 0-324-40597-9
  1. Corporations—Valuation—United States. 2. Corporations—United States—Finance. 3. Marketing—United States—Management. 4. Brand name products—United States—Marketing. I. Title.
   HG4028.V3C66 2006
   658.15'2--dc22

                                                            2006002628